History of American Thought and Culture

Paul S. Boyer, *general editor*

James L. Machor

PASTORAL CITIES

Urban Ideals and the Symbolic
Landscape of America

The University of Wisconsin Press

Published 1987

The University of Wisconsin Press
114 North Murray Street
Madison, Wisconsin 53715

The University of Wisconsin Press, Ltd.
1 Gower Street
London WC1E 6HA, England

First printing

Printed in the United States of America

Library of Congress Cataloging-in-Publication Data
    Machor, James L.
    Pastoral cities.
    (History of American thought and culture)
    Bibliography: pp. 257–263.
    Includes index.
    1. American literature—History and criticism.
2. Cities and towns in literature.   3. City and town life
in literature.   4. Landscape in literature.   5. Pastoral literature,
American—History and criticism.   6. Nature
in literature.   7. Cities and towns—United States—
History.   8. United States—Civilization.
9. Urbanization—United States—History.
I. Title.   II. Series.
PS169.C57M3   1987   810'.9' 321732   87-2171
ISBN 0-299-11280-2
ISBN 0-299-11284-5 (pbk.)

for Lawrence and Helen

Contents

Illustrations

All illustrations are reproduced by permission of the I. N. Phelps Stokes Collection, The New York Public Library, Astor, Lenox, and Tilden Foundations.

Preface

As the subtitle of this book suggests, this is not primarily a study of the American city or of American urbanization. Its concern is not with the social patterns of cities or the historical development of urban America. Rather, it is a study of a conception of America's urban environment that has played an important role in our culture and literature. I have called this conception urban pastoralism.

Since a major part of my purpose is to trace the history of an idea, a word about the meaning of the term *city* is in order. Modern definitions of the city, with their emphasis on demographic characteristics and networks of social structures, have only limited value for the history of ideas because they cannot take into account the more visionary patterns informing past conceptions of urban life. Nor can such definitions serve as a basis for deciding which of these visions actually are urban. For the notion of urbanity is itself a product of changing historical contexts. Before 1750 in America, perhaps only Boston would qualify as urban by modern standards, but the inhabitants of Philadelphia, New York, Charleston, Salem, New Haven, and a score of other places perceived themselves as living in cities, and this perception is what is important to the historian of ideas. Since any definition of the city, including a modern sociological one, is itself a concept predicated on the values and ideas of its own time, the wholesale application of such a definition is finally anachronistic. Rather than proscribe the past through the present, I have left the term undefined, allowing its meaning to emerge from the historical documents examined.

Because the shape of any idea, moreover, is a product of an extended historical process, understanding that idea requires some delineation of its antecedents. The majority of American ideas did not spring spontaneously from native soil but developed through the interaction between American conditions and the suppositions transported from Europe. The history of urban pastoralism is no exception. Thus, Chapter 1 of this book examines the European origins of this concept as it was applied to and affected by the startling facts of the New World. The relations between American and European ideas, as both sources for and transforming agents of urban pastoralism, form an important part of this study.

These relations, however, ultimately mean little unless we accept the premise that ideas are important to an understanding of culture— a premise by no means universally assumed. In particular, social historians over the past twenty years have challenged the notion that ideas significantly influence history. Arguing that thought is primarily a ploy for justifying class interests or for satisfying emotional needs, those historians have emphasized the role of environmental forces, both physical and social, in shaping culture and have fashioned a social history based on the behavior patterns reflected in quantifiable evidence. As some social historians have begun to recognize, however, experience and behavior (what we might call "reality") do not exist independently of the perceptions brought to them. Because physical events and their records are bound up with the meanings ascribed to them, culture constitutes a matrix of interconnected experiences and shared patterns of thought. A full understanding of a culture or a subculture requires a study of that matrix in a way that both describes and analyzes those interrelations. To do so necessitates going beneath formal systems of thought to discover the deeper ideational regularities and rhythms that form cultural myths—those shared patterns of belief, often in the form of tacit premises, by which a group gives order and significance to experience.

Delving into a part of that matrix has been the object of this study. I have sought to explore certain conceptual patterns and forms of behavior, especially written behavior, as cultural embodiments of a particular recurrent idea about urban America. Because those phenomena are complex, I deliberately have avoided simplistic claims that this idea has determined a given set of events. My concern has been to document and analyze what shapes this idea has taken and why it has assumed those shapes at different times and for different people. My emphasis is less on the way urban pastoralism has impelled actions and more on the way it has been invoked, sometimes without conscious intent, to give meaning to the American environment. Both the concept of rural-urban synthesis and its changing manifestations in formal and symbolic expressions of thought are the subjects of this study.

A moment ago I invoked the term *myth,* not only because it is an important component of culture, but because an examination of urban pastoralism as myth lies at the center of this book. While my general approach has been that of a student of ideas, my method has consisted of a particular type of intellectual history usually referred to as myth-symbol analysis—a method that has determined my choice of written documents as the primary source of data. Because myths are thematically constituted in symbolic actions, and because language is the most symbolic of human expressions, discourse provides the richest source for studying the actualization of myth. For myth-symbol analysis does not assume a platonic realm of timeless ideas independent of individual expression; just as experience does not exist apart from our apprehension of it, ideas, including myths, exist only by virtue of the semiotic behavior, especially language, in which they are actualized. And just as we can extrapolate from a relatively finite collection of discourses an underlying system of language, we also can infer from a collection of cultural expressions an infrastructure of tacit premises or myths that guide the coherent expression of ideas.

This union of mythography and discourse analysis is particularly valuable for clarifying the relation between literature and culture and for guarding against simplistic approaches to literature itself. Because literature is discourse, an understanding of its relation to culture must begin with an understanding of its relation to the verbal expressions of nonliterary culture. Since nonliterary discourse provides an important avenue into mythology, it becomes a medium by which the image patterns of myths are identified in a way that allows us to see their presence and forms in literature. For the mythographer, cultural expressions thus serve as a means for illuminating literature, with myth acting as the connecting filament between the two. Because myth-symbol analysis asserts that myths are embodied in form, moreover, it requires that the mythographer pay due regard to the relation between structure and content. Such analysis, performed with the tools of literary criticism, treats literature as more than a collection of discursive statements and so facilitates an understanding of the degree of complexity with which myths are embodied and presented in literature. For sophisticated literature such an approach is especially productive because it discloses how this literature differs from the general culture in its articulation of a particular myth. This theory of reciprocal illumination has informed the structure of this book and especially the discussion in Chapters 5 and 6.

Yet the question that remains is what "general" culture is being talked about. One of the problems of myth-symbol analysis has been its eagerness at times to claim that the myths it examines are characteristic of American people as a whole. That is not my assertion, but in eschewing it I have not attempted to identify exactly which elements of the culture have been affected by the urban-pastoral myth and which have not. Because this is not a sociological study, I have not sought to explore the role of this myth in subcultures defined by criteria of occupation, gender, income, or region. Rather, my choice of material has determined *a priori* the subgroup on which I have focused: the white, predominately middle-class, articulate members of our culture, who historically have been the self-appointed spokespeople for the values of "mainstream America." Although I use the term "mainstream America" advisedly here because there may be no such beast, the point is that I am not claiming that urban pastoralism is a characteristically American value in the sense of being systemic in the culture. Nor am I asserting that it is shared by all middle-class Americans; it is not even shared by all members of this articulate subgroup. As I note in the Prologue that follows, urban pastoralism has constituted only one of the many conceptual patterns through which Americans have viewed their cities. However, because it has appeared among members of this articulate group from a wide variety of occupations, backgrounds, regions, and time periods, this myth has displayed a pervasiveness that makes it a significant component of American values. I have undertaken this study because I believe that if we wish to understand the history of urbanization in America, we need to examine this component of our culture.

When I use the terms "general culture" or "culture at large" in the following pages, therefore, I am referring to the group I have just identified. My concern has been with the public discussion of rural-urban synthesis, not with the private conceptions held by the great cross section of Americans. Yet having specified that focus, I should add that other phenomena indicate that this myth has not been limited to an articulate subgroup of Americans. When possible I have drawn on additional types of data, such as demographic patterns, to try to suggest where in the culture these lines of continuity extend.

In a study such as this, one incurs more obligations than he can hope to acknowledge. This book would not have been possible without the previous excellent work done on American urbanization and myth-symbol analysis, and my intellectual debt to these studies probably goes deeper than I realize. For particular individuals and institutions I can be more specific. I am grateful for the thoughtful criticism and helpful suggestions of John Hellmann, Edward Davidson, A. Lynn Altenbernd, Thomas Cooley, and William Angel, who read all or parts of the manuscript in various drafts. To Francis Hodgins goes my deep appreciation for his perceptive advice and encouragement during the years when this project began to take shape. I want to extend special acknowledgments to Paul Boyer for his steady support of this project in its later stages and to Barbara Hanrahan of the University of Wisconsin Press for her editorial expertise and advice.

Part of this study was supported by a fellowship from the University of Illinois and a grant from Ohio State University, and I thank these institutions for their assistance. The curators of the rare book rooms at the University of Pennsylvania and the University of Illinois libraries and of the special collections at The New York Public Library and The American Antiquarian Society were extremely cooperative in providing access to their valuable holdings; Betty Milum of the Ohio State University Library was untiring in helping me obtain important materials. Among those who aided in preparing the final manuscript, none contributed more than Judy Von Blon.

Since portions of this book have appeared previously, I wish to thank the following journals for permission to use that material: *American Literature,* for my article "Pastoralism and the American Urban Ideal: Hawthorne, Whitman, and the Literary Pattern" (in *American Literature* 54:3, pp. 329–353, copyright © 1982 Duke University Press), which was revised and expanded as Chapter 6; *American Studies,* for my essay "The Garden City in America: Crèvecoeur's *Letters* and the Urban-Pastoral Context" (copyright © 1982 Midcontinent American Studies Association [Mid-America American Studies Association], from *American Studies,* Volume xxiii, Number 1) which was incorporated in Chapter 3; the *Pennsylvania Magazine of History and Biography,* for "The Urban Idyll of the New Republic" (April 1986 issue, pp. 219–235) also used in Chapter 3; and the *South Atlantic Quarterly,* for my "Urbanization and the Western Garden: Synthesizing City and County in Antebellum America" (in

South Atlantic Quarterly 81:4, pp. 413–428, copyright © 1982 Duke University Press), which served as the basis for Chapter 4.

Finally, my greatest thanks go to my wife, Nancy. Without her patience, understanding, editorial assistance, and friendship this work would never have been completed.

Pastoral Cities

Prologue
The Rural-Urban Synthesis

Although American writers over the past two hundred years increasingly have made urban life the focus of their imaginative explorations, the image of the dark, threatening city has been so common that our literature, particularly in the nineteenth century, has seemed to be almost anti-urban. Reinforcing this impression is the fact that even our most urbane artists have made the impulse to withdraw from society into an idealized rural landscape a cardinal theme of their works, suggesting that a more meaningful life is possible closer to nature beyond the constraining, complex, and corrupt city. Yet even a brief survey of America's literary history reveals that such antagonism has formed only a part of the artistic response to urbanization. In addition to the tendency of mid-nineteenth-century popular novelists to laud the excitement and opportunity of the city, many of our major writers have gone beyond a simple antipathy toward the urban milieu to recognize it as an important component of the American scene. When Emerson wrote that "the test of civilization is the power of drawing the most benefit out of cities," he was not reproving his countrymen for participating in a misguided process but expressing an idea shared by other American romantics including Whitman, Hawthorne, and Cooper: that the city was a valuable factor in individual and national development.[1] A similar attitude appears in the fiction and poetry of James, Howells, Dreiser, Sandburg, Fitzgerald, Dos Passos, Hart Crane—and the list could go on. Though willing to depict the callousness, duplicity, and artificiality of the urban milieu, many American writers have incorporated in their works an appreciation of the city's rich diversity and interesting complexity.

The divergent attractions to rural and urban values have not, of course, been unique to literature. For much of our history Americans as a whole repeatedly have displayed a fascination with nature and the open countryside. In the eighteenth and nineteenth centuries in particular, the native experience was highly colored by what historians have referred to alternately as the "agrarian myth," the "pastoral ideal," and the "myth of the garden," a way of thinking which, in Perry Miller's words, identified "the health, the very personality of Americans with Nature, and therefore set it in opposition to . . . the city."[2] That such a fascination has continued into our own age is evident from phenomena as diverse as the back-to-nature movements of the 1960s, the myriad advertisements for commercial products and real estate equating the good life with rustic settings, and the recent, increasing trend among urban dwellers to abandon the city for country homes. Our culture, as well as our literature, has tended continually to perceive environment through a pastoral filter.

Although a fondness for country life closer to nature has been especially strong in America, other societies clearly have shared the same inclination. As Schiller once remarked, "all people who have a history have a paradise, a state of innocence, a golden age."[3] But our experience as a nation undoubtedly has invested the idea with immense moral significance. Here was a new continent offering an opportunity, never before equaled, to begin life anew by returning to a simpler rural past. Little wonder that America was defined for so long as "nature's nation," establishing a set of values that remain today in our nostalgia for rusticity and our repeated efforts to slough off the demands of urban existence.

Despite the prominence of this ideal in American life, however, we have not remained a rural society—an indication that not all Americans have felt a repugnance toward urbanization. Over the past fifty years revisionist historians such as Carl Bridenbaugh, Sam Bass Warner, Jr., Charles Glaab, John Reps, and Richard Wade, among others, have been stressing this fact while demonstrating the importance of the city as a source of economic, political, educational, and artistic advancement since the seventeenth century.[4] Nor is this awareness a distinctively modern phenomenon. When Henry Tappan in 1855 wrote that "cities [are] the center of intelligence, enterprise, and education," he articulated a conviction shared by many of his contemporaries, who also would have acquiesced to his conclusion that "the human being dwelling alone, or in sparsely settled districts, without any communication with cities, remains unacquainted with his own capabilities and . . . deteriorates in prejudice and ignorance." From articles in nineteenth-century periodicals such as *DeBow's Review*, *Putnam's*, and *Hunt's Merchants' Magazine* back to the writings of the Puritans comes substantial evidence that Americans long have been aware of urbanization's ameliorative effects and have been quite willing to champion the city against the attacks of rural advocates.[5]

There is no denying that a belief in the superiority of either rural or urban environments has been central to America, for beneath their divergence these two ideological strains share a common assumption informing much of our history: the conviction that city and country embody diametrically opposed values. Whether the subject has been the preference for the open landscape of fresh possibilities as symbolized by the image of the American Adam, or the development of the garden image of America, or the special role of the city in fomenting political revolution, the preeminence of this dialectical opposition in American conceptions of the two realms has been tendentiously affirmed, explicitly or implicitly, by social, intellectual, and literary historians. Such an emphasis, unfortunately, has largely obscured the fact that an equally significant strain of thought has conceived of the American scene as a place where that dialectic finally could be synthesized. Drawing on the promise of the open landscape and pastoral sensibilities and rhetoric, proponents of this perspective have linked city and countryside to describe or envision America as a healthy, harmonious urban-pastoral society combining the best of both worlds.

In our own day this way of thinking has taken a number of forms. At its most simplistic it appears in the renewed interest among city dwellers in tending gardens and cultivating tropical plants as well as in the frequent meetings of sensitivity groups where alienated urbanites seek to "get in touch with" their "natural" feelings. But it also is present in the recent calls for a Jeffersonian simplification of the Washington bureaucracy, in the tree-planting projects that constitute an almost obligatory concomitant of urban renewal, and in the mass exodus to the suburbs after World War II. The proliferation of these purportedly unencumbered environments, with their large lawns and well-spaced houses, providing nevertheless many advantages and services of urban life, attests to the inexorable grip such an idea has upon many Americans.

But it would be a mistake to assume that this desire for synthesis has been limited to our own age. The pathway of American history is marked by recurrent signs of the same longing. We find it in F.D.R.'s recovery program, which included creation of greenbelt towns, and in Henry Ford's belief that establishing fifty thousand gardens in Detroit would help urban factory workers become more content, morally fit, and self-sufficient. Before that, it appears in the planning theories of architects such as Frank Lloyd Wright and, at the turn of the century, in the efforts of liberal reformers, including Henry George and Jane Addams.

Although this concern with integrating rural and urban forms and values has not gone completely unnoticed by historians, those who have mentioned it usually have done so only incidentally, as though it were an insignificant and ephemeral phenomenon in America. Even the few individuals who have gone beyond occasional remarks have reinforced this trend either by examining a particular version of the ideal, as if it occurred in a cultural vacuum, or by concentrating on its manifestation in a narrow historical period.[6] The Progressive Era and the two decades before have received most of the limited attention devoted to this ideational pattern, with historians such as Scott Donaldson, John L. Thomas, and Peter Schmitt asserting that this epoch inaugurated the quest for a fusion of city and country.[7] However, the ideal of an urban-pastoral society no more originated among Progressive reformers than it did among the vanguard of the park-planning movement just before the Civil War. Rather, both represented versions of a way of thought already widespread in America during the first fifty years of the nineteenth century. Playing a role in efforts to establish benevolent societies and houses of refuge and in urban temperance movements, the idea of the pastoral city also informed the histories, travel narratives, and promotional literature about the urban West. One repeatedly finds it in the writings of intellectuals, in popular fiction and periodicals, and in the iconography of the period. Nor is it surprising that such an interest heated up in antebellum America, given the romantic fondness for nature that developed at this time. But the concept did not burst spontaneously into a flaming enthusiasm in the early 1800s.[8] The new interest in organicism only fueled a habit of thought that had burned brightly in the seventeenth and eighteenth centuries.

The ideal of an urban-pastoral synthesis appears, for example, in Pierre L'Enfant's design for Washington, D.C., in which he sought to create a national metropolis which also would be, as he explained, a "compleat garden."[9] Influencing beautification projects at Newport, Boston, and Philadelphia in the late 1700s, the ideal also surfaced during the early years of the century in the histories and promotional tracts of Virginia that linked the benefits of agricultural development to town building. Hector St. John de Crèvecoeur made the ideal a central theme of his *Letters from an American Farmer*, particularly in his depiction of Nantucket, and Franklin employed it in his *Autobiography*, presenting himself as an urban version of Jefferson's self-reliant, noble husbandman. We can continue into the past to discover forms of it in William Penn's 1683 plan to make Philadelphia a "green country town"; in the early Puritan township pattern of settlement; and even in John Winthrop's lay sermon aboard the *Arabella*, where he defined the Puritan community of New England as a "Citty upon a Hill" that would be built according to the "lawe of nature."[10] Many other examples exist, but the point is that all these instances are related by an underlying impulse that has constituted an important, though frequently overlooked, component of our culture since the age of settlement. Until we recognize that relation and the shape of the ideational pattern informing it, our understanding of this urban-pastoral vision will remain fragmented while our conception of its history will be truncated.

I

If we have not as yet paid adequate attention to the prevalence of urban pastoralism and extensively explored its variations, part of the reason seems to lie in the nature of the ideal itself. Like Proteus, it can take a number of shapes, making its central features and continuity difficult to recognize. Its idealism causes it to be easily confused with utopianism, and because it so readily draws on bucolic images, it may appear at first glance to be just a variant or outgrowth of pastoral ideals. Hence the recent assertion of one historian that "the urge to be near nature nurtured a rural ideal in Jeffersonian America that was gradually transformed into a suburban ideal . . . in the nineteenth century."[11] Yet a deeper reason for the lack of extensive attention is a discernible uneasiness among historians regarding claims that a particular view of the city is characteristic of the "national mind." Sensitive to the distortions created by studies arguing that American culture has been anti-urban and rural oriented, historians such as Charles Glaab have warned that "it would be unfortunate if urban history were merely to become a means of arguing the other side of a supposed urban-rural dialogue, which earlier historians artificially imposed on our past."[12]

Ironically, however, urban historians inadvertently have contributed to such a situation. Grounded in the belief that the city has played a distinctively significant role in America's past, much urban historiography, from analyses of town planning to discussions of the city's social, economic, and political structure, has constituted an implicit obverse of our culture's fascination with the rural world. The result has been the kind of insufficient concern, already noted, for the vision of these two realms not as opposites but as complements that need to be combined. Certainly Glaab and others are correct in one sense: It would be a mistake if urban history became only a study of urban pastoralism. As great an error (and one containing its own irony), however, would be to neglect this response to environment in an effort to keep urban studies a broad and flexible field.

Any exploration of urban pastoralism nonetheless must be alert to potential pitfalls, one of which is the assumption that this ideal somehow is characteristic of the "national mind." As historians of ideas increasingly have recognized, the concept of "national mind" is at best misleading, since culture constitutes a collection of beliefs, some of which are shared by certain members and some by others, with considerable differences and overlappings. Americans have viewed themselves and their world in many ways, and it is impossible to claim that one perspective has dominated our history. Consequently, not all Americans have embraced the urban-pastoral ideal, nor has it had relevance for all social groups. Recognizing that this idea has existed simultaneously with a distrust of cities and with a defense of their political and economic advantages, therefore, can prevent oversimplification and distortion of the role of urban pastoralism in American ideas. Oversimplification of another sort, however, constitutes a second danger. Though the ideal's continuity has seminal importance, significant differences among its manifestations, both within a period and from one age to another, cannot be ignored. Preventing reductionism requires an understanding of urban pastoralism flexible enough to allow for this diversity but precise enough to differentiate the ideal from other conceptual patterns. Unless we go beyond saying that urban pastoralism seeks to synthesize city and country, discovering the difference between it and utopianism or pastoralism will be impossible.

The first step is to recognize that the ideal of a pastoral city is not tantamount to utopianism, if by that term we mean a vision of or attempt to build a perfect society. For one thing, all utopianism is not urban, as the transcendentalist experiments at Brook Farm and Fruitlands testify. Nor is urban pastoralism merely a subclass of utopianism. While communitarian societies, such as those at New Harmony and Nauvoo in the early nineteenth century, and numerous fictional utopias, like those in Edward Bellamy's *Looking Backward* (1888) and Henry Olerich's *A Cityless and Countryless World* (1893), do embody the ideal, such perfectionist versions constitute only one category of urban pastoralism. [13] Certainly there is nothing utopian in most civic tree-planting programs or in L'Enfant's plan for Washington, D.C., nor did the Puritans expect to build a heaven on earth in Massachusetts. Only if utopianism is taken in a much broader sense to mean a commitment to creating what it conceives of as the best possible society can urban pastoralism be seen as utopian. But by this definition, Marxism, utilitarianism, pastoralism, and most other "isms" also fall in this category. Identifying the ideal of a pastoral city as utopian in the larger sense, therefore, in no way facilitates an understanding of its distinctiveness, especially in relation to bucolic ideals.

This last distinction is imperative because urban pastoralism is so easily confused with a purely pastoral vision. In *The Machine in the Garden* Leo Marx has provided perhaps the most incisive discussion to date of this latter ideal. Marx explains that pastoralism in Western culture, and in America in particular, has existed in two forms. The first, which he calls the "complex pastoral," is a literary structure of Greco-Roman origin that creates an ideal natural landscape but uses a pattern of disruption to identify that landscape as a fiction incapable of exisiting in reality. The second and more pervasive, however, is a *cultural* form of pastoralism that posits a particular conception of the good society as an achievable goal, and it is this form that we must be careful to distinguish from what I call urban pastoralism. [14]

This cultural version of pastoralism, according to Marx, constitutes a reaction to the world engendered by the desire to withdraw from the complexities of a structured civilization toward a natural environment promising individual freedom and instinctual spontaneity. Not advocating a complete retreat to a primitive life-style, the impulse envisions a mild, cultivated terrain, a "middle landscape" in which the conflicting values of art and nature, civilization and primitivism merge into a characteristically rural environment located between the poles of untamed nature and the city. Incorporating a moral geography—in effect, an ideography—by ascribing value to the middle ground of integration while opposing it to the primitive and urban realms, the landscape of pastoralism possesses a symbolic dimension in that it represents a state of mind or ethical attitude as much as a literal place. Because cultural pastoralism is a flexible concept, however, it is not always anti-urban. At times it takes the city, as an institution, into account as something more than a location to be eschewed, displaying even a conciliatory attitude toward the urban world.

Though appearing infrequently, this broad kind of pastoralism seems to embody a vision of synthesis suggesting that urban pastoralism is not a separate concept. Yet even in its widest configuration, pastoralism is markedly different from the ideal of rural-urban synthesis. To clarify that difference let us compare two representative examples, one containing this expanded version of pure pastoralism, the other incorporating an urban-pastoral vision. Although the two share certain features, each rests at bottom on a distinctive ideational pattern.

In 1815 George Troup of Georgia delivered in the U.S. House of Representatives a speech embodying the pastoral ideal in its broad form. Celebrating the victory of Andrew Jackson at New Orleans, Troup's oration is in many ways typical of the times, which produced numerous paeans valorizing Jackson and his troops by linking them to nature and rural values. Accordingly, when Troup addresses the question of how such a triumph occurred, he answers by invoking the talisman of native conditions, declaiming that the prodigious success of the Americans came from their ability to "judiciously employ the means which God and Nature have bountifully placed at our disposal." The landscape has made possible the creation of a people who, "committing themselves to the bosom of the mother of rivers," are intrinsically connected to the land they defend. The men under Jackson, notes Troup, were not professional soldiers but "the yeomanry of the country marching to the defence of the City of Orleans[,] leaving their wives and children and firesides at a moment's warning." Owing to their tenacity, native ingenuity, and, he implies, dedication to the land they defended, "the farmers of the country [were] triumphantly victorious over the conquerors of the conquerors of Europe." As he repeatedly invokes the image of "the *American husbandman*, fresh from his plow," Troup all but overtly claims that the very condition of the

American farmer, whose "freshness" comes from a life close to nature, kept New Orleans out of enemy hands.[15]

Although Troup's speech pivots on the conventional homage to the noble husbandman, it does so quite differently than, say, Jefferson's *Notes on Virginia*. For Troup, the farmer is not merely a peaceful tiller of the earth isolated in a rural retreat; he has the capacity to become involved in political issues that bring him into contact with the larger world, in this case the forces of European urban power. More important, he rescues a city. In Troup's moral geography the pastoral ideal in no way clashes with his joyous contemplation of New Orleans' salvation. The city is not opposed to the rural world but is enfolded in the overall scheme of victory.

In its ideal of a harmonious relation between city and country, Troup's speech appears to contain an urban-pastoral vision. In actuality, however, it consists of a substantially different conceptual paradigm. For in Troup's oration no doubt exists as to what merits praise. Far less than the idea of rural-urban harmony, the image of the noble husbandman stands as the token of value. No synthesis, in the sense of a cooperative partnership between rural and urban, ever comes forth. The country saves the city, but the city gives nothing in return. New Orleans functions primarily as a backdrop or vehicle through which the good farmer displays his patriotism. Any union is at best perfunctory, since Troup leaves little doubt that after the battle the American husbandman will return to his rural world of virtuous peace. His involvement in the battle has been primarily an effort to maintain the America he epitomizes: a simple rural world free from corrosive European urban power. Despite its wider vision, Troup's pronouncement still adheres to a standard pastoral ideography, which identifies the middle landscape as the source of inspiration. Typifying the broader version of pastoralism, it says, in effect, that cities are acceptable but only as minor functionaries subordinated to the dominant rustic character of society.

The difference between this ideational pattern and urban pastoralism becomes clearer when comparing Troup's perspective to that of a work such as Henry George's *Progress and Poverty* (1879), which builds toward a climactic vision of society epitomizing the urban-pastoral ideal. To do so it invokes a symbolic geography, but one much different from Troup's, for George is not celebrating victory but seeking a remedy for the distorted landscape he faces.

George focuses much of his study on the current scene, particularly

the vast urban poverty that paradoxically has accompanied civilization's progress. The problem results, he explains, from monopolistic
land ownership, especially through speculation. The fact that "labor
is thus shut off from nature . . . can alone explain the state of things
that compels men to stand idle" and remain impoverished. Such social maladjustments, he insists, "spring from a denial of justice," and
since "justice is the natural law," blocking access to land "ignore[s]
natural laws." While seeing this problem throughout Western society,
George finds it especially unconscionable in America, not only because this country was founded on natural law but also because "this
public domain, . . . the enormous common to which the faces of the
energetic were always turned, has been the great fact that, since the
days when the first settlements began to fringe the Atlantic Coast, has
formed our national character and colored our national thought."[16]
Current conditions, therefore, contradict the very ethos of America,
which nature itself indelibly has inscribed. To correct this parlous situation George advocates a procedure that has become almost synon-
ymous with his name. A single tax on all owned property, he argues,
will discourage speculation and monopoly and so make land once
again available to Americans.

In urging his method George does not expect or even desire America to become once again a predominantly rural society. Harboring no
illusions about the supposed nobility and superiority of rustic ways, he
notes that "the life of the average farmer is now unnecessarily dreary.
He is not only compelled to work early and late, but he is cut off by
the sparseness of population from the conveniences, the amusements,
the educational facilities, and the social and intellectual opportunities that come with the closer contact of man with man." Though recognizing that "the development of the country . . . makes the city
grow," George sees the relationship as reciprocal. The urban world
contributes to the country because "the great manufactory; the
carthorse and the locomotive; the fishing boat and the steamship"
have produced "the blessing of material progress." Equal cooperation
of the two must eventuate, and the single tax has precisely that purpose. Its implementation

> would tend to diffuse population where it is too dense and to concen-
> trate it where it is too sparse; to substitute for the tenement house,
> homes surrounded by gardens, and to fully settle agricultural districts
> before people were driven far from neighborhoods to look for land.

The people of the cities would thus get more of the pure air and sunshine of the country, the people of the country more of the econom-
ies and social life of the city.

With its rural urbanity and homes amidst gardens, America would
become "a great co-operative society" in which "government would
. . . be vastly simplified" even as sophistication increased through
"material progress, which would go on with greatly accelerated
rapidity."[17]

The salient feature of George's vision, when set against even the
broad pastoralism of Troup's speech, is its emphasis on integration.
Though also invoking the exceptional conditions of native geography,
George's landscape, in its symbolic role as an index of value, is one
with cityscape. Not subordinated to rural ideals, the city is united to
the country, each an equal partner of a society defined by its urban-
pastoral synthesis. Unlike the pastoral ideal with its emphasis on
individual freedom in a landscape separated from the continuing demands of corporate society, George's vision combines personal fulfillment with cooperative identity. Even as "individual interests [would]
be subordinated to general interests," each person would have "leisure,
and comfort, and independence, the decencies and refinements of
life, the opportunities of mental and moral development. . . . Talents
now hidden, virtues unsuspected, would come forth to make human
life richer, fuller, happier, nobler."[18] To be sure, George's claim rests on
the possibility of developments to come, but that very emphasis underscores an important difference between the pastoral ideal, exemplified by Troup's speech, and urban pastoralism. While the former
looks toward a simpler past in an effort to maintain its existence in the
present, the concept of urban-rural integration, epitomized in
George's book, combines such nostalgia with an energetic commitment to future development of the city. This look-both-ways attitude
gives urban pastoralism an emphasis on advancement virtually absent
in the rural ideal.

That future orientation frequently appears even in descriptions of
the present as a realization of the urban-pastoral ideal. Such is the
case, for example, in Joel Barlow's *The Vision of Columbus* (1787). In
this epic poem Barlow has the aging Columbus experience a vision of
America as a harmonious blend of cultivated fields and active urban
centers—a future that has become the reality of Barlow's own day.
Unlike the despotic urban Europe he has known, Columbus views a

free, peaceful America where "gardens, vales and streets and structures rise," where "fields . . . bloom" and "towns and empires claim their peaceful sway." In this world, "Each rustic . . . turns the furrow'd soil," seeing his "rights secured," while the "growing throngs" from cities, which Barlow calls "seats of art," spread the developments of civilization to "bid dire diseases cease, / Or sound the tidings of eternal peace." In the poem's last book, moreover, Barlow allows Columbus to see how this bountiful blend will continue beyond the author's time owing to the "future progress of society with respect to commerce, discoveries, the opening of canals," and further advances in "philosophical, medical and political knowledge" until, through America's leadership and example, the harmony will embrace "all nations."[19]

Taken together, the visions of George and Barlow share a general pattern that constitutes the archetypal core of urban pastoralism—a core that differs considerably from that of the pastoral ideal as defined by Leo Marx. In addition to its unification of past and future, the idea of rural-urban synthesis possesses a distinctive moral geography which modifies the ideographic triptych of pure pastoralism by interposing a fourth term. Viewing pastoralism as inadequate in itself, the urban-pastoral vision conceives of an alternate "middle" realm in which the city blends harmoniously with the countryside or contains within its own boundaries urbanity, complexity, and sophistication combined with the physical or social attributes of simple rusticity. This synthesis might take a number of forms, from a preservation of open green spaces in the urban topography to an "organic" relationship among the inhabitants. At the base of the ideal lies an impulse to provide the urban dweller with some means to renew continually his elemental connection to his spontaneous, natural self while remaining a member of society, of the city, in a word, of civilization. Because of this orientation the ideography of urban pastoralism retains a dialectic structure, but it substitutes for the rural-urban dichotomy an opposition between the overcivilized city, cut off from nature, and the organic city that maintains contact with pastoral values.

Urban pastoralism thus is more than an attempt to infuse into cities touches of greenery and rural virtue, as though cities are necessary evils that must be purified with nature. Although at times it has taken this shape, the ideal also constitutes a vision of environment in which city and country are equally valuable components in an evolving landscape best served when those components operate in harmony. Moreover, as it has developed in this country, urban pastoralism has embodied a concept of unification predicated on the very conditions of America. As the examples of Barlow and George indicate, the ideal has hinged on the belief that the native terrain has provided a unique opportunity to create on a national scale an urban pattern that is one with the cultivated landscape. In its most ambitious form, the moral geography of urban pastoralism has been a moral geography of America, tied to the collective belief that this country, by its very nature, can yield a new, more harmonious society embracing the entire American scene.

Not all these generalized features, it should be noted, appear in every phenomenon displaying urban-pastoral traits. What we are considering is a conceptual pattern which, like all paradigms, evinces significant variation from one instance to another. Nor does every manifestation overtly display its urban-pastoral components. At times, as in Franklin's *Autobiography* or Jane Addams' *Twenty Years at Hull House*, the ideal may obtain even though physical nature or an explicit invocation of rustic ideals plays no direct role. Such subtle instances are among the most interesting, however, because they suggest just how deeply some of the features of the ideal have ingrained themselves in our culture, from daily actions to the writings of political leaders and social theorists.

These subtle versions of urban pastoralism are especially worth exploring when they appear in imaginative literature, primarily because of what our best artists have done with them. Like the culture at large, American writers have been attracted to the vision of a complementary relation between urban and rural—a fact that helps explain the otherwise paradoxical mixture of prourban and anti-urban images in their work. Not opposed to cities per se, many native writers have directed their censure against a particular type of city: the overcrowded, hypercivilized urban monster that crushes bucolic hopes. Hence Emerson, for one, could warn against the dangers of untempered urbanization yet proudly proclaim, "Let the river roll which way it will, cities will rise on its banks."[20] Extolling the potential of urban America to take its character from nature, he urged his countrymen to build towns that would express the latently inherent relationship between cityscape and landscape. This image of reconciliation has been a recurrent feature of our literature, salient in the synthesized landscapes of Barlow's *Vision of Columbus* and Freneau's *Rising Glory of America*, subtle in the novels of Cooper and

Hawthorne, where characters shuffle between city and country seeking some kind of balance—in short, present in the works of some of our most compelling writers including Whitman, Dreiser, James, Fitzgerald, and William Carlos Williams. American artists, however, have done more than simply champion the ideal with visionary expectations or denounce the failure of cities to accommodate pastoral values. Beginning with our first significant literary generation in the 1830s and 1840s, a number of leading writers have turned the ideal upon itself and in the process disclosed its contradictions. Probing it with a perceptiveness rarely found in the society at large, they have fashioned sophisticated responses to urban pastoralism that illuminate both its limitations and value as a cultural ideal. Significant in themselves, their insights nonetheless can be appreciated only in light of the development and staying power of urban pastoralism for Americans in general.

II

Although a number of writers deliberately have incorporated the ideal in their imaginative journeys through our society, not every manifestation of urban pastoralism in the general culture has stemmed from an intended involvement with it. Certainly few urbanites who plant gardens consciously seek to unite such abstractions as urbanity and rusticity or think in terms of a moral geography. This unconscious feature thus suggests that urban pastoralism functions as a myth, one of those many ideological structures which embody values shared consciously or unconsciously by a significant portion of Americans. A collective phenomenon, myth works, as anthropologists have shown, by reconciling antithetical cultural ideas in a way not always recognized by members of that culture. Similarly, urban pastoralism operates by fusing, sometimes on a subconscious level, divergent values central to American life: specifically, the continued nostalgia for rusticity amidst a tenacious striving for a more advanced urban civilization. While such a fusion may be important for all societies, it has seemed especially necessary in America where, as Michael Kammen has cogently argued, "unstable pluralism on a scale of unprecedented proportion" has engendered a pervasive inclination toward contradictory combinations and "paradoxical coupling[s] of opposites."[21]

This capacity to relieve cultural tension in part accounts for the continual appeal of urban pastoralism in America, but its strength can be explained only in part by its ability to satisfy collective needs. Because ideas are not entirely extrapersonal, getting at the attraction of urban pastoralism entails looking at the individual, and doing so suggests that the ideal draws a portion of its energy from the same source as the purely pastoral vision—the impulse to withdraw from an overly complex civilization into a life closer to nature. But as Freud pointed out in *Civilization and Its Discontents,* this impulse to return to nature, to the pristine conditions of isolated independence born of the desire for "the happiness of quietness," is only one of the drives influencing the individual, who also is impelled by the power of Eros and what Freud called the "reality principle" or awareness of external necessity—factors that he elsewhere suggested may have precipitated the development of early communities.[22] The individual thus is pulled simultaneously away from society and toward it. To balance these polarizing impulses he may choose an alternative to withdrawal; he may desire to remold the existing society in a way that eliminates or mitigates its oppressive elements and replaces them with others consistent with his wishes. As Herbert Marcuse has noted, drawing on Freud, the battle between discontent and the reality principle, between individual desires and group orientation, frequently "generates the wish that the paradise be re-created on the basis of the achievements of civilization."[23]

More recent developments in psychoanalytical theory suggest further reasons for such a choice. In his study of narcissistic personality disorders, Heinz Kohut reveals that many individuals suffer from "a deep sense of uncared for worthlessness" because they have failed to receive the kind of empathic reassurance required for the development of an integrated personality. Each individual, Kohut explains, needs to identify himself in group contexts available only within the social structure. Without such group identification, the individual remains in a solipsistic state, feeling isolated and experiencing an inner deadness.[24] To achieve or maintain emotional stability, the individual must try to fulfill this need for communal involvement even as he strives for individual freedom.

As both Freud and Kohut suggest, the healthy individual will successfully balance within the ego the conflicting desires for self-gratification and social identification by discovering a method for synchronizing those inward longings with the inevitable demands of the group to which he belongs. Concluding that "a good part of the struggles of mankind centre round the single task of finding an expedient accommodation . . . between the claim of the individual and the claim of the group," Freud, however, was not overly optimistic about the possibilities. "One of the problems that touches the fate of humanity," he explained, "is whether such an accommodation can be reached by means of some particular form of civilization or whether the conflict is irreconcilable." Leaving the question open-ended, Freud's comment reminds us of the very precariousness of the balance when achieved. As long as things go well with a person, such harmony is possible, but when things go wrong, when the polarization of desires intensifies acutely, the visionary impulse resurfaces. Whole peoples have responded to crises in such a way, noted Freud, particularly when the feel they are a chosen group or inhabitants of a chosen land. [25]

This polarizing tendency thus applies to cultures as well, as Karl Mannheim has argued. Dividing culture into two modes of ideation, to which he assigns the terms *ideology* and *utopia*, Mannheim identifies the very tension which powers the social dynamic. As he defines it, ideology constitutes a habit of mind which tends to view the present society complacently, obscuring its real conditions to entrench and stabilize its structure. By contrast, the utopian mentality, a product of discontent, opts for change by remaking society to fit its fantasies. Often motivated by a belief that the present way of life somehow has fallen away from a purer past, it seeks to reestablish that society by transferring its location to the future. Its ultimate goal is to synthesize the dialectic, making its utopian viewpoint the dominant ideology. When successful it is in turn subject to new utopian pressures, rein-stituting the dialectical struggle and repeating the process *ad infinitum*. [26]

Armed with these theories of self and society, we can begin to see where the appeal of urban pastoralism resides. By conceiving of cities that unite the best of urban activities with pastoral values, it addresses the desire for a way of life in which the personal conflict be-tween self-fulfillment and group identification and the cultural ten-sion between change and continued stability are reconciled. Though such thinking is contradictory, the ideal is especially engaging and believable because it does not renounce the demands of the group and the undeniable significance of urban life. Embracing the city and much of what it stands for, especially its sophisticated order and commitment to advancement, it seems more credible than pure pas-toralism with its overtly static, retrospective orientation. Indeed, the most compelling element of urban pastoralism may be that it wraps the ideal's own stasis in a progressive cloak. Combining wish fulfillment with an ostensibly realistic attitude, offering simultaneous visions of equilibrium and progress, the ideal possesses a mythic capacity for uniting antitheses on a personal as well as a cultural level.

Given this capacity, it is easy to see why the image of the idyllic city has played a role in thoughts about America almost from the moment of discovery. However, the psychological and mythic nature of its appeal suggests that such thinking is not uniquely American, and examples abound to support this assumption. The Garden City movement, which enjoyed a brief vogue in this country in the early twentieth century, actually originated in Europe, and if we go back to the seventeenth and eighteenth centuries, we can find that L'Enfant's plan for Washington and Penn's design for Philadelphia both drew on European precedents for including small parks and gardens in urban design. But if Americans have shared this ideal with others, it has displayed an intensity in this country rarely found elsewhere. Several reasons for this are implicit in what already has been said about native conditions. The exceptionally strong hold of urban pastoralism has resulted in part from the acute need for such myths in a culture characterized by an inordinate number of conflicting values. Then, too, the geography of America has encouraged such visions. For much of our history the untouched terrain, like a new Eden, beckoned with opportunities for fresh beginnings, for new ways of life that included new types of cities intimately connected to nature. Though that open landscape now is gone, the passionate commitment to ideas it inspired about urban life has become an integral part of our culture. But the difference in intensity between the American and European versions has resulted from more than the appeal of landscape and paradoxical inclinations. It is related also to the historically different functions of the city in each locale. In Europe the city developed as a socializing institution, the product of a settled landscape. In America the city, for the most part, was a domesticating influence, a foregone conclusion seen as necessary to tame and develop the land. As a result, the very function of urbanization in America, defined in relation to nature, encouraged urban-pastoral projections and lent to the American city an *ad hoc* quality attuned to visionary expectations.

Despite such differences in degree, however, it is impossible to ignore the parallels between Old and New World instances of urban pastoralism—parallels implying that American versions have drawn on a conceptual pattern extending beyond our own history. Freud's ideas about the origins of society indicate that such a way of thinking may have a long tradition stretching back to the mythologies informing early cultures. If so, then the history of urban pastoralism constitutes one example of the trend that historians such as Carl Becker have pointed to: the transformation in Western thought of religious and mystical values into secular social theories, made possible since the seventeenth and eighteenth centuries by a new ontology and novel vocabularies.[27] Stripped of their topicality, accordingly, American versions of urban pastoralism, including George's and Barlow's, reveal certain elemental ideas about the relation between urban and rural that have existed in Western society for over two thousand years. But unlike the rural ideal, which developed from Greco-Roman sources, the roots of urban pastoralism lie in the biblical visions of a reconstituted city, the New Jerusalem.

III

Appearing in a number of early prophetic books in the Old Testament, the New Jerusalem is an image of hope, a development promised to a people ravaged by turmoil, and nowhere is this image more central than in the Book of Isaiah. Written in the eighth century, Isaiah reflects the political conditions of the time, during which Aram, Assyria, and Egypt were engaged in a cataclysmic struggle for domination of the Fertile Crescent. Wedged precariously between were Israel and Judah, and the writer of Isaiah describes the effects of this holocaust on the chosen land: "Your country is desolate, your cities are burned with fire; your land, strangers devour it in your presence, and it is desolate, as overthrown by strangers" (1.7). According to the prophet, however, the true cause of its defiled cities and its desolate, infertile landscape is Israel's own internal corruption. God's chosen have immersed themselves in material pleasures, displaying a haughty demeanor and indulgence in adornment symptomatic of a great spiritual malaise. Because the faithful have put their trust in idols and the powers of earthly allies such as Egypt, to the neglect of Yahweh, they must be punished by pestilence, famine, and dispersal. Yet out of the catastrophe will emerge a new Israel and a New Jerusalem that will be called "the city of righteousness, the faithful city" (1.26).[28]

This renovation will be the work of Yahweh himself, but the people of Israel will play a part. Most of the prophetic books possessing this image depict the faithful on a spiritual journey in which they must foreswear the guilty past and return to a faith in their God to inherit the new Israel and a new world at the end of time. In its most pronounced versions, this revised environment will be nothing less than a paradise on earth. Beasts of prey will mingle with the lambs, fertility of the soil will be unmatched, and deserts will "blossom as the rose." At the center of this edenic landscape, atop a mountain, will be the New Jerusalem as the seat of authority from which the Lord will reign and to which all nations shall flow (Isaiah 35.1 and 2.1–3). In espousing this thought, several of the prophetic books repudiate the military state and conceive of a garden city dominated by peaceful, humble farmers.[29] Since the words *Jerusalem* and *Israel* are sometimes employed interchangeably in these writings, the implication is that the two will be inextricably related, each taking on the character of the other. Interestingly enough, in the eleventh century Urban II, while proclaiming the First Crusade, would draw the same conclusion, describing Jerusalem, "the royal city . . . situated at the center of the earth," as "the land . . . fruitful above all others, like another paradise of delights."[30]

Though the Old Testament image of the New Jerusalem has had an impact on subsequent Western ideas, its importance would not have been as great as it was had it not been absorbed so readily in Christianity. Most scholars agree that the vision of the Old Testament prophetic books played a significant role in early Christian writing, particularly in the Revelation of John, which uses similar imagery to render a vision of "a New Jerusalem, coming down from God out of heaven," as the center of a refertilized new earth following the millennial reign of Christ's second coming.[31] Whether the author of Revelation intended such a vision literally or figuratively has been a point of controversy for over two thousand years, but just how far it could be taken as a description of an actual future is evident from the response of early Christians such as the Montanists of Phrygia and church fathers such as Tertullian and Lactantius. In his *Divine Institutes* the latter maintained that with the millennium God would reign from a new holy city at the center of an edenic earth, where "rocky mountains shall drop with honey; streams of wine shall run down, the rivers flow with milk." The same type of chiliastic paradise was described by Irenaeus, who asserted that for God's faithful the blessings described in Revelation and the older prophetic books "shall have their fulfillment after the coming of Antichrist, and the Resurrection, in the terrestrial Jerusalem."[32]

Nor did belief in the millennial promise disappear when official church doctrine, guided by Augustine's arguments in *The City of God*, proclaimed that the redeemed city of prophecy was to be viewed as a metaphor for a purely spiritual state. Throughout the Middle Ages and into the Reformation, belief in the eventual reconstruction of an actual redeemed city situated amidst a renewed paradisiacal earth continued to hold sway among sectarians and splinter groups and even in some orthodox circles right up to the discovery of America.[33]

While historians long have recognized the prominence of the New Jerusalem as a recurrent metaphor or symbol for righteousness and salvation in Western thought, paramount for our purposes is the ideographical content of the image. When we consider the prophetic vision alongside such works as George's *Progress and Poverty* and Barlow's *Vision of Columbus*, the general correspondence in the design and values of each is striking. All employ a similar moral geography pivoting on an opposition between a fallen urban world cut off from nature or nature's God and a reformed one in which the union is restored. Displaying a future orientation, each has as its locus of value an urban milieu that merges with the surrounding countryside and even takes on the latter's characteristics, promising peace, prosperity, and freedom. Finally, all share an emphasis on corporate identity reinforced by an assumption of divine favor or uniquely endowed environmental advantages. The urban-pastoral archetype undeniably lies at the center of each.

This is not to say that differences are absent, since the visions of Judeo-Christian prophecy and the urban-pastoral pronouncements of Americans remain worlds apart in several ways. While the former proclaim a synthesis at the end of time, works like George's and Barlow's speak of a realization within a historical continuum. In place of a providential design, the latter draw on a progressive theory of history with man as the guiding hand. With the prophetic books in mind, we thus can see that American versions of urban pastoralism, such as those of Barlow and George, have adapted the ideal, passed down through Western thought, to the particular circumstances of their own ages and to the native scene in general. Some advocates of the ideal even have shown a partial awareness of that conversion, as did George near the conclusion of *Progress and Poverty* when he explained that the America he foresaw would fulfill "the glorious vision which has always haunted man with gleams of fitful splendor. It is what he saw whose eyes at Patmos were closed in a trance. It is . . . the City of God on earth."[34] That most Americans who have subscribed to the ideal have not been so conscious of the connection merely attests to the way the basic image has become endemic to Western, and especially American, belief. That it has taken such different shapes underscores the importance of paying due regard to the interplay between that persistence and the sometimes subtle, sometimes volatile transformations of the image.

The influence of urban pastoralism on American thought, therefore, cannot be understood solely by identifying its origins in Old Testament cosmology. To appreciate its centrality and power entails an awareness of its historical modifications, particularly in relation to New World conditions. Understanding that process and its ramifications, in turn, can illuminate the complicated explorations of the ideal by some of our major literary artists. For such writers were responding not to an antiquated ideal but to an image that continued to hold power, in new forms, for their contemporaries. The resulting dialogue between the culture and its artists over the viability of fusing the city and the garden has woven an important and richly textured pattern in the history of American ideas.

PART ONE

Geography and
the New Jerusalem

I

The Pastoral City
of Man and God

America and the European Imagination

America was discovered before it was conceived, but the conception
or identification of America consisted of more than a recognition that
this previously unknown land did indeed exist. To become a reality
America had to become a state of mind as much as a place, an entity
whose identity and existence depended upon its meaning. That
meaning emerged only slowly in the sixteenth and seventeenth centuries as Europeans responded to discovery and exploration by gradually applying traditional conceptions of place to construct several
different and sometimes conflicting images of the New World. For Europeans a number of Americas emerged, and one of them was a new
land where the dream of the pastoral city was a tantalizing possibility.

I

Although Columbus and Vespucci had described the New World as a
prelapsarian garden, an Englishman writing at home was the first to
conceive of it as a setting for a full-scale description of an ideal city
and commonwealth. There is little doubt that Thomas More's *Utopia*
(1516) was inspired in part by reports of the early explorers. The proof
lies not only in the references to Vespucci's voyages in the work but in
its overall mood: the exotic atmosphere that surrounds Hythloday's
narration and particularly the sense of wonder and awe with which
More invests his character's response to the new land. Anyone who
knows Columbus' journals, for example, cannot help noticing the parallels in the emotional constellations of each. While the inspirational
sources for the feelings in the two differ, the impulses are essentially
the same—the desire for fresh beginnings, for spiritual and emotional

rebirth in a new landscape radically different from that of the Old World. In *Utopia,* however, that landscape is not Columbus' untouched garden but an informing presence making possible the ideal urban society that forms the subject of Hythloday's impassioned narrative.

More's New World commonwealth is a literal urban garden, uniting city and country on the territorial level through its spatial arrangement. At a time when the enclosure laws had begun to remove open fields and displace rustics in England, More allows for substantial grazing and tilling space while allying it to the urban world of which all Utopians are members. Each city possesses at least twelve miles of arable land per side, making it entirely self-sufficient, though it is close enough to other cities to ensure comradeship and cooperation among them. Such spaciousness combined with an interdependent network of cities creates a stable society free from the internecine squabbles and expansionist ambitions of Europe so severely criticized by Hythloday in book 1. Although More is able to depict this stability only by minimizing or ignoring the effects of population growth upon available land—a problem already present in Europe in the early sixteenth century—he succeeds because, as Hythloday implies, the problem is irrelevant to the New World. When the Utopian population grows too large, the surplus plants a colony on the mainland where "the natives have much unoccupied and uncultivated land."[1] What More invokes here is a value that was to become central to American visions of the ideal city: a faith in the natural abundance of the New World and its capacity for ensuring that its cities will remain wedded to a rural order.

The synthesis of country and city on the territorial plane is replicated by the Utopians on the municipal level in their urban plan, originally drawn up by Utopus. Internal spaciousness mirrors the external expansiveness. Houses are built in blocks, the center of each square being devoted to a "broad garden" which the inhabitants till in common. What is interesting about the configuration is that it suggests a grid pattern for laying out streets at a time when that method of urban design was not yet widely used in Europe. The blend of grid and garden, of civilization and nature in the Utopian city, figures in a very concrete way the fulfillment of the urban-pastoral ideal expressed only vaguely in prophetic visions of the New Jerusalem.

The urban-pastoral topography of Utopia is complemented in the social arrangements of More's commonwealth. Recognizing the defects of his own land, particularly the fragmentation of society induced by a social smugness and sense of exclusiveness that had been developing among city dwellers since the Middle Ages, More extracts the root of the problem by eliminating specialization of trades. Although an agrarian economy is the cornerstone of Utopia, no one farms exclusively. As Hythloday explains, each citizen receives a country education, and while "men who take a natural pleasure in agricultural pursuits obtain leave to stay several years," most Utopians serve only a two-year tenure of husbandry before moving to one of the cities where they learn urban trades.[2] All Utopians thus lead lives that combine city and country backgrounds. By such an arrangement, More incorporates an agrarian life-style into the predominately urban world of Utopia.

For Utopia is an urban society despite its agrarian base. An elaborate system of trade and a commitment to technological advance, to poetry, philosophy, architecture, and astronomy, in addition to the simple pleasures of gardening, constitute essential elements of Utopian existence. Yet these elements are consistently integrated into a simplified life-style and freedom from luxury that epitomize the balanced goal of urban pastoralism: complexity without confusion, control with freedom, simplicity through sophistication. Although life is regulated, ordinances are few, allowing every Utopian to be an expert in the law. An essential feature of city life in Utopia is its lucidity. It is a giant urban village in which each citizen knows exactly where he stands in relationship to the society at large. No city or part of it remains sequestered since each person lives "under the eyes of all." In Utopia, the collective eye of the group replaces the eye of God in the apocalyptic visions of the New Jerusalem.[3]

Even the communal economy of Utopia is related to its urban-pastoral synthesis in that More's emphasis on economic sharing stems from an impulse common to most urban-pastoral visions: the desire to restructure present and future cities by recapturing a purer past. Just as the topography and social patterns of Utopia reintegrate the older agrarian ideals with urban life, the communal economy constitutes More's attempt, as Lewis Mumford has noted, to restore "the sharing and largesse that were common in simple communities before the introduction of a money economy."[4] Because of the great abundance in the New World, as exemplified in the society of its supposed inhabitants, the Utopians, communal sharing becomes plausible as a potentially workable social system.

In positing such an environment, More assuredly was influenced by a number of sources. Several elements of his utopia, especially its communal economy and its emphasis on justice, clearly have their roots in classical tradition, particularly in the ideal society described by Plato in *The Republic*.[5] Nonetheless, other factors suggest that Judeo-Christian eschatology also influenced the shape of More's urban-pastoral society.

As a devout Christian proficient in Latin and well read in the bible, More certainly was familiar with the visions of Isaiah, Amos, Ezekiel, and Revelation. To have lectured on Augustine's *City of God*, which More did in 1501, would have required a knowledge of millennialism and apocalyptic tradition, a supposition supported by his discussion of Antichrist and the day of judgment in the *Dialogue concerning Heresies*.[6] Though these facts and inferences in themselves do not prove that More was thinking of the prophetic books while designing his ideal commonwealth, when we consider them in conjunction with certain features of his imagined society, several connections appear.

Unlike *The Republic*, *Utopia* has no provision for a privileged warrior class. While the Utopians have wars, they have, literally following the biblical injunction, beaten their swords into plowshares. Even when they engage in conflict, their main tactic is psychological rather than physical, using agents to plant dissension among the enemy. In Utopia, the goal of peace that defines the New Jerusalem of Isaiah and Revelation assumes equal weight with the goal of justice defining the ideal cities of Plato and Aristotle. Additionally, More does not limit his vision to an enclosed, localized city-state. By encompassing an entire nation that subscribes to the ideal of human brotherhood, More's Utopia moves closer to the eventual universality of Judeo-Christian eschatology than to the isolationism of ancient Greece.[7] This extension, coupled with New World discoveries, allows More to create an air of geographical authenticity in his commonwealth. In *The Republic*, Plato never connects his ideal city to a terrestrial location; its existence is confined to its own articulation of an ideal. In contrast, *Utopia* and the prophetic visions of the New Jerusalem contain no such limitation. Both the Old Testament prophets and Christian millenarians always assumed the New Jerusalem to be a future manifestation in a specific location. Although literally "nowhere," More's Utopia similarly is located in space—in the New World. While More's geography is purposefully vague and the society projected upon it a fantasy, it is a fantasy imposed upon an actual place.

Even as he incorporates a verisimilitude paralleling millennialist visions, however, More repeatedly warns his readers that Utopia is finally no more than an imagined ideal by which to judge the present. Nor do the clues that he provides need extensive elaboration here. As numerous commentators have noted, there are continual contradictions and ironic implications in Hythloday's narrative.[8] More also utilizes the resources of language as a check against delusion by assigning Latinate names, with their etymological denotations of nullity and vapidity, to the commonwealth, its rivers, and its leaders. Even the name of the narrator, Raphael Hythlodaeus, reveals More's attitude since *Hythlodaeus* means "expert in trifles" or "well-learned nonsense." Equally telling is the structure More employs to frame Hythloday's narrative. By prefacing the description of Utopia with a dialogue between Hythloday and himself as a character, More creates a dialectic of ideas and values which remains with the reader as a continual critique of Hythloday's ideas. Fittingly, More allows his persona to comment briefly at the close of Hythloday's narrative that the features of Utopia are "easier for me to wish for in our countries than to have any hope of seeing realized."[9]

Though More was attracted to the idea of a society that fused rural and urban life, his decision to present Utopia as a pure fantasy stemmed from several factors. One was his personal conviction about the nature of man. As a sixteenth-century orthodox Christian, More simply could not believe that the evils plaguing humankind were entirely the products of political and economic institutions. Tempering his humanistic faith with a strong Augustinian strain of piety, More was convinced that man was a corrupt creature whose sinful nature made it impossible to reform society to create the ideal city. His other writings both before and after *Utopia* reveal More's belief that earthly situations, given man's fallen state, were beyond human control.[10]

While this conviction is important to More's ideas, it does not, however, account fully for his ironic qualification of his urban-pastoral society as a New World projection. After all, several of the reports up to that time had implied that the conditions of the new lands seemed to alter radically man's worldly state—to change almost his very nature. To understand More's skepticism we must turn to what can be called phenomenal reasons: the circumstances of the New World as they were known to More and his contemporaries.

What finally makes a poignantly ironic comment on Hythloday's report is the fact that in 1516 none of the news from America contained any information to warrant such extravagant visions of urban possibilities. Despite intense exploration, Europeans had discovered no magnificent cities nor had they built any of their own. While some port towns such as San Domingo had been established, they remained little more than makeshift outposts. The problem of credibility ran deeper, however, than the doubts resulting from an absence of examples. It flowed into the murky question about the very nature of the New World at the time.

In the age of discovery two of the most common European images of America involved contradictory interpretations of its natural conditions. To some the New World seemed to be a paradise restored, a veritable pleasure garden; to others it was a hideous wilderness where the European found himself, at best, uneasy.[11] But despite their ostensible difference, these two perspectives share a common feature—an anxiety about the New World, which remained only latent in its depiction as a paradise. The image of a garden continent had darker implications, and one who recognized them was Columbus.

Although the version of his journal which has survived deprives us of many of Columbus' exact words, the epitomizer (probably Las Casas) has managed to preserve the reactions of the admiral as he apparently recorded them originally. As he describes Columbus' response to the virgin beaches, he recounts how the admiral had thought himself returned to paradise. In Columbus' own words, the attraction of the landscape was so strong, "the songs of the birds . . . so pleasant that it seemed as if a man could never wish to leave the place." In itself the passage reflects a conventional response in the face of nature, conveying the sense that in that position a person somehow is restored to the sources of spontaneity, freedom, and joy. Under such conditions he becomes a different sort of individual whose values begin to change. Yet in this very idea of change and redefinition rumbles an uneasy implication. Implicit in the passage is a polarization of values which the epitomizer makes clear when he notes that "the Admiral was attracted on the one hand by the longing and delight he felt to gaze upon the beauty and freshness of those lands, and on the other by a desire to complete the work he had undertaken." Though we possess his insight only in paraphrase, we find in the journal Columbus' recognition of a startling fact about the New World: If, as a garden, it promised much that man lacked, it also threatened to obliterate what he valued. So powerful was the delight to "gaze upon the beauty and freshness of those lands" that the admiral found himself forgetting the "work he had undertaken." So compelling were the feelings engendered by the terrain that he discovered in himself the unconscionable desire to retreat from the responsibility and fidelity to which he had pledged his life and his voyage. Nor, Columbus records, were these feelings peculiar to him: "Many people [i.e., his crew] had asked me to give them leave to remain" rather than return to Spain.[12]

No doubt it is difficult for us today to imagine this strange mixture of delight and anxiety which Columbus evidently felt as he faced the green gaze of the virgin land. Nothing in our own experience can compare. It is the response of a man who recognized that the very fulcrum of civilization is responsibility, honor, and loyalty; who felt himself part of it; yet who was attracted to the opportunity, on a scale unmatched before or since, to withdraw from it. Though Columbus suggested the disturbing implications of that opportunity for someone like himself, he was especially suspicious of the havoc it could play in Europeans like Martin Pinzon, who were driven by greed and the desire for power. As Columbus recounts the irresponsibility of the captain of the *Pinta* in his maniacal quest for gold, his story becomes a sober warning of the dangers of freedom and plenty promised by the absence of restraint.[13]

The experiences of explorers such as Columbus revealed a startling fact about the newly discovered lands: If their wilderness conditions posed a danger, so did the enticements of their edenic freedom. Such a picture of the New World, by nature alien to a civilizing order, hardly could inspire unqualified belief that it would be the site of a reconstituted, redeemed urban civilization. That doubt, in turn, helped engender uncertainty about the meaning of America in the overall scheme of things. Without a clear sense of what the New World might become, it was impossible to develop precise conceptions of its significance in divine history. Why had God delayed its discovery for so long, and what was to be the relation of the New World to Christian Europe? Though these questions were asked, before 1520 no satisfactory answer had come forth. The absence of a providential context severely undermined the credibility of urban-pastoral projections upon the new land.

Considering these facts, we need not wonder that More withheld final approbation from his ideal commonwealth. Rather, in light of events, what is impressive was his ability to pay tribute to the ideal by investing it with a verisimilitude missing from earlier literary utopias. As the first attempt to confront the idea of urban pastoralism in an

American setting, his *Utopia* offered a vision of the New World that as yet lacked plausibility. In a hundred years the situation would change markedly.

II

The ideal of material plenty that More made central to his work reminds us that, from the start, this element of America had captivated Europeans. Long accustomed to limitation, they now faced a new land of abundant resources, enchanting flora and fauna, and idyllic pleasures. Yet the explicit uniqueness of the New World also announced the absence of many of the elements and values through which Europeans had come to identify life: the cities, arts, rudimentary technology, and monotheistic religion regarded as the hallmarks of civility. Even in its most appealing moments, the New World described in explorers' accounts seemed to be disturbingly antithetical to the environment Europeans knew.

In the 1520s and after, however, these reports started to change. Though some continued to stress a sense of alienation, others began to present a more conciliatory picture of the New World. Extensive exploration reduced anomie through discoveries, or so the explorers believed, that the New World was not entirely alien to the Old. Important factors were the stories told by Indians (and repeated by explorers as if they were truths) of spectacular kingdoms recalling the great urban civilizations of Europe and suggesting, perhaps, that the ideal city might be found in the New World. In the early 1530s Jacques Cartier recorded that the Indians around the St. Lawrence had spoken of the prodigious kingdom of Saguenay to the west, where "there are many towns and tribes of honest folk who possess great store of gold and copper," where "the natives go clothed and dressed in woolens like ourselves," and where "the men . . . are white as in France."[14] Nearly a decade before, similar claims about America has been verified to the south with Pizarro's discovery of the Incan Empire. But by far the most influential accounts equating the New World with the ideal city were the dispatches of Cortes, describing the discovery and conquest of Tenochtitlan.

In validating previous stories of a great civilization, Cortes' letters evince both childlike awe and calculated commitment to confirming the existence of everything which Europeans, in their fancies, had projected upon the New World. Repeatedly Cortes emphasizes both the wonderful uniqueness and reassuring familiarity of what he encounters. In coming upon the capital of the Tlascans, for example, he exclaims: "The city is indeed so great and marvellous that though I abstain from describing many things about it, yet the little that I should recount is, I think, almost incredible." What he does recount is the manner in which the city, in size and form, resembles Granada and is in fact superior to it. The city market, which attracts "more than thirty thousand people daily," contains utensils, earthenware, produce, and garments of "excellent quality, as fine as any in Spain." In the city are barbers and public baths and an "efficient police system" which maintains "good order." Cholula, another smaller city, possesses many of the same attributes. In addition, its topography allows Cortes his first opportunity to evoke the image of the ideal city with its blend of natural sufficiency and urban splendor. As he describes it, Cholula figures a complete harmony of the natural and civil—a "city [that] is very fertile, with many small holdings, for there is an abundance of land which is for the most part well irrigated."[15]

Even the greatness of these cities pales in comparison to the capital of the dominant tribe, the Aztecs. Everything about it, as Cortes records the details, suggests that here seems to be manifestation of the apocalyptic dream. Its very location recalls the archetypal image: protruding atop a great mountain plain, it nonetheless blends into the landscape, epitomizing the harmony of art and nature. Surrounding Tenochtitlan is a saltwater sea, which nurtures the city by providing food, while nearby is a lake of fresh water for drinking. The former has become an extension of the city through four man-made causeways leading over it to the mainland. As Cortes describes it, Tenochtitlan appears as a world in which the urban and the natural merge almost imperceptibly into one another.[16]

This synthesis is paralleled by the interior of the city. There Cortes finds replicated the best elements of European "high" culture:

> The city itself is as large as Seville or Cordova. The principal
> streets are very broad and straight, the majority of them being of
> beaten earth, but a few and at least half the smaller thoroughfares
> are waterways along which they pass in their canoes. . . .
> The city has many open squares in which markets are continually
> held and the general business of buying and selling proceeds. One
> square in particular is twice as big as that of Salamanca and completely surrounded by arcades where there are daily more than sixty

thousand folk buying and selling. . . . There are street porters such
as we have in Spain to carry packages.

The markets themselves are what attract Cortes' interest initially.
Their abundance is so great that the entire countryside seems contained therein. The Spaniard explains how "all kind of vegetables
may be found there," among them leeks, watercress, garlic, arti-
chokes, and maize. He describes "many different sorts of fruit including cherries and plums," fresh- and saltwater fish, pastries made from
them, eggs and fowls, and even "omelettes ready made." Indeed, he
concludes, "There is nothing to be found in all the land which is not
sold in these markets, for over and above what I have mentioned there
are so many and such various other things that on account of their
very number . . . I cannot now detail them." In one sense, this catalogue of plenty is not unusual; by Cortes' time it already had become
a standard device for describing the natural bounty of the new land.
What is unique in this case is that Cortes uses the device not to describe raw nature or even a rural landscape. While the imagery suggests the immense fecundity of the surrounding land, that fecundity
is linked to the city in the daily phenomenon of the market. Cortes
describes an urban world containing a garden of natural delights.[17]
· Nowhere is this image more evident than in the description of one
of Montezuma's chief residences, a magnificent palatial garden and
zoo. This palace, Cortes writes, "had a magnificent garden with bal-
conies overhanging it, the pillars and flagstones of which were all jas-
per beautifully worked." Within the garden are pools of water which
keep "every kind of waterfowl known in these parts" and an aviary
containing every type of bird "that is known in Spain, from kestrel to
eagle, and many others which were new to us."[18] An architectural
marvel stocked with the bounty of the local floral and fauna, the royal
palace epitomizes the kind of urban garden made possible by the abundance of the New World.

Less the exotic and more the blend of the familiar and exotic cap-
tures Cortes' imagination. He carefully notes how the cities and fields
resemble those of Spain yet, by their very uniqueness, are superior to
anything Spaniards have known. The Aztec capital especially im-
presses him with its hospitality to Europeans. There the entire "manner of living among the people" recalls "that in Spain." His recurrent
analogies between its facilities, size, and layout and those of Seville,
Cordova, Salamanca, and Granada only strengthen the connections.

Completing the parallels are the fashion and architecture of the Aztecs. Continually referring to their dress as "Moorish" and "Moslem," Cortes calls their temples "mosques." Surely such images evoked in Spaniards at home an idea of their own land, with its traces of Moorish culture. Far from representing a unique or alien environment, the geography of the New World becomes in Cortes' idiom an idealized version of Spain. Although part of what glitters in Cortes' eyes is the immense wealth of the Aztecs, which he foresees filling Spanish coffers, he embodies his description of this opulence in a larger pattern justifying and encouraging European settlement. [19]

Justification is the crux of Cortes' letters. If this new urban milieu seems to be an idealized Spain, the mention of the mosques also recalls the holy city in Palestine, long held by the Moslems. Cortes himself cultivates the association by noting that the city is so splendid "that not even the sultans themselves or other eastern potentates were surrounded by such pomp and display." Such connections allow Cortes to embellish his experiences by placing them firmly in the context of the quest for a redeemed Jerusalem. Tenochtitlan possesses all the salient physical features of the ideal vision of that city in the prophetic books, but like the actual city its spiritual center is rotten. Inhabited by infidels and idolators, it demands to be purged with a divinely inspired effort analogous to the Crusades. As Cortes relates it, the future of Tenochtitlan in relationship to Europe becomes tied to the fate of Christianity itself, and Cortes becomes a latter-day Crusader. Depicting the battle for the city as one between "Christians" and "pagans," Cortes' account takes the form of the *chansons de geste*, recalling the deeds of Christian knights. His troops, "fighting for our faith," attack under "the banner of the cross," the traditional symbol of the Crusader's vow. Their very success results from providential intervention in destroying Indian defenses, as Cortes explains at a crucial point in the battle: "Had not God broken their ranks twenty of them might have stopped a thousand men from mounting the tower." The corporate image of these passages is that of an army of God, divinely selected, achieving sacramental ends—a panorama which assumes the proportions of apocalyptic myth. Its message is that the ideal city will exist in the New World only after its pastoral topography has become part of the Christian hegemony—only, that is, after the European has made it his own. To be sure, such a conception of the European role in America was hardly the product of one mind. The crusading spirit, as Charles Braden has explained, was rampant among most Spaniards in the New World. But never before had any European confronted events which allowed such an explicit series of connections among the belief in a providential mission, the idea of the pastoral city, and the quest for a New Jerusalem.[20]

Just how much Cortes believed in what he wrote and how much was a conscious effort to employ the language of myth in justifying the capture of the city is difficult to say. Whether sincere or not, however, Cortes' letters presented both a justification for conquest and settlement and a paradigm for European ideas about America's providential appointment as a possible location for the ideal urban environment. The appealing implications in part account for the tremendous popularity which the second and third letters were to enjoy. Made public soon after they reached Spain, both were copied and printed in 1522. Shortly thereafter, they were translated into Latin and Italian and sold in Germany and Italy.[21]

Although they created immediate excitement, the most visionary pronouncements they inspired occurred later in the century. One Franciscan, Gerónimo de Mendieta, referred to Cortes as "another Moses in Egypt," the instrument of God "for opening the door and preparing the way for the preachers of the gospel in the new world." De Mendieta even went so far as to prophesy that Spain, led by the efforts of Cortes, would help inaugurate the millennial kingdom of Revelation in the New World. Interestingly, de Mendieta employed the opposition which later was to become standard in American conceptions of their special role: To the New World he assigned the creation of the true City of God while he relegated Europe, the haunt of the "accursed Luther," to the role of the City of Man.[22]

By 1600, largely because of reports like Cortes', such projections became more frequent in Europe, and literary men were quick to take advantage of them in their works. In their *Eastward Ho* (1605), George Chapman, Ben Jonson, and John Marston included a dialogue between one Sea Gull, a sea captain recently returned from America, and Scapethrift, soon bound for Virginia, which encapsulates this revised image of the New World:

> SEA GULL: I tell thee, gold is more plentiful there than copper is with us; and for as much red copper as I can bring, I'll have their weight in gold. Why, man, . . . all the chains with which they chain up their streets are massy gold . . . and for rubies and diamonds they go forth on holidays and gather 'em by the sea-shore to hang on their children's coats and stick in their caps. . . .

SCAPETHRIFT: And is it a very pleasant country withall?

SEA GULL: As ever the sun shined on; temperate and full of all sorts
of excellent viands: wild boar is as common there as our tamest
bacon is here: venison as mutton. And then you shall live freely
there, without sergeants or courtiers, or lawyers, or intelligen-
cers. . . . Then for your means to advancement there, it is simple, and not preposterously mixed. You may be an alderman there,
and never be a scavenger: you may be a nobleman, and never be a
slave. You may come to preferment enough, and never be a pan-
der; to riches and fortune enough, and have never the more vil-
lany nor the less wit.[23]

Here is a place where nature is both prodigious and completely domesticated (boars are equated with "tamest bacon"), where a man
can be part of society but nevertheless remain aloof from it, where
preferment and morality are not at variance, and where sophistication
(social advancement) and simplicity coalesce. In short, it is a pastoralized urban environment of streets paved in gold.

Of course, the conventions of the satiric genre in which they were
working indicate that the authors, far from offering Sea Gull's description seriously, were in fact deriding its assumptions. Their decision to include the scene at all, however, suggests that such an image
of the New World was popular enough to be ridiculed. It was, for instance, held by at least some of those who ventured settlement in
America, as William Wood affirmed in 1634:

I have myself heard some say that they heard it was a rich land, a
brave country, but when they came there they could see nothing but
a few Canvas Boothes and old houses, supposing at the first to have
found walled townes, fortifications and corn fields, as if townes could
have built themselves.[24]

By the second decade of the seventeenth century, the irony and
skepticism of More's Utopia were yielding to a conviction among Europeans that the New World could be the sight of thriving towns and
well-planted fields existing in idyllic harmony. The extent of this
change is especially apparent in the difference between More's stance
and that of the next major utopia set in the new lands: Tommaso
Campanella's The City of the Sun (1623). Though sharing certain features with his predecessor's work, Campanella's text, drawing upon
the revised conception of the New World, projects upon it an urban-

pastoral society unencumbered by the qualifications that had been unavoidable only a hundred years before.

As in *Utopia,* we learn about Campanella's society from a traveler, one of Columbus' Genoese sailors, who recently has returned from a voyage of discovery and whose narrative is rendered in a dialogue with a Knight Hospitaler. As the Genoese describes it, the topography and society of the City of the Sun display a compelling harmony of art and nature, with pastoral life-styles and values incorporated into an advanced urban environment. Built as it is on a promontory, which recalls the New Jerusalem, the city is laid out so that art carefully is married to the shape of the hill, allowing the inhabitants to move about on steps so formed that ascent is practically effortless. Even the seven walls, which separate the various levels of the city, testify to the inhabitants' skill in this area. Each wall is an impressive piece of architecture decorated by natural objects. The second wall is adorned with precious and common stones and metals, while on the third circuit "every kind of herb and tree to be found in the world is represented" and "specimens of each are grown in earthen vessels placed on the ravelins." On the fourth appear "all kinds of birds, their characteristics, sizes, and habits" as well as all sorts of reptiles and insects; the fifth has all "the perfect animals [i.e., mammals] of the earth in such great variety as to amaze you." The inhabitants are so adept in their art of drawing out similarities between natural and synthetic objects that the Genoese must confess his astonishment over the resemblances he saw. [25]

As with the Utopians, agriculture is an important pursuit among these citizens: "All the people go out into the fields with banners flying, with trumpets and other instruments sounding, equipped according to the occasion whether to hoe, plow, reap, sow, gather, or harvest." Their methods, however, are hardly backward or rustic since "everything is accomplished in a few hours." They have a knowledge of mechanics and currents which they have used to build field wagons "driven by sail; and when there is no wind, one beast is enough to draw even a large one—a wonderful thing!" In a like manner, the inhabitants tend small kitchen gardens around the city. [26] The result is a populace well exercised and strong of limb, whose beauty is purely natural.

While the inhabitants live in a pastoralized environment, their lives are not circumscribed by that way of existence. Although they regard agriculture as the noblest activity, "they consider the noblest man to be the one who has mastered the greatest number of skills," including masonry, blacksmithing, and architecture. The Solarians are urbanites who understand the need for power and learning, but what distinguishes them from their European contemporaries is the manner in which they exercise power. Because values and manners are so homogeneous, authorities rarely if ever must repress contumacy. There is literally no competition within the society and thus no need to turn power against another to exploit him. Strictly speaking, there are no poor and no rich, since all goods are held in common. Thus "all [are] rich and poor at the same time—rich in that they possess everything, poor in that they do not have possessions to serve, while all possessions serve them." All this is possible because the immense abundance of their land makes the City of the Sun economically self-sufficient. Through the Genoese's account emerges a composite impression of a society in which the autonomy and economy of rural culture is welded to the protective and ordered structure which Europeans traditionally ascribed to the city. It is an archetypal image reaching back through *Utopia* to the Old Testament prophetic books.[27]

Amid these parallels, however, a major difference exists between More's and Campanella's works, particularly in the overall tone of the latter as it emerges from the techniques and details. Gone, for example, are the Latinate proper names which More used to undermine the ostensible reality of his commonwealth. Gone as well is the strong countervailing incredulity that More incorporated through his persona. While Campanella structures his work as a dialogue, it contains no countervoice to undermine the credibility of its narrator. Campanella's Hospitaler functions only as a vehicle to prod the Genoese into chronicling the particulars of this delightful society. The wealth of detail the latter provides, unchallenged as it is by his interlocutor, suggests that such a society might actually exist in the New World.

This degree of credibility is perhaps the salient feature of the entire work, and Campanella enhances it in several ways. The most obvious is the manner in which he has his traveler come upon this urban garden. In *Utopia* we never quite learn how Hythloday has discovered the lands he tells about. We simply are informed that "after traveling many days" he and five companions "found towns and cities and very populous commonwealths with excellent institutions." In *The City of the Sun*, however, the Genoese's discovery is invested with particulars endemic to the age of exploration. In the course of his journeying, he tells the Hospitaler, he was "forced to put ashore" and to hide in a forest "to escape the fury of the natives." Even when he first comes upon some of the inhabitants of the city, he is wary, for the crowd he meets consists of "armed men and women."[28] The mood that emerges is hardly one suggesting immediate benevolence and incredible ease, as in *Utopia*. Instead, Campanella weaves into the situation the very tension recorded by explorers who saw the New World as a place of terror. The beginning of Campanella's *City*, that is, reads with the credibility of an actual explorer's log.

Yet the most compelling and important quality of Campanella's book—and the one that implicitly ties it to the hundred-year change in the conception of the New World—is the geographical realism of his depiction. In locating his city in Taprobana, Campanella had chosen to set his ideal environment in an actual place. Although Renaissance maps generally placed Taprobana in Sumatra or Ceylon, the parallels between certain details of Solarian society and the depictions of the New World contained in explorers' accounts indicate that Campanella was thinking about America when constructing his urban-pastoral vision.

The parallels first appear in the very name Campanella gives to his city. Although scholars disagree about its implications, one interpretation repeatedly offered is that Campanella was thinking of the cult of sun worship in Mexico. If so, then Campanella was deliberately connecting his city to an actual society described first by Cortes. That the plausibility of his own city increases through such a technique scarcely needs mentioning. Of course, this one allusion hardly proves that Campanella was relying specifically on Cortes' descriptions of Tenochtitlan as a model for his city. Cortes refers to sun worship only once in Letter 3, and there only obliquely. Furthermore, Campanella might have drawn on any number of other works which contain the same information in more detail, including the histories of Bernal Diaz and Las Casas. Specifically, scholars cite Giovanni Botero's *Relationi Universali* as the primary source for Campanella's information about the New World. But when we compare the topography of the City of the Sun and that of Tenochtitlan, as Cortes describes it, the relationship between the two works becomes evident.[29]

Both cities are built on an extensive plain. Just as Tenochtitlan is linked to the mainland and other smaller cities around it by four causeways, so too are the separate sections of Campanella's city connected "one to the other . . . by four avenues and four gates." Even more striking is the parallel between Cortes' description of Montezuma's palace and Campanella's account of the rings of his city. Montezuma's aviary, filled with more birds than Cortes can name, reappears along the fourth wall of Campanella's city in the form of paintings of "all kinds of birds" known to man. Whereas the Aztec emperor has zoological gardens of tropical plants and caged "lions and tigers," the inhabitants of Campanella's city have live specimens of every plant along the third wall and pictures of all the larger animals of the earth on the interior of the fifth.[30] Simply too close to be fortuitous, these parallels indicate that Campanella conceived his pastoral city in the context of American developments. By borrowing images from Cortes, who had connected his venture to the mythic quest for a New Jerusalem, Campanella is able to imply that his own utopia constitutes another chapter of that saga, now carried to the New World.

Campanella, however, does not stop there; he takes these details as the basis for ascribing to his city a strongly European character. Absent among the inhabitants are the rich ornamentation, loincloths, and delicately wrought capes of feathers characteristic of the Aztecs. Instead, the solar citizens wear undergarments, socks or half-buskins, and boots as well as togas. Their technology is exemplarily European: they build cannons and water clocks and use gears to drive machinery. Their intellectual life is modeled on the classics of Greece and Rome, while in spiritual matters they worship one "God in the Trinity" and conceive of sin, in an Augustinian manner, as the absence of good.[31] By interweaving these elements, Campanella suggests that his city is not just Tenochtitlan. It is a city blending the best of the New World with that of the Old—a city which, if not yet manifest, nonetheless could emerge in the new-found land.

Yet when we consider these implications in relation to Campanella's own comments about his work, a question emerges. In other writings Campanella refers to *The City of the Sun* as "a dialogue on his own state"—an imaginative model by which the shortcomings of Naples could be delineated and reforms urged.[32] Given that purpose, what are we to make of the authenticity with which he invests his narrative and the apparent contradiction between its ostensible setting in Taprobana and its borrowings from those very reports that promulgated a new mythology for America?

To answer that question, I believe, we must dispense with any notion that for Campanella the condition of Europe, events in America, and worldwide exploration were unrelated. Although concerned with the condition of Naples, Campanella was heavily invested both in the westward-looking tendency of the age and in the more mystical and eschatological elements of Christianity. In his *Monarchia Messiae* (1633) he affirmed that soon would "appear that golden age which Christ came to restore, as predicted by prophets, poets, and philosophers." Asserting that "this age already exists at the present time, even though it does not appear to be so," Campanella expected a physical manifestation of that state on earth—a harmonizing of discordant elements into the golden world promised by the prophetic books. Appropriately enough, Campanella's Solarians hold much the same view as they "await the renewal of the world" when "the world will be uprooted and cleansed, and then it will be replanted and rebuilt."[33]

For Campanella that renewal was intimately related to extensive exploration and American developments because all were part of an overriding providential design. Nothing makes this clearer than the final pages of Campanella's book where his interlocutors become complementary voices articulating the larger meaning of what the Genoese has narrated. Both identify the opening of new lands, through the efforts of Columbus and "the Spaniards [who] discovered the rest of the world," and the spreading of the true faith, made possible by men like "Hernando Cortes, who established Christianity in Mexico," as a divine plan for the earth "so as to unite it all," as the Hospitaler explains, "under one law." What he has learned about the City of the Sun, adds the Genoese, helps confirm "the great changes that will be produced"—changes that will "transform the world completely and renew it." Having the Hospitaler conclude from what he has heard that "we know not what we do but are instruments of God," Campanella suggests that the fates of Europe and previously unknown lands are united.[34] The ultimate value of New World cities of the sun will be their role in establishing a millennial new earth where the urban-pastoral promise will be fulfilled.

Such a claim was possible because, by 1620, America had been conceptually transformed. Surmounting the doubts of the early explorers, some Europeans foresaw the New World as a future ideal environment in which sacred and secular history would unfold conjointly. For them the vision of the garden city was not confined to expectations of urban development redeemed by rustic touches. In their conception, the New World offered a pathway, charted by Providence, to a future society uniting the advantages of urbane, communal existence with the bounty of a domesticated natural paradise.

Latent in the American strand was another, better Europe, where the dream of the pastoral city could be realized.

III

Though increasingly embraced in the early 1600s, the urban-pastoral vision of the New World raised a question that no European was capable of answering: just how and when this new environment would eventuate. Among the more sober-minded, moreover, such visions seemed little more than fantasies. These individuals, despite the increasing hopes about America, recalled reports describing "this land as the one God gave to Cain," a land of "boisterous Boreal blasts mixed with snow and hail in the months of June and July."[35] But even among those who fancied themselves realists appeared a growing proclivity for describing America as an edenic environment hospitable to advanced European civilization. By 1611, one of the most skeptical, William Strachey, was accounting a stretch of Virginia as "ample and fair country" precisely because the terrain seemed to invite urban development. To Strachey, the value of Kecoughtan lay in its potential to become a "delicate and necessary seat for a city, . . . being so near,—within three miles by water of the mouth of our bay,—and is well appointed a fit seat for one of our chief commanders." This call for the construction of cities was to be a recurring theme in the writings of Virginians through the seventeenth century, some of which display flights of rhetoric recalling millennialist visions. To one concerned cleric, writing in 1662, the settlers' "dispersed manner of Planting themselves" had resulted in a failure to conduct worship, build churches, and establish an ordered environment. To redeem this spiritual and social desert, the cleric urged the bishop of London "to acquaint the King with the necessity of promoting the building [of] Towns in each County of *Virginia*." Through this effort, he believed, "the poore Church (whose plants now grow wilde in the Wildernesse) [will] become like a garden enclosed, like a Vineyard fenced, and watch'd like a flock of Sheep with their lambs folded by night, and fed by day; all which are the promised fruits of well ordered Towns." Although the images here are extravagantly poetic, they describe not an atemporal or aspatial arcadia, but an actual environment of the future. Amidst the peculiar conditions of the New World, the language implies, the felicity and harmony previously confined to pastoral poetry become the "promised fruits of well ordered Towns."[36]

Drawing on the conceptual paradigm first applied by Cortes to an actual location in the New World, Europeans in general and Englishmen in particular were arguing the same point with increased frequency in the first three decades of the century. Although the Spanish example had provided the impetus, the British began asserting that Spanish efforts were a mere prelude to the truly successful work to be done by England. As William Haller has demonstrated, since the last three decades of the sixteenth century, the British had been developing a sense of themselves as a nation specially selected by God to carry out his work, and promoters such as Richard Hakluyt began in the early 1600s to identify colonization as an extension of England's divinely appointed mission.[37] If the Spanish, Hakluyt argued, "in their superstition, by means of their planting in those parts, have done so great things in so short space, what may we hope for in our true religion." John White was to make the same argument the controlling theme of his *Planter's Plea,* declaring that "this Nation is in a sort singled out unto that worke; being of all the States" most fit for the task.[38]

Inspired by such rhetoric, some Englishmen began entertaining the idea that their efforts could lead to the millennium. White himself felt that colonizing America and converting it to Christianity assuredly would be a prelude to "the coming of Christ in the flesh." Several years later a similar idea was put forth by the Reverand William Twisse. While thinking about "our English Plantations in the New World," Twisse inquired, "Why may not that be the place of the New Jerusalem?"[39] Repeatedly one finds working its way into the literature of colonization in England the belief that the fulfillment of sacred history attended upon British settlement of the New World.

The striking repetition of values and images that constituted such mythologizing of America in the sixteenth and seventeenth centuries resulted because Europeans were drawing on a common legacy: the language and millennial expectations of a paradisiacal New Jerusalem. Inspired by a lush, fresh landscape that seemed like a new promised land, they borrowed biblical images to envision a future in which the garden and the city would be harmonized. As the imagery was buttressed by invocations of providential design that united sacred and secular history, Europeans created a theography for the New World that made such descriptions increasingly credible. In the transatlantic ideography that developed, the New World had supplanted the Old as the place God had ordained for the creation of an urban-pastoral society.

II

New England's Jerusalem
Millennialism and the Puritan *Urbe in Rus*

Among those who looked to the New World with expectations of an urban-pastoral society, none had greater hopes than the Puritan settlers of New England. Although the harsh treatment they received in Britain from Anglican bishops, coupled with the threats of James I to harry them out of the country, made their move to America as much a necessity as a choice, the Puritans of the Bay seized upon the situation as a divinely appointed opportunity that would lead to the New Jerusalem. Identifying their migration as a religious errand, "a heavenly translation from corrupt to more pure churches," they buttressed this sacred obligation with a worldly sense of mission. [1] Conceiving of themselves as God's elect, charged with a task of reformation that included social regeneration, they envisioned their churches as part of a society built according to the revealed will of Providence. When the Puritans spoke of their New Jerusalem, therefore, they meant it in several senses: at once a spiritual state of individual regeneration, a holy congregation of visible saints, and a social construct attuned to the prophetic promise.

The Puritan definition of their errand as a divine mission of a chosen people moving toward the New Jerusalem had several advantages, not the least of which was its usefulness in providing them with an identity that justified their errand. But the idea of mission also enabled them to reconcile the hitherto conflicting images of the New World. For the Puritans brought with them a fluid conception of environment that went beyond identifying America as a wilderness. Although historians repeatedly have emphasized the horror in Puritan reactions to New England, the idea of the New World as a garden—

47

and hence as a fit site for the pastoral city—also played a role in their response to the land.

John Winthrop, for one, recorded his first reaction to America in his journal with words that hardly convey a sense of a man facing a hideous wilderness. While still aboard ship, he noted how "we had fair sunshine weather, and so pleasant a sweet air as did much refresh us, and there came a smell off the shore like the smell of a garden." If this were the only instance of such a response among the Puritans, we might dismiss it as a momentary indulgence in fancy. But two days later, after landing in New England, the governor-elect repeated the image more explicitly in a letter to his son:

> For the Country it self I can discerne little difference betweene it and our owne. we have had only 2 daies which I have observed more hot then in England here is as good land as I have seene there but none so bad as there Here is sweet aire faire rivers and plenty of springes and the water better than in Eng[land] here can be noe want of any thinge to those who bring meane[s] to raise out of the earth and sea.

Far from finding New England an impenetrable desert, Winthrop described it as superior to England in its edenic splendor. A similar response came from the Reverend Thomas Welde for whom America was "as goodly a land as ever mine eyes beheld. Such groves, such trees, such an air as I am fully contented withal and desire no better while I live." Nor were these remarks confined to the earlier settlers before they experienced the harsh winters of New England. Nearly a decade after the first arrivals and only one year after the bloody Pequot War, George Wiswall lauded New England as "a fine land, good for corn, . . . good for pasture, and good hay land, [with] plenty of wood. It is a pleasant country to look upon." By the third generation, Cotton Mather could repeat the claim, extolling "the brave Countries and Gardens which fill the *American Hemisphere.*"[2]

These examples do not imply that the Puritans were essentially primitivists, expecting a life of relaxed solitude in a natural garden. As Winthrop's remark reveals, they recognized that "noe want of any thinge" will come to "those who bring meane[s] to raise out of the earth and sea." The words suggest that for the Puritans America was a *potential* garden—a world requiring human activity guided by providential design. The American wilderness was not just a static territorial obstacle for them but a theographic threshold inviting development as part of God's plan for his chosen people in a chosen land. Through such a perspective they were able to resolve the tension between the images of America as a wilderness and as a garden, between its hostility toward civilization and its hospitality to it. Edward Johnson was to make the point this way in 1654: Though New England had begun as a "desolate and barren Wilderness," through "the Lord in his wonderful mercy" the land had "becom a second England for fertilness in so short a space, that it is indeed the wonder of the world." For Johnson and other Puritans, however, the Lord's work did not end with the transformation of forests into cultivated fields. Nine years after Johnson's remarks, John Higginson pointed out that the progress of New England from "small beginnings to great estates" included not only agricultural growth but the creation of towns and seaports filled with "shops and ships." If the new land seemed at first inimical, events proved that it was being turned into a "well-ordered Commonwealth" blending fertile farms and thriving towns.[3]

Into such a developmental concept of a malleable America fit perfectly the urban-pastoral ideal in its original biblical context. Through such an application the Puritans could read their errand as an enactment of the biblical quest in all its salient details. If the New World was to become a new Canaan, a veritable land of milk and honey, it nonetheless contained dangers as did the original promised land. But those dangers need not deter. To those who spoke "ill of this Countrye, of the barrennesse etc. of it," Winthrop replied, "so did the Spyes of the lande of Canaan," yet Canaan had become the site of the holy city. Now New England (and by extension America) was to enjoy the same blessing. "We cannot imagine," wrote Cotton Mather, "that the brave Countries and Gardens which fill the *American Hemisphere* were made for nothing but a *Place for Dragons.*" On the contrary, he continued, "There are many arguments to persuade us, That our Glorious *Lord*, will have an *Holy City* in *America.*" What was necessary was a purgation of the new land analogous to that enacted by the Israelites. As a result, the Puritans would themselves be cleansed. Just as God had "carried his people into the wildernesse, and made them forgett the fleshepottes of Egipt," wrote Winthrop, he was now leading them to America away from the "fleshepottes" of Europe.[4] The Puritan quest for the New Jerusalem thus became a reenactment of an archetypal journey pattern: a movement away from corruption, through the wilderness and its attendant hardships, toward social and spiritual redemption. But as the Puritans saw it, their errand, read typologically, was to be the final mission of God's elect to build the foundation of the ideal city which had eluded humankind for so long.

Nonetheless, the Puritan desire to leave behind the fleshpots of the Old World did not mean abandoning their commitment as English Protestants. Anxious to avoid the charge that their errand was a mere hegira, they defined themselves as the vehicle by which England and ultimately the rest of the world would be renovated. New England, proclaimed Cotton Mather, was the vanguard of the providential plan for "the *General Restoration of Mankind* . . . and the opening of that scheme of the *Divine Proceedings,* which was to bring a blessing upon all the *Nations of the Earth.* "[5] On the map of God's global history, the Puritans charted their journey toward the pastoral city of visible saints.

I

Perhaps in no single document do so many of the Puritan ideas about the ideal community coalesce than in Winthrop's *Model of Christian Charity,* delivered aboard the *Arabella* before the first major wave of settlers had landed. It is here that Winthrop invokes the "Citty upon a Hill" to describe the Puritan community and in the process affirm the dual nature of the Puritan quest: to "seeke out a place of Cohabitation and Consortshipp under a due forme of Government both civill and ecclesiasticall."[6] Instructing his charges in the efforts needed to achieve that end, Winthrop constructs what amounts to a symbolic geography defining the special form and position of this new community.

In "these extraordinary times" of carving life from the new land, explains Winthrop, many will find their "brothers [to] be in want" and so must be ready to practice a charity far beyond the ordinary. Although Winthrop identifies the landscape as a rugged wilderness against which a breastwork of corporate communal action must be raised, he also defines the wilderness as a malleable environment that can become a new Canaan where "the Lord will be our God and delight to dwell among us, as his people." A "community of perills calls for extraordinary liberallity and soe doth Community in some speciall service for the Churche," especially when it is formed "by a mutuall consent through a speciall overruleing providence." *Community* is the operative word for Winthrop in his repeated emphasis that "the care of the publique must oversway," though not eradicate, "all private respects."

With this emphasis, Winthrop clearly does not envision New England as a collection of isolated farms or as a place of independent, individualized opportunity—the pattern of value eventually embodied in the agrarian ideal. Conceiving of settlement as an enterprise in cohabitation, Winthrop identifies the Puritan community as a collocation of urban social structures. The untouched landscape demands a civilizing order that will be at once collective and hierarchical to ensure "the preservacion and good of the whole." In this society some people will be "highe and eminent in power and dignitie; others meane and in subieccion" so as "to hold conformity with the rest of his [i.e., God's] workers."[7]

When Winthrop, by this last association, incorporates the city on the hill into the entire texture of God's creation, he defines it as more than a product of human civilization. It becomes in his vision a component of God's synchronized order that includes nature as well. The very language he uses reinforces the connection. Despite his awareness that the wild terrain of this new world presents dangers, he invokes natural imagery to illustrate the form of this future society, identifying it as a construct which must follow the combined imperatives of the "lawe of nature" and the Gospel. The community, he explains, is a body, a biological organism, and "the ligementes of this body which knitt [it] together are love." Though conventional, the choice of such a trope and the fact that it appears in more than one phrase signal an implicit conceptual pattern. The images suggest that for Winthrop the Puritan community is to be an organic entity, metaphorically duplicating natural processes. As such it will achieve a harmony among God's works, including nature and civilization, in accordance with providential design.

When Winthrop, therefore, explains that the Puritan settlement "shall be as a Citty upon a Hill," he means it in several senses, informed by an underlying urban-pastoral geography. At once a literal city and a holy community, populated by God's own people, it also will be a complete milieu, reconstituting the entire New England landscape. Moving between a literal and figurative meaning of *city*, Winthrop brooks no division between town and cultivated field, city and country, human society and natural law. His "city" is at once a single settlement and the entire colony, all being part of the community of love. What will make it possible is providential guidance and human effort wedded to New World opportunities. For if the untouched landscape is a danger, it also is a boon, since it enables the Puritans to build their society "not . . . with the ordinary meanes whatsoever wee did in England" but with resources that will lead to a truly cooperative society. Divine direction united to the American promise of a fresh start, geography merged with urbanity—these provide the hinges on which Winthrop hangs his idea of the holy, organic city.

By taking this position Winthrop is able to define Puritan settlement in terms of its relation both to the primitive landscape of New England and to the Old World, which becomes the "corrupt city" where the "enemies of god" are waiting for the Puritan experiment to fail. But if, in Winthrop's urban-pastoral geography, the Puritan community is symbolically central, located between the hypocritical, worldly civilization of Europe, where truth remains "in profession onely," and the unimproved terrain for which a dispersed pattern of rural settlement will not suffice, the city on the hill is also morally prior. As Winthrop makes clear with his closing statements, the "model" of which he speaks is the Puritan community itself. Since "the eies of all people are uppon us," the city on the hill can serve as an example to the rest of mankind, an illuminated precursor in God's overarching plan. Echoing in these last remarks the words of Isaiah, who prophesied that the new Israel and the New Jerusalem would be "a light to all peoples to open eyes that are blind," Winthrop firmly connects his vision of settlement to its biblical roots. In his lay sermon resides the Puritan belief that the fulfillment of sacred history depends upon the creation in New England of a divinely ordained urban-pastoral society.

What is compelling about these ideas is the way the Puritans, for a time at least, managed to translate them into social actualities. Part of the success lay in the relative homogeneity of the population. In New England there were no Court and Country parties to foment regional antipathies as in England. The presence of Indians and some Negro slaves, as Richard Slotkin has explained, "made racial difference a more obvious and important source of social distinction than that between farmer and city man."[8] The need for collective cooperation in the early years especially contributed to a deemphasis of geopolitical distinctions that had caused discontent in the Old World. Services provided by the towns, including road building and the maintenance of adequate wheelwrights, cobblers, and blacksmiths, made them essential to the lives of the farmers.

Beyond the fortuitous homogeneity of the group and its common purpose, New Englanders also took deliberate action to guarantee that their society would blend the most agreeable features of the New World (its space and abundance) with those of the Old (its pattern of order and habitation). By 1635 they had superimposed the latter upon the former to produce a new type of city plan and political unit: the township. The distinctiveness of the township as a political construct lay in its operation. Consisting of the united resources of several towns, villages, and the open country surrounding them, it provided an effective cooperative network for performing civic and governmental functions while abrogating the usual division between rural and urban. It also furnished a method of promoting a reasonable degree of conformity in religious polity. As a plan for laying out towns, apparently developed by Thomas Graves, it was a device particularly suited for harnessing the bounty of the open land by employing social patterns with which the Puritans were familiar. The township consisted of a central meetinghouse surrounded by the inhabitants' houses arranged in a grid pattern. Farm lots belonging to the residents formed a contiguous boundary around this inner square; farthest from the meetinghouse were commons for grazing. The major advantage of the plan, which served as the basis for a number of towns including Cambridge, was that it was oriented toward an agricultural economy while still providing the solidarity, security, and order that Elizabethans associated with city life. Most important, the township symbolized concretely the social and even metaphysical values which informed the Puritan quest for a city on a hill. For the Puritans, as Sylvia Fries has suggested in her study of colonial urban development, may have derived the rectangular shape of the township from biblical descriptions of the New Jerusalem contained in Ezekiel and Revelation.[9]

The success of the first ten years of Puritan settlement encouraged them in their venture and prompted echoes of Twisse's question about New England: "Why may not that be the place of the New Jerusalem?" But if Twisse's words revealed an immense hope, they also suggested an important qualification intrinsic to the biblical version of urban pastoralism—a qualification shared by New Englanders in the seventeenth century. No one—not even the Puritans of the Bay, despite their confidence in their errand—knew for certain what kind of success (or failure) Providence had determined for the saints within human history. Even Increase Mather, one of the staunchest exponents of the mission, could wonder in his more dolorous moods whether New England would become, not the New Jerusalem, but "the woefullest place in all America, as some other parts of the World once famous for Religion, are now the dolefullest on the Earth, perfect emblems and Pictures of Hell."[10] More than the inscrutability of Providence, however, determined the New England version of the New Jerusalem. The belief that man was a fallen creature, incapable of his own salvation, and the accompanying conviction that nature had been corrupted by Adam's sin, placed important restrictions on the Puritan vision of the ideal city as a product of human history.

Because of these factors the Puritans did not conceive of their effort to build the New Jerusalem as an attempt to achieve a harmony with nature per se. The city on the hill, conceived as an environment uniting rural and urban forms, possessed significance as a symbol for the kind of harmony promised in the New Jerusalem. While such a design may have embraced nature in its desire for completeness and balance, it was not predicated upon a faith in nature as a touchstone of value. When Samuel Danforth set out to define again in 1671 the purpose of the Puritan errand, he argued that New Englanders had departed from their homes just as John the Baptist had gone out into the desert to withdraw "from the envy and prosperous zeal of such as were addicted to their old Traditions"—to move "off from worldly pomp and vanities" epitomized by the urban societies of the Old World. As Danforth defined it, the migration had been a movement, not toward nature, but *away* from "Babylon." For the Puritans, the American landscape was valuable primarily as a context for an opportunity, the success of which depended on providential favor.[11]

Although such a conception allowed the Puritans to conflate sacred and secular history by measuring their errand on the scale of divine time, it did so only up to a point. While they applied the prophetic symbol of urban-rural harmony by referring to all of New England as a "holy city" or a "New Jerusalem," the place of peace promised to the faithful, they recognized that "New England," as Jonathan Mitchell reminded his congregation, "is but earth and not heaven and therefore not exempt from the machinations of the devil" or the terrors and strife of penury. As long as the colony and its center, Boston, existed in a fallen landscape and remained a part of secular history—a history marred by sin and turmoil—it would be impossible for it to become the New Jersualem. At best, wrote Cotton Mather, the record of New England would constitute merely a "history of some *feeble attempts* made in the American hemisphere to anticipate the state of the New-Jerusalem, as far as the unavoidable *vanity of human* affairs and *influence* of Satan upon them would allow of it."[12]

Apologists of the New England way, however, could not believe finally that the fate of God's people could end in such abysmal stultification, since they conceived of defeat as a prelude to victory. To be resurrected one must first die, and the Puritans envisioned the ideal city in similar terms—a variation of the archetypal death-to-life journey implicit in the Judeo-Christian version of urban pastoralism. For the Puritans, the ultimate journey was not spatial but temporal, ending in an exodus from the confines of human history. Drawing on the prophetic tradition and new methods of biblical exegesis, they invested their errand with significance by describing it as a prelude to the apocalypse, which would eradicate secular time and initiate a new world and new city in the millennium.

II

Although renewed interest in millennialism had been developing in orthodox Protestant circles since the early 1500s, it became feverish in the seventeeth century owing to several factors. One was the growing dissemination of Protestantism, which seemed to signal the downfall of Antichrist (i.e., the papacy and Satan) and the imminence of apocalypse. Another was the discovery of the New World, which, in exposing the entire globe to Christianity, appeared to fulfill one of the primary requirements of Revelation for the descent of the New Jerusalem from heaven. A common assertion in Europe and New England was that the discovery and settlement of America were the workings of God in "this last age."[13] Equally important were novel techniques in biblical exegesis evolving back in Europe, especially through the work of Joseph Mede. Drawing on Mede's writings, particularly his *Clavis Apocalyptica* (1627, translated into English in 1642), biblical exegetes in England devoted such efforts to John's book that by 1649, according to one contemporary source, over eighty full-length studies on the apocalypse and millennium had been published in that country alone.[14]

In New England, the growing interest in millennialism constituted an essential component of Puritan ideas from the very beginning of settlement. Because of their convictions about human limitations and their countervailing belief in being a chosen people, in fact, the Puritans were impelled toward the apocalyptic promise, particularly in the form historians have come to call premillennialism. By maintaining that the New Jerusalem would materialize only after a divinely directed cataclysm had remade the world to produce a regenerate nature and a beatific city, premillennialism provided them with an eschatology that promised fulfillment outside the ravages of a secular history stained with sin.[15] Apocalyptic expectations thus enabled the Puritans to retain faith in their errand as a necessary final stage before the coming departure from history.

In the early years, several Puritans sought to affirm the connection between the Massachusetts colony and the paradisiacal holy city of millennial prophecy. In his *Wonder-Working Providence of Sion's Savior in New England* (1654), Edward Johnson identified the building of the Bay Colony as a prelude to the last great battle between the forces of Christ and Antichrist, which would precede the creation of a new earth and new society. Then, Johnson explained, invoking the traditional image of rural-urban synthesis, "shall the time be of breaking Speares into Mattocks, and Swords into Sithes," as a "universall Government will then appeare" administered in the holy city established upon earth. Above all, averred Johnson, New England "is the place where the Lord will create a new Heaven, and a new Earth in, new Churches, and a new Common-wealth together." What is noteworthy is that Johnson's ideas were neither eccentric nor idiosyncratic. As several historians have noted, the convictions of the *Wonder-Working Providence* were representative of the time. In the early years, many New Englanders expected their capital to be the site of the New Jerusalem on a reconstituted earth to which "Christ would come in person and live with them for a thousand years."[16]

Despite these facts, in the first thirty years of the colony millennialist texts did not appear with the frequency one would expect. In general, extended discussions of last things are confined to Johnson's book, a few works by John Cotton, and texts such as Ephraim Hurt's *Whole Prophecie of Daniel Explained* (1644), Thomas Parker's *The Visions and Prophecies of Daniel Expounded* (1646), and William Aspinwall's *A Brief Description of the Fifth Monarchy* (1653).[17] Only after 1660, and especially near the end of the century, did millennialist themes and visions of the New Jerusalem begin to appear in a large number of works by New Englanders.

Occasionally during the last forty years of the century, a layman would broach the subject of the apocalypse with a fervor epitomized by Samuel Sewall's *Phaenomena quaedam Apocalyptica* (1697). There Sewall set out to demonstrate *"that the set Time draweth very near for our blessed Lord Jesus Christ to be Recognized and Crowned KING of Kings & LORD of Lords"* and that the *"New World . . . stands fair for being made the Seat of the Divine Metropolis."* Sewall, in fact, seems to have been obsessed with the idea of the New Jerusalem and the need to prove that America would receive it. His diary makes references to conversations with ministers such as George Burroughs concerning its eventual appearance, and his activities included the formation of a club which addressed itself to the arcana of biblical prophecy.[18]

Among the ministry occurred the greatest increase in expectations of a millennial new earth and a beatific society. John Davenport spoke of *"a Political Kingdom of Christ* to be set up in the *last times,"* while Thomas Shepard confronted the question of last things in his *Parable of the Ten Virgins Opened & Applied.*[19] The ministers who had the greatest hand in inaugurating a period of intensive and extensive prophetic speculation were the two Mathers, Increase and his son Cotton. Neither, however, got all his ideas on this subject together in one place, not even Cotton in his massive (and unpublished) "Triparadisus." Instead, both kept returning to it again and again, circling old ground and adding new landmarks as they delimited their visions of the final days.

To ascertain the Mathers' ideas of apocalypse, accordingly, requires piecing together a number of their works, although giving separate accounts of their millennialist perceptions is unnecessary, because their beliefs and ways of expression were essentially similar. Both men held that in the last period of human history, which "is near," Christ will descend from the heavens, chain the devil and his "Eldest Son" (i.e., the Roman See or Whore of Babylon), and commence a terrible conflagration of the earth. Neither the faithful nor the earth, however, will be exterminated. The former will be raised for a time above the flames, which "will not be [for] the *Destroying* of the Earth, so much as the Reforming of it." After the purgation, the saints will return for a "thousand years of holy rest" upon earth, which will have undergone a "glorious renewal" in that it *"will be restored to its Paradise state."* Both Mathers believed that the new earth "will be a true *Eutopia*" for the saints, who will enjoy a life free from disease, hunger, and suffering in an agricultural paradise that will constitute "something better than, *A Golden Age.* " Concurrently, according to the two Mathers, *"Jeru-*

salem shall be Literally Rebuilt." But the holy city will not appear just anywhere. "When New Jerusalem should come down from heaven" to be the center of this urban-pastoral milieu, "*America* will be the seat of it."[20]

These millennialist visions of a New Jerusalem wedded to a paradisiacal earth are significant not because they contain elements which were unconventional (the sequence of images had become rather standard by the last quarter of the century), but because of the intensity and frequency with which both Mathers promulgated their visions. The array of titles denoting works by the two dealing with last events is, in fact, staggering: Increase's *The Day of Trouble Is Near, Ichabod, The Mystery of Israel's Salvation, A Discourse concerning the Uncertainty of the Times of Men*; Cotton's *Theopolis Americana, Remarks upon the Changes of a Dying World, Things to Be Look'd For,* "Triparadisus," and numerous others. For father and son alike, a literal holy city situated amidst the lush green landscape of a renewed earth was imminent in America at the end of time. Indeed, for Cotton, belief in the New Jerusalem of "a thousand years" was more than a personal creed; it was central to the true Christian canon, to the entire Reformation, and to the meaning of New England.[21]

Although constituting the most strident version of millennialism in New England, the Mathers' disquisitions reflected the interests of a substantial number of clerics during the last third of the seventeenth century. The sermons, tracts, and pamphlets issuing from colonial presses in this period reveal a rising tide of anticipation, an intensification of apocalyptic emphasis, which made it central to the ministerial concept of New England's future. What is remarkable, however, is that visions of final events grew to such significance in the last years of the century even as New England was enjoying immense prosperity. The wilderness had been subdued, Boston had developed into a provincial metropolis of 6,700 souls, the fishing and shipbuilding trades were flourishing, and agriculture was thriving. Nowhere in history had there been a more dramatic instance of sudden growth from an almost primitive settlement to a semi-urban society. Nor were the ministers blind to this change. The Synod of 1679 included in its message a statement marveling at the manner in which "the Lord (by turning the Wilderness into a fruitful land) brought us into a wealthy place . . . having cast out the Heathen." "If we look abroad over the face of the whole earth," asked the collected voice of the ministry, "where shall we see a place or people brought to such perfection and

considerableness in so short a time?" On the religious plane, the ministers had hammered out an effective congregational polity and the
church was thriving. By the 1680s the number of full church members
had grown significantly.[22] Such facts, indeed, suggested the very fulfillment of the dream which had impelled the first settlers.

Given New England's situation after 1665, no one answer can explain the clergy's expanded interest in millennialism. In part, the fervor can be attributed to the delay between the development of new
exegetical techniques and their dissemination in America. Then too,
contemporary events, including the English Civil War and the great
London fire of 1666, fomented rumors that the apocalypse was drawing near. Perhaps more important, however, was the very success New
Englanders were enjoying in the New World. Paradoxically, that success was beginning to raise doubts among divines about the fate of the
colony—doubts causing them to meditate increasingly about a paradisiacal earth and godly city beyond human time.

III

Although signs of success in New England might reasonably have
been construed as indications that God was preparing his people for
the new earth and holy metropolis they would inherit in the coming
millennium, apocalyptic writings after 1665 display no such sanguine
interpretations. In the last three decades of the century, few ministers
were willing to claim that the current state of New England showed
signs of progress toward the millennium.[23] Instead, many of the clerics
complained that religion was being made subservient to worldly interests. According to Cotton Mather, New England was confirming
the old adage that "Religion brought forth Prosperity, and the *daughter*
destroyed the *mother*."[24] As they surveyed their thriving colony, the
ministers contended that its mission was degenerating beneath a
growing materialism and emphasized the need for a divine cataclysm
to cleanse the world in preparation for the New Jerusalem.

Since the story of New England's declension has been frequently
told and often debated by historians, the question here is not whether
declension was actually as extreme as the ministers claimed or
whether they truly believed that it was. The first probably cannot be
determined definitely, while the written record suggests that the clergy
was convinced its assertions were valid. The point, rather, is that belief in declension, as a function of New England's prosperity, pro-

foundly contributed to increased interest in the chiliastic version of urban pastoralism after 1665. A major theme of millenialist writings and the jeremiads, those sermonic diatribes castigating degeneration while affirming the special role of the colony, was the lament that New England had departed from the idea of the harmonious, integrated society articulated by Winthrop and epitomized in the township plan. Facing a changing environment, the ministers alleged that their towns were becoming overcivilized Babylons. Instead of producing a cooperative effort to build a holy city and turn the wilderness into a garden, growth and prosperity were dividing rural and urban, rending the social fabric of New England, and creating a playground for Satan. "The Devil was never more let *loose* than in our *Dayes*," warned Cotton Mather, "and it proves the *Thousand Years* is not very far off.[25]

Although the clergy saw the threat of declension everywhere, Boston bore the brunt of their harangues partly because, by the 1660s, that city had become something of a social and topographical oddity on the New England landscape. As Darrett Rutman has shown in his history of Boston's first forty years, the early settlers had intended to establish a single town as a localized embodiment of the city on a hill.[26] Unfortunately, in the first year that goal was frustrated when the Puritans, threatened by French attack from the north, had to abandon their initial settlement at Charlestown and scatter to a number of locations. One of those was the Shawmutt Peninsula, the eventual site of Boston, capital of the colony and new embodiment of the goal. Despite its growth, however, Boston never succeeded in drawing back all the scattered settlers, though an attempt was made in 1631.

Part of the problem was that the Shawmutt Peninsula lacked sufficient arable land to accommodate the goal of establishing an urban society based on an agrarian order, as conceived in the township plan. The failure to maintain a single, integrated community was further compounded by the arrival of new settlers at the capital. The limited land did not provide enough space for all the new families, and by 1635, as William Hubbard related retrospectively, the peninsula was so "overpressed with multitudes of new families, that . . . there was a necessity that some should swarm out" into the hinterlands.[27]

If Shawmutt's limited land helped frustrate a primary goal of the first New Englanders, it was to have an even greater impact on Boston itself and its relation to the rest of the colony. As Boston grew into the center of the New England economy, its lack of land, coupled with its strategic position, impelled its inhabitants to turn increasingly away

from agriculture to the occupations of shipbuilders, tradesmen, arti-
sans, and merchants. The transformation from a sparsely populated
rural settlement to a bustling commercial seaport had proceeded so far
by 1650 that only in the Common and in an area to the south remained any traces of a rural order. By 1660 the town had grown to a
population of three thousand and had assumed the characteristics of
an English port city. One writer, John Josselyn, went so far as to compare it to London, an analogy that undoubtedly disturbed those who
continued to view that city as an embodiment of "the fleshepottes of
Egipt."[28] Boston, with its twin satellites of Salem and Charlestown,
was becoming a community vastly different from the rest of the
colony.

In particular, the presence of a thriving, upwardly mobile merchant
class was beginning, by the 1660s and 1670s, to produce effects
highly disturbing to apologists of New England. As the merchants'
wealth grew, so did the display of power and luxury. Attempting to
emulate their London connections, merchants and others growing in
affluence began to build stately mansions, don periwigs, have their
portraits painted, and ride about in sedan chairs and spring carriages,
the latter being the latest trend in transportation from Restoration
England. Although by today's standards periwigs and sedan chairs
hardly seem disturbing signs of social deterioration, to the ministers
and certain laymen of seventeenth-century New England such phenomena graphically bespoke a swelling material pride—signs of overcivilization traditionally identified as a threat to the urban-pastoral
ideal. And by the 1660s and 1670s, spokesmen for the New England
way were saying as much. "Surely this day *New England* is sick," exclaimed Thomas Walley, and "the great reason many are *Unquiet* is
because they do not think they are high enough." Though the increasing prosperity of the entire colony was creating a material pride "that
doth abound everywhere," particularly disquieting to a minister like
Increase Mather, himself a well-respected Bostonian, was the marked
prevalence of that "iniquity" in "a particular manner in this great
Town."[29]

The merchants, however, were not entirely to blame, if that is the
correct word, for the secularization and transformation of Boston. As
it grew, the capital began to take on a heterogeneity distinct from
both the inland rural settlements and its own homogeneity in the
early years. The effects of the Restoration, particularly the Crown's
desire to consolidate its colonial holdings, included the influx into

New England of a new group of royal agents not particularly sympathetic to the goals of the Puritan founders. Because their concern was to regulate and exploit the economic products of the colony, most of these individuals settled in the coastal trading towns, particularly Boston. Its role as a seaport also exposed that city to a growing number of transients, notably sailors, who were hardly pious or model citizens. "The Seafaring part of the Flock," recorded Cotton Mather in his diary in 1717, has "degenerated into all possible Stupidity and Malignity" and "come to such a tremendous Degree of Desolation, there must be more attempts to awaken them unto due notice thereof."[30]

Money was to be made from this worldly-minded clientele, however, and a number of Bostonians quickly seized the opportunity, further promoting the transformation. Taverns, inns, and alehouses increased in number, and a new species of vice, the brothel, made its appearance in 1672—all to the consternation of the ministry. Although authorities tried to regulate these "iniquities" in Boston, the problem went deeper than mere regulation. There was, quite simply, no way to reverse the complex flow of events which was changing the face of Winthrop's city on a hill—no way, that is, if the colony wished to survive economically and politically. That fact, however, did not stop New Englanders from lamenting those changes or their results, as William Bradford did when he complained that a major "cause of our decline here / Is a mixed multitude, as doth appear."[31] Although Bradford was bewailing heterogeneity throughout the colony, there can be little doubt that he was thinking especially of Boston, where that diversity was most pronounced.

Bradford, in fact, was one of the first to employ a theme that was to become common by the end of the century: the idea that Boston had regressed from the golden days of its early years. According to Bradford, in a verse entitled "Boston in New England," that city began humbly, during which time the inhabitants

> drank freely of thy spring
> Without paying of anything.
> We lodged freely, where we would.
> All things were free, and nothing sold.

But now, because "trade is all in your own hand," Bostonians are enamored of "sordid gain" to the point where Bradford must admonish them to "oppress not the weak and poor" in the rest of the colonies.

Greed, "drunkenness," and "excess," he warns, are propelling Boston down a precipitous path away from "truth and justice." What is interesting in these lines is Bradford's tendency to depict the early life of town and colony in images of pastoral, almost semiprimitive felicity, contrasting it to the overcivilized, avaricious urban society of the present.[32]

Cotton Mather struck a similar note almost fifty years later in his *Magnalia Christi Americana*, particularly in "The Bostonian Ebenezer," which begins his monumental history of New England. According to Mather, the "sins of Sodom," including "ignorance, profaneness, and bad living," have gotten footing in Boston, creating a nefarious atmosphere. "Can't you remember," he asks the older generation, "that *in your days* those abominable things did not show their heads that are now *bare-faced* among us?" Marveling that God has not yet destroyed Boston as he did Sodom, Mather accentuates the theme of degeneration by placing this sermon just before he begins his lives of the founders—lives rendered as examples of simple, almost rustic virtue. Winthrop, for Mather, becomes a paragon of temperance who "abridged himself of a thousand comfortable things," while John Norton is depicted as living at a time when Boston had been a "garden." In the *Magnalia*, builders of the Bay Colony are the pillars of an urban-pastoral society in luminous contrast to the divisions, apostasy, and worldliness of the present.[33]

If Cotton Mather marveled at the absence of divine wrath poured upon the city, however, Solomon Stoddard out on the frontier saw with clearer eyes. For Stoddard, the outbreak of King Philip's War in 1674 bore the imprint of divine judgment upon all of New England in retribution for "that intolerable pride in clothes and hair; the toleration of many taverns especially in Boston." Later, in surveying the state of the colony, including its material preoccupations and the depressed economic conditions among the western farmers, he indicted the merchants of coastal towns such as Boston for "sell[ing] their goods at excessive Rates" and cheating country buyers.[34] According to Stoddard, Babylon had reappeared in New England, and the whole countryside was suffering for it.

What ministers like Stoddard and magistrates like Bradford were pointing to was the replication in New England of a problem supposedly left behind in the Old World: a political, economic, and social opposition between rural and urban environments. Their statements implied, too, that the old distinction between the fallen and redeemed cities had a disturbing relevance to Massachusetts. Nor was this awareness confined to these two figures. The bewailing of regional divisiveness was a major theme in such jeremiads as John Higginson's *The Cause of God and His People in New England* (1663), Thomas Walley's *Balm in Gilead* (1669), and Urian Oakes's *New-England Pleaded With* (1673), which excoriates the "*bitter Contentions and unchristian Distances and Divisions* among us" and the "*sides* and *parties* and factions" in the various "Societies amongst us." It surfaces also in Cotton Mather's *Present State of New England* (1690) and in his *Magnalia*, which bemoans the "*piques* between some leading men . . . [which] had *misled* all the neighbors far and near into unaccountable *party-making*." Like the other ministers, Mather identified regional contentions, antithetical to Winthrop's goal of an organic society, as a major flaw of New England. [35]

Without getting into the full problem of declension as fact or fiction, it should be noted that the subject of these laments was not entirely the product of overactive imaginations in the ministry. Bernard Bailyn, Richard Bushman, Michael Zuckerman, and other historians of the colonial period cogently have demonstrated that antagonism between town and country and among regions, exacerbated by increased movement to the outlands which weakened communal cohesion, grew as New England moved into the eighteenth century. The merchants of the coastal towns, because of their trade, felt a much greater affinity with England than with the western settlements, while the settlers of the west, resenting their economic subservience to the urban east and adhering to a tradition which T. H. Breen has called "persistent localism," increasingly resisted Boston's control and sought instead a local political autonomy. Apparently the situation had become so disturbing by 1689 that the General Court had to publish a declaration instructing "the several towns within the jurisdiction" of Massachusetts and their rural hinterlands to "take care to avoid factions and quarrels." [36]

The central irony in New England's changing scene was that the ministers who bemoaned the divisiveness, materialism, and moral reprobacy were themselves partially responsible for the manifestations. That responsibility involved more than the contradictions Perry Miller identified in the Puritan code preached by the ministers—a code which, by encouraging diligence in labor and the creation of a prosperous society, helped foster social mobility, cultural heterogeneity, and concern with worldly gain. It inhered as well in the inflammatory effects of the conflicts and denunciations in which the ministry was engaged. On the theological front Solomon Stoddard and the Mathers, all of whom stridently denounced regional contention, nonetheless promoted it by engaging in a ten-year battle over open communion: Stoddard speaking for the Connecticut valley, the Mathers for Boston and Cambridge. In 1700, when Cotton Mather urged greater control of the churches, country parsons denounced the plan as a tyrannical presbyterianism foisted by a benighted Boston ministry.[37] When addressing economic and social matters, the clergy indirectly created their own version of a moral geography of oppositions within New England, as exemplified in Stoddard's remarks on the exploitation of yeomen by the urban merchants and Cotton Mather's diatribes against Boston. Since Mather himself was a staunch Bostonian, his harangue in no way can be construed as that of a rural advocate, yet it contained many of the same implications. Because Mather argued that Boston had fallen away from the simpler, more pastoral life of its first years, he indirectly lent credence to the belief that the lives of the western inhabitants, whose rustic settlements more closely resembled those of the founders, were in greater harmony with the original purpose of the colony. Such intimations, published at a time (1700) when regional differences were becoming more and more pronounced, undoubtedly reinforced the idea that Boston had taken the wrong path and that true piety and morality remained alive in the villages and isolated farms far removed from the capital.

Yet few if any of the ministers saw the role they were playing in fomenting regional antagonism. Instead they saw only the results. Faced with a colony which, they felt, was becoming increasingly fragmented and devoted to carnal ends, not a few ministers came to believe that presenting the specter of apocalypse might motivate a return to the ideal. If, as Thomas Shepard posited, "carnal security" was the first sign of "spiritual slumber," "one special way to prevent and remove security" was "by daily setting before" the people "the last and great coming of the Lord." Of course, ministerial interest went beyond using the apocalypse as a mere rhetorical prod. Divines such as Shepard, Davenport, and the two Mathers were firmly committed to the promise. The Bible had prophesied that the pattern of history was part of a larger, providential plan ending with success, and the ministers ardently believed that New England was to play a prominent role in that pattern. Faith in a millennial New Jerusalem, therefore, could serve as a psychological balm, as Cotton Mather admitted: "And until the

Peaceable Kingdom of our Lord Jesus Christ arrive, let the prospect of it, *comfort us,* under all the *Sufferings of this present time.* " If New England was divided, if ungodliness abounded, these phenomena only confirmed the long-standing conviction about man's inability to make things right and the need for divine intervention.[38] With one final act, God once again would unite the saints in a holy urban-pastoral community, centered in the New Jerusalem, and achieve what humankind on its own was powerless to produce.

In this sense, the millennialism of the last part of the century marked a departure from the earlier apocalypticism of men like Cotton and Johnson, who viewed the current scene as a positive prelude to the new earth. Although continuing to affirm the nexus of sacred and secular history, the ministers of the last three decades in effect weakened the link by stressing that the New Jerusalem would appear only after human time had been obliterated. Even as they maintained that America was a fitting site for the holy city, they argued that contemporary degeneration demanded nothing short of a divine purgation before the urban-pastoral paradise of Revelation could commence.

Of course, no one knew for certain when those events would transpire, but the inscrutability of Providence did not preclude conjecture. Cotton Mather, through careful correlation of Revelation and historical events, boldly predicted that the millennium would commence in 1697. When it did not, Mather was not despondent; he merely juggled his authorities to announce 1716 as the year of the apocalypse.[39]

Needless to say, history was to have the final word. The millennium did not arrive in 1716 nor in 1724, despite Mather's claim in that year "that there is nothing [now] to hinder the immediate Coming of our Savior." By that time, however, it was becoming increasingly evident that millennialist expectations were losing their relevance for the majority of New Englanders. Instead, the major concern of the colonists manifested itself more clearly in a 1720 tract by John Colman. Colman, too, decried the dissipations of Boston but not because they signaled a religious decline or betokened the apocalypse. In lieu of the ministerial response, Colman denounced these habits as hazardous to the New England economy because they produced a deficit in the balance of trade. Meanwhile, in an unpublished manuscript, Cotton Mather confided that New Englanders "will have no more Apprehension of any mighty and sudden *Change* to come upon the world," pri-

marily because others were "deluding them into an Imagination, of
Happy Times to arrive, & be Long Enjoy'd . . . upon earth, before the
coming of the Lord. In a word, *All* [are] *fast* asleep!"[40]

Looking back from the vantage point of nearly three hundred years,
we can decipher fairly clearly what had gone wrong. The problem,
which ministers like Mather seemed unable to perceive, was that the
old millennialist idiom had become outworn, inadequate for expressing feelings commensurate with the developing life in America.
While millennialism would continue to play a role in sermonic literature well into the next century, though in a new form conventionally
referred to as postmillennialism, it would not be the driving force behind future urban-pastoral projections. For even as postmillennialism
posited a thousand-year reign of peace achieved through human action, without a cataclysmic intervention by Providence, it assumed
that future would result, not from man's initiative, but from the infusion of divine grace through mass conversion. It remained an essentially passive ideology, relying on a more subtle but nonetheless
essential intrusion by Providence. While man could act to inaugurate
the thousand years of peace, his actions were in no way independent
nor would they eventuate in new types of social institutions or reconstituted physical landscapes. As a result, postmillennialism lacked
the elements needed to function as a catalyst for environmental
change.[41] Continuing to emphasize spiritual regeneration in an
increasingly secular age, the ministry simply was incapable of defining a meaningful alternative to the apocalyptic version of urban
pastoralism.

What was necessary was a fresh context for the ideal, based upon a
new attitude toward history and an entirely different concept of nature and man's relationship to the world. During the eighteenth century such a context would be formed—one that would free the urban-
pastoral ideal of America from its apocalyptic moorings and place its
achievement within the province of human history.

PART TWO

The Garden and the Secular City

III

Civilization and the Order of Nature

The Eighteenth-Century Ideal

The eighteenth century witnessed a change in the conception of urban pastoralism from an essentially ahistorical accomplishment of Providence to a secular, historical possibility. As we have seen, in the sixteenth and early seventeenth centuries, writers had begun to appropriate for depictions of America the biblical imagery of the millennialist city and some of the feelings connected with it. But when presented without connections to divine history and millennial expectations, that image had been shrouded in irony or satire. It was impossible to take the idea seriously as a social goal as long as nature and man remained tainted with the idea of sin. For a new concept to emerge both nature and man had to die and be phenomenologically reborn.

Although Europeans had been developing a new fondness for nature and landscape during the Renaissance, not until the late 1600s did these feelings receive a theoretical framework. Through the early efforts of natural scientists such as Francis Bacon and astronomers such as Galileo and Copernicus, nature was beginning to lose its identity as an opaque, fallen substance beyond human ken. Employing direct, empirical observation that revealed a magnificently ordered cosmos behind and within natural phenomena, the new sciences led Europeans by the end of the seventeenth century to redefine the universe as a great mechanism permeated by rationality and reflecting a divine, unchanging God. As a result, nature achieved an ascending dignity as a tutelary phenomenon equal if not superior to holy writ. To confront the great book of nature was to peer into the divine mind and read its immutable laws recorded there. By the eighteenth century the old assumption of nature's corruption was anathema, inconsistent with the idea of an unalterable, rational God and the discoveries of the new sciences. But if nature was becoming the new bible, the new priests were men like Newton and Boyle, individuals who revealed the power and integrity of human intellect and became almost demigods in the mythology of the age. As Alexander Pope was to announce, getting the prevailing feeling into a couplet, "Nature, and Nature's Laws lay hid in Night. / God said, *Let Newton be!* and All was *Light.*"[1]

Implicit in Pope's couplet was a new idea about man himself, one which was evolving in England by way of France and Germany. As early as the end of the sixteenth century, thinkers such as the Catholic priest Pierre Charron began to redefine humankind, not as inherently corrupt, but as morally regenerate because of its very nature. "Men are naturally good, and follow not evil," wrote Charron. "Nature in every one of us is sufficient, and a sweet mistris and rule to all things, if we will harken unto hir, employ and awaken hir." Among Protestants a similar idea started to unfold, particularly in England. By the middle of the next century, Anglicans were dispensing with rigorous predestination and the idea of man as intrinsically reprobate, to the point where Richard Cumberland, an Anglican bishop, asserted in 1672 that "man has a natural tendency toward benevolence by virtue of his physique, his intellect, and his affections."[2] But if these writers were providing a philosophical plinth for a new idea of man, it took John Locke to construct the theoretical mortar and brickwork for a fully developed concept based on the new empiricism.

Though raised a Puritan, Locke had come to believe, through his association with Arminians and Remonstrants in England, that Adam's legacy consisted solely in the curse of mortality. To assume more, Locke contended, was simply inconsistent with the idea of a rational, logical deity. Employing this belief in conjunction with the new empiricism, Locke argued in his influential *Essay concerning Human Understanding* (1698) that man receives knowledge totally through sensory perception and that the human mind at birth lacks innate ideas, being simply a blank slate waiting for an imprint. In effect, Locke's theory implied that all men, of godly or ungodly parents, are equal at birth and begin life with commensurate opportunities. The difference for each individual is the environment to which he is exposed.

A short jump from such a theory, particularly as deists and other rationalistic philosophers seized upon it, lay the assumption that humans were not just ideationally neutral at birth but ontologically neutral, or even moral, as well. Because man's faculties are free and not determined, these thinkers claimed, man is capable of reasoning logically and acting morally. Supported by Lockean epistemology on the one hand and the writings of liberal divines on the other, English deists such as William Tindall proclaimed that "Man, as our Divines maintain against Hobbes, is a social creature, who naturally loves his own species, and is full of pity, tenderness, and benevolence." Such a belief, as Carl Becker has noted, became the sine qua non of eighteenth-century philosophes, deist and nondeist alike, who "knew instinctively that 'man in general' is naturally good, easily enlightened, disposed to follow reason and common sense . . . above all a good citizen and a man of virtue."[3]

A corollary of the new faith in man and nature was the growing tendency to view human history as an ever-increasing spiral of accomplishment and to postulate the perfectibility, within time, of both man and his institutions. Even before the work of Locke and Newton, this idea had surfaced in some intellectual circles. Recent work in the history of progressive thought, especially by Robert Nisbet, amply has demonstrated that forerunners of the idea existed as far back as the eighth century BC and that other antecedents can be found in the writings of the early church fathers and in the Middle Ages. Yet as Nisbet himself points out, not until the Enlightenment and the decades leading up to it do we find articulated the modern idea of progress with its belief that steady, continuous advancement was probable and even inevitable as a product of man's own capabilities. By the early eighteenth century, owing primarily to the advancements in science and the new faith in human nature, intellectuals were confident enough to claim, as Leibniz did, that "a perpetual and unrestricted progress of the universe as a whole must be recognized."[4]

Under the aegis of this progressive theory, past failures or occasional regressions could be explained away, not as the products of sin in man and nature, but as momentary irrationality and superstition caused by man's failure to follow natural law. For the enlightened mind, man's sin thus became a "sin" against himself, an anthropological error which he could expiate by bringing his institutions—including his most notable one, the city—in line with the laws of nature. For the eighteenth century, the goal of a pastoralized urban milieu, freed of its biblical-millennialist moorings and buoyed by the theory of progress, began to attain an immediacy and historical credibility it never had possessed before.[5]

74

I

Although the new ontology of man and nature and the progressive theories emanating from Europe were to have a profound effect throughout America, the colonies to the south of New England were the first to experience their impact. Part of the reason for this greater receptivity was that those colonies were settled primarily by Anglicans, who did not hold as tenaciously to the idea of predestination and human depravity. Because they maintained that the law of nature and nature itself were as significant as the Bible for revealing God's will, the Anglican clergy in Virginia and the Carolinas were much more amenable to the fashionable, liberal philosophy emerging from England. When the College of William and Mary was founded, it immediately became a bastion for the new ideas about man and nature almost a decade before they were "corrupting" the undergraduates at Harvard.[6] Additionally, these colonies, despite their Anglican majority, collected a much more heterogeneous group of inhabitants from the very beginning, making it ostensibly more difficult for southern settlers to conceive of themselves as an elect people operating under a unified religious purpose.

I say "ostensibly" here because the difference between the North and the South was not as sharp as it first appears. In the early decades of Virginia's settlement, the immigrants were as sedulous as New Englanders in anchoring their colony to the providential rock, as is evident from a letter from the Company and Council of Virginia, which described settlement as "an action concerning God, and the advancement of religion." Similarly, an anonymous promotional tract entitled *The New Life of Virginia* claimed in 1612 that by colonizing Virginia, Britons would be "preparing the way of peace (so much as lies in you) before the second coming of that King of peace." These words are striking in their thematic similarity to those issuing from New England. Both posit colonization as a stairway to an exit from history and conceive of settlement as a religious activity of an elect people. As stridently as Cotton Mather could Virginians such as Alexander Whitaker ascribe success of the colony to "the finger of God [which] hath been the only true worker here."[7]

We are closer to an understanding of the times if we view the difference between Virginia and New England as one of degree and not kind. Both infused the secular with significance by linking it to the sacred, both assumed that they were a specially chosen people, and both were impelled by visions of an ideal society. The distinction between the two colonies involved the amount of weight placed on each side of this secular/sacred balance and the time at which the balance began to shift toward the secular as the new values of the Enlightenment were laid upon it. It is unnecessary, however, to speak abstractly of that shift, particularly as it relates to urban pastoralism. At least one work, written by a native Virginian, embodies it concretely—not consciously through its subject matter but half-consciously through its form. That book is *The History and Present State of Virginia* (1705) by Robert Beverly.

Beverley's spirited but finally disjointed book begins with the conventional reference to settlement as a component of England's mission as an elect nation. In its pristine splendor Virginia was "a Scene laid open for the good and gracious Q. *Elizabeth*, to propagate the Gospel in, and extend her Dominions over." Echoing the words of the first explorers and settlers as well as those of New England clerics, Beverley asserts that the land seemed to be "purposely reserv'd" for the English "by a peculiar Direction of Providence, that had brought all former Adventures in this Affair to nothing." Reflecting the idea that sacred history attends upon the English settlement of the New World, Beverley subscribes as well to the assumption that fulfillment of the English mission requires the establishment of towns, and he directs much of his attention in book 1 to colonial efforts in this matter. During the governorship of Sir William Berkeley, he explains in one breath, "the Church of *England* was confirm'd the established Religion, the Charge of the Government sustain'd, Trade and Manufactures were encouraged, [and] a town [i.e., Jamestown] projected."[8] But as Beverley relates this and other efforts at town building, he indicates that the results have been less than satisfactory.

Despite Berkeley's laudable intentions, Beverley explains rather disappointedly, Jamestown failed to develop beyond a few houses of entertainment. What little success it achieved was undermined when the provincial capital burned to the ground during Bacon's Rebellion. As a result, the town "now . . . is almost deserted." But isolated instances such as the firing of Jamestown are only symptoms of a larger problem which Beverley locates in the whole settlement pattern of the colony. Owing to the abundance of land and "the Advantage of the many Rivers for Shipping at every Man's Door," Virginians have fallen into "such an unhappy Settlement and course of Trade; that to this

Day they have not any one Place of Cohabitation among them, that may reasonably bear the Name of a Town."[9]

To a degree, Beverley's statements about failure in town building are not new. In 1662, we should recall, the anonymous author of *Virginia's Cure* had employed similar rhetoric to lament Virginians' "dispersed manner of planting themselves." What is new, rather, is where Beverley places the blame for the failure. While seeming to indict the settlers themselves and the tempting charms of the landscape, he locates guilt less in the colonists and more in the selfishness and greed of interfering Englishmen from the Old World. Although an "Act for Cohabitation" was passed by the Virginia Assembly in 1679, Beverley notes that it "was kindly brought to nothing by the opposition of the Merchants of *London*." And while ascribing Jamestown's abandoned condition partially to dispersed settlement, he cites royal governor Francis Nicholson as the true culprit. According to Beverley, shortly after Virginia had become a royal colony in 1698, Nicholson "caused the Assembly, [and] the Courts of Judicature, to be remov'd from *James-Town*, where there were good Accommodations for People, to *Middle-Plantation*, where . . . he flatter'd himself with the fond Imagination, of being the Founder of a new City . . . call'd *Williamsburg*." Unfortunately, "this imaginary city," remarks Beverley rather sardonically, "is yet advanced no further, than only to have a few Publick Houses and a Store-House, more than were built upon the Place before."[10]

Although his ownership of a large tract of land in Jamestown may have helped inspire his attack on Nicholson and Williamsburg, Beverley's assignment of blame was otherwise well grounded in social and political facts. Because tobacco, the money crop of Virginia, could be grown most effectively and economically on large plantations, both the English Crown and the Lords of Trade and Plantations were wary of promoting town development in Virginia. When the first edition of Beverley's history appeared, the English commissioners of customs were completing a report warning that building towns would be "detrimental by drawing the inhabitants off from their planting tobacco in the country to the cohabiting and setting up handicraft trades."[11]

By opposing the well-being of Virginia to the goals and actions of the court and London, however, Beverley moves far away from the premises with which he opens his history. Additionally, when he turns in the second of his four books to a discussion of natural conditions, he completely abandons his ardent support for town building. Instead, he begins to depict the landscape in hyperbolic language delightfully matched to the bounty it describes. In sparse but rhythmic prose he explains how "Honey and Sugar Trees" grow "spontaneous" along the river deltas and how grapes are of "unusual Bigness." "As for fish," he avows, "no Country can boast of more Variety, greater Plenty, or of better in their several Kinds." Especially enticing to Beverley is the way the landscape seems to be an anodyne for the spiritual ills of tired Europeans. With a joyous tone recalling that of the first explorers, Beverley's prose suggest that in the presence of the natural bounty people are refreshed with a delightful feeling of wonder and well-being, and this panegyric to nature continues in the rest of the history. Recording in book 3 his admiration for the Indians, particularly their spontaneity, innocence, and generosity, Beverley describes Virginia as a virtual paradise regained. "Certainly it must be a happy Climate," he asserts almost nonchalantly, "since it is very near of the same Latitude with the Land of Promise." Near the close of this exuberant depiction, however, Beverley once again displays chagrin. Although "a Garden is no where sooner made than there," the settlers of Virginia, he explains, have not taken advantage of the opportunities nature affords. Instead of turning this primitive bounty into a cultivated agricultural landscape, they have made so few improvements that "they han't many Gardens in the Country, fit to bear that name."[12]

No doubt Beverley was discomfited by this failure of his fellow Virginians, but it is difficult to see the relationship of this disappointment to the emphasis of book 1. While both speak of failures, they are of different sorts. Far from his emphasis on town building in book 1, the rest of his history focuses on the lack of agricultural development. He mentions colonial urban development only once in books 2 and 3, merely in a passing remark about the use of coal. Beverley's *History*, that is, reads as though it were two separate texts—a fact that Beverley may have recognized, for he attempts to draw the two halves together in the final pages. "By reason of the unfortunate Method of the Settlement, and want of Cohabitation," he asserts there, Virginians "cannot make a beneficial use of their Flax, Hemp, Cotten, Silk, Silkgrass, and Wool, which might otherwise supply their Necessities, and leave the Produce of Tobacco to enrich them, when a gainful Market can be found for it."[13] That is, if Virginians "han't many Gardens in the Country," the reason is, paradoxically, that they have no cities.

Again it is necessary to note, however, that Beverley's assertion here is not entirely new. In the same year, Francis Makamie, a Presbyterian clergyman from Accomack County, had adopted a similar position in arguing that "Towns, and nothing but Cohabitation, would soon fill our Country with people of all sorts . . . [who] would inhabit and cultivate, or plant those Lands, which now are Waste and Useless." Beverley's importance, rather, lies in the relationship he sees between cities and cultivation of the landscape. To say, however, that he simply is arguing for a marriage of art and nature—the hallmark of the pastoral ideal—only obscures the point, since his interest extends beyond creating a rural middle landscape. For Beverley, town building, agricultural development, and the natural order are equally important as reconcilable sources of value.[14]

To understand Beverley's idea of reconciliation and the way he effects it requires a return to book 3, where he discusses the Indians and their society. Although he extols the natives' moral character, comeliness, and spontaneity, equally important to him are their modes of habitation and their method of government. Unlike the white settlers, the Indians reside "altogether by Cohabitation, in Townships, from fifty to five hundred Families in a Town," which enables them to act collectively in emergencies. Because their huts are part of one town, they can construct a "Palisado," which they reinforce when attack seems imminent. Such patterns of habitation also facilitate an effective and unified government, since each town possesses a vicegerent who acts as governor, judge, and chancellor for the king, who in turn rules over several towns. In this manner the Indians have developed an effective chain of authority which can mobilize the people and ensure social cohesion.[15] Beverley does not gloss his description with any moral evaluation, but it is clear that in the context of the entire history he intends the Indian society to stand in laudable contrast to the white man's. Though he describes their lives as instinctual and unmannered, Beverley implies that somehow the Indians have learned the lesson of social development better than white Virginians.

Beverley's implications here begin to make greater sense if we consider them in conjunction with a work that appeared twenty-two years later. In his *History of the Five Indian Nations*, Cadwallader Colden used a modified form of the same idea more explicitly when he wrote that "the present state of the Indian Nations exactly shows the most Ancient and Original Condition of almost every Nation; so I believe, here we may with more certainty see the Original Form of all Governments" and all societies. Colden, that is, wrote his history in accordance with the social-compact theory of the previous century, stated most explicitly by Locke. According to the theory, in his original state of nature man existed in isolation, free of social controls, but shortly thereafter he congregated with his kind to form the first societies. Accepting that theory allowed Colden to explain how the Indian, on his own, had begun to evolve a civilization without the help of the white man.[16] The implications of the theory, however, went beyond this particular application. Supported by books such as Colden's, which seemed to offer concrete illustration, the theory suggested that society was progressive, not static, and that complex civilizations were not opposed to the natural order but immanent in it.

In his obscure, halting way, Beverley seems to have been following the same logic. Since Colden was drawing on the Lockean environmentalism of the previous century, it is not unlikely that Beverley, twenty years before Colden, did the same thing. We know, for example, that as a youth Beverley was educated in London, where he probably was exposed to the new ideas of the Enlightenment, and that he spent some time in England among the booksellers' shelves in 1703. Then too, such ideas were being disseminated in the colony itself through the curriculum at William and Mary. The point is, Beverley's implicit argument allows him to incorporate an urban structure into his central symbol of natural felicity. Far from being artificial, Beverley implies, towns are part of nature's plan. In settling in a dispersed manner, Virginians have failed to follow the model of nature, supplied by the Indians, and paradoxically have moved further from the natural order.[17] So preoccupied with profits—or so inhibited by English commissioners and London merchants—the settlers have ignored the landscape's wordless message: in Beverley's idiom, the value and necessity of cohabitation.

Within the *History*, Indian towns ultimately serve, not as an urban-pastoral blueprint for the white man, but as a vehicle for furthering Beverley's central assertion: Embedded in the land is an immanent garden waiting to exfoliate if only Virginians would adopt an ordered communal organization validated by nature itself. In the opportunity afforded by native conditions—both the vegetational abundance and the social example provided by the Indian towns—Beverley finds the resources the settlers can use to turn their colony into an agricultural paradise predicated on urban development. In the process, town life itself would benefit from this edenic bounty. Beverley's urban-pastoral ideography is neither localized nor unidirectional. For him, towns and fields would be interdependent components contributing to each other's growth and well-being throughout the colony.

That conception, of course, rests on Beverley's ability to ignore an important question: Will not urban life in America yield the same type of overbearing courtiers and unscrupulous merchants who have proved the bane of Virginia? In a very real sense, however, that question is irrelevant to Beverley even though he knows that since the arrival of the English the Indian communities have been torn by greed for a "thousand things, they never dreamt of before."[18] For Beverley identifies greed itself as the culprit, equating it, not with cities per se, but with the overall social and environmental conditions of the Old World. If European civilization has produced a race of omnivorous settlers, it is only because, habituated to limited land and scarce resources at home, Englishmen have been bred to self-indulgence and rapine. Accordingly, in America the whole question of town building takes on a different coloration. If left alone to settle randomly, Englishmen will continue in their corrupt ways. But with regulation through a careful pattern of cohabitation—a pattern sanctioned by nature—that greed will disappear.

What makes all the difference for Beverley is his unwavering faith in the sanative influence of native geography. The theory that Emerson would announce over one hundred years later—that "the land is the appointed remedy for whatever is false or fantastic in our culture"—Beverley tacitly accepts already.[19] Both assume that in America there is enough for everyone, but for Beverley that abundance requires community, cooperation, and central control—qualities conventionally attributed in Beverley's time to urban life.

Yet if Beverley's point is that America can be the site of a new urban society based on close contact with nature and if he believes that gardens will not flourish until towns develop, why does he not say so overtly? Part of the answer is that Beverley wrote his history to encourage settlement. Had he openly argued that few gardens would exist until towns were built—a procedure opposed by the British Crown—he would have rendered a rather hopeless picture to prospective immigrants. But a more important reason is that in the two halves of the History Beverley employs two distinct idioms and speaks from two different ideological bases. When he projects urbanization as essential to subduing and Christianizing the wilderness, he is using the old language of national election and providential history. When he places towns beneath the auspices of the natural order and the beneficent conditions of American geography, however, he begins to employ the language of the Enlightenment in which environment accounts for everything. If Beverley's ideas appear inchoate or confused, the reason is that he switches value systems, apparently quite unconsciously, in the midst of writing. Nevertheless, in doing so he helped lead the way for the more fully developed expressions of a pastoralized urban America that would appear later in the century. In the intervening years, meanwhile, Western thought would continue to move in the direction mapped out by Locke and Newton, allowing for further refinement of the structure and vocabulary for such an idea.

II

By the third decade of the eighteenth century, the fruits of the scientific revolution had begun to yield both a new knowledge of nature's intricacies and an awareness of the vast powers in the natural world which lay at man's disposal. No longer content to speak of natural law in the abstract as they responded to the world "out there," philosophers and aestheticians began to promulgate nature as a moral and aesthetic norm. Whole treatises on the efficacy and correctness of natural religion were being written by such men as William Wollaston and Lord Kames, and writers and painters turned as never before to the landscape as a subject for art. A certain "preromantic" quality also began to modify the conventional stylized treatment of nature. As observation disclosed not only a magnificently ordered world but one of infinite variety, aestheticians began to prize irregularity, imbalance, and asymmetry over the old values of proportion and uniformity. Now when theoreticians such as Francis Hutcheson wrote about beauty, they defined it as a harmonious blend of uniformity and variety, a delicate mixture of art and nature in accordance with the patterns of the flora and fauna. For Hutcheson, and for writers such as Pope, Joseph Addison, and James Thomson, a natural scene enhanced by art was significant as both a pastoral retreat and a mode of aesthetic pleasure which could elevate man's very soul.[20]

Such theories contributed immensely to the rising interest in gardening and the increased estimation of agriculture which developed in England, France, Holland, and America in this period. The idea that a cultivated landscape somehow restored one to a natural contentment became a commonplace, with writers such as Addison claiming that "a garden . . . is naturally apt to fill the Mind with

Calmness and Tranquility, and to lay all its turbulent passions to rest." By the last quarter of the century the great fashion was to live in the country and play at being a farmer. A penchant for gardening appeared everywhere, from isolated villages in England and France to the courts of Louis XVI and George III. Added to this passion was the theoretical argument, first propounded by the French physiocrats, that agriculture was the true source not only of increased virtue but of a nation's economic well-being. Though disagreement existed over the credibility of the physiocratic claims, most economists of the age supported the idea. Even Adam Smith, despite his trenchant opposition to much of the French doctrine, argued that the wealth of a country was "a very precarious and uncertain possession, till some part of it had been secured and realized in the cultivation and improvement of its lands." Contending that the farmer was more intelligent, more moral, more physically fit, and in general nobler than his urban counterpart, Smith and the physiocrats, as well as popularizers such as Arthur Young, seemed to be saying that the best of all possible societies would be one devoted exclusively (or almost exclusively) to agriculture.[21] Moreover, if any country seemed to be following this lead, it was America. Despite the skepticism of the Abbé Raynal, Count Buffon, and other physiocrats toward the healthfulness of the American climate and flora, a cadre of Europeans, including Richard Price and Voltaire, and divers native spokesmen led by Jefferson and Jedidiah Morse asserted that the conditions of America were creating there a race of happy, independent husbandmen.

Though American writers had been exploiting that idea for some time, in the last three decades of the eighteenth century the image of America as a benevolent rural society was promoted with increased frequency. "The great Business of the [American] Continent is Agriculture," wrote Benjamin Franklin in his essay "The Internal State of America." "For one Artisan, or Merchant, I suppose we have at least 100 Farmers, by far the greatest part Cultivators of their own fertile Lands." In his poem "The American Village," Philip Freneau employed a variant of the same idea, extolling the native rural scene, with its "fields waving with eternal corn," as a place of "ev'ry joy and ev'ry bliss." There "fair Charity puts forth her hand / And pours her blessings o'er the grateful land." Since the farmer seemed to be the primary force behind civilization's advance across the uninhabited landscape, the noble husbandman became something of a cult figure, embodying many of the significant values of the age. Finding they could privilege cultivation by cultivating a privileged image of the farmer, native writers made him the subject of some of the most impassioned pronouncements of the century. Perhaps the most famous is the one Jefferson wrote to John Jay in 1785, in which he identified "Cultivators of the earth" as "the most valuable citizens. They are the most vigorous, and they are tied to their country, and wedded to its liberty and interests by the most lasting bonds." For Jefferson and other defenders of the rural order, liberty, democracy, and agriculture were closely related. [22]

Accordingly, at the close of the War of Independence, there came into vogue the myth that the war was conducted primarily, if not exclusively, by farmers. In his "Epistle to the Patriotic Farmer," Freneau styled that republican figure as the one "who first aimed a shaft at George's crown, / And marked the way to conquest and renown." Several years earlier, Franklin wrote that, though the major cities in America were captured by the British during the Revolution, "their being in the Possession of the Enemy did not necessarily draw on the Subjection of the Country [i.e., the rural areas], which bravely continued to maintain its Freedom and Independence notwithstanding." [23] In native lore, the farmer came to symbolize more than virtue and civilizing order; he was enshrined as the essence of the political system for which the Revolution was fought.

Around the middle of the century, however, ideas and events began to challenge the entire value system of agrarian supremacy. The Industrial Revolution was under way in Europe, and with it came a massive increase in population and urban growth. In France, the population soared from 18 million in 1715 to 24 million in 1770, most of this increase being absorbed by the larger cities. In England, London was growing to well over a million souls, and manufacturing cities such as Manchester and Birmingham were expanding rapidly. For the most part, Western Europeans experienced in this period a rather sudden conversion from rural to urban life. Even in America appeared signs of the same phenomenon in the last three decades of the century. Though the growth of cities lagged behind that of the country as a whole, every major city displayed a dramatic increase in the number of inhabitants from 1700 to 1790. Boston's population grew from about 6,700 to 18,000; New York's from 4,400 to over 32,000; and Philadelphia's from 4,500 to an amazing 42,500. New cities such as Albany and Baltimore had begun to develop; the latter, with a population of 200 in 1750, had mushroomed to over 13,000 by the year of the first federal census. By 1790 there were twenty-four incorporated places of 2,500 inhabitants or more (the official definition of an urban location until 1950), giving the new nation a total urban population surpassing 200,000. For the first time, Americans as a people were encountering a substantial growth of cities.[24]

Simultaneously, observers on both sides of the Atlantic were beginning to see the benefits of these changes. As a result of urban manufacturing, innovative machinery was raising British agricultural productivity beyond anything known before. The new factory products meant increased opportunity for trade, while the expanding urban centers multiplied markets. In America urban growth was likewise significant. Though the markets were much smaller than Europe's, they nonetheless served as enlarging points of exchange for the farmers' raw goods and imported finished products. Just as significant were the symbolic implications of urban development in America. As one resident of Baltimore noted, "a Boston, a New York, and a Philadelphia add lustre and dignity to the colonies to which they belong, and are advancing with rapidity towards perfection in arts and sciences, commerce and mechanics."[25] The speed with which American cities were developing seemed sublime validation of the growing faith in progress and the first substantial fruits of the American promise.

That faith was further supported by the new "conception of civilization" which began to emerge in Europe after 1750. Growing from the social-compact theory of the previous century, the idea appeared first in rudimentary form in the writings of Turgot and Rousseau. But it was Condorcet's *Esquisse d'un tableau historique des progrès de l'esprit humain* (1790) which set forth the conception explicitly. Translated into English shortly after publication, Condorcet's treatise argued that all societies naturally moved upward through a series of stages from primitive hunting and gathering, through herding, to agriculture. Theoretically at least, this conception implied that the more humankind improved nature (i.e., the greater its progress), the more civilized it became. Civilization, therefore, was the "ultimate state of nature," an equation which the American judge Nathaniel Chipman announced only three years after Condorcet's theory first appeared.[26] If cosmopolitan trading cities were the most advanced form of civilization, it followed, moreover, that they were man's best and most "natural" type of society.

Since such a concept, together with the ideas of unlimited progress and the visible benefits of urban growth, directly contradicted the pre-

vailing reverence for agriculture and rural life, the question of reconciliation inevitably arose. Admittedly, a partial accord existed in
the idea that the city was part of natural development, but even there
a paradox emerged. For if the city was a natural, "superior" product
of evolution, such a concept implied that urban society was destined
to supplant, not harmonize with, the "inferior" rural domain. No
doubt the tension implicit in the idea was partly responsible for the
tendency of much late-eighteenth-century writing, as Lois Whitney
has shown, to champion the values of a static pastoral order while simultaneously affirming unlimited progress.[27] Yet attempts at reconciliation did occur. For over two thousand years the Western world had
been drawing on the urban-pastoral image to embody its social and
spiritual ideals, and now in the eighteenth century the idea of an urban middle landscape seemed eminently suited to mediate between
the agrarian philosophy and the new concepts of civilization and
progress.

Literary attempts at such mediation assumed a number of forms. In
Pope the reconciliation appears in various parts of *Windsor-Forest* and
in his epistles "To Bathurst" and "To Burlington." Although the greatest proportion of the latter poems is devoted to life on the rural estates
of the two earls, Pope manages to present the central figures addressed
as individuals who move easily between the urban and rural worlds,
incorporating the best of both. For Pope, the future development of
the English empire, including its increased urbanization and trade,
harmonizes with rural life because it emanates from the good estates
of moral figures such as Bathurst and Burlington. Both poems confidently imply that the country, through its raw materials and beatific
inhabitants, can yield buildings, navies, and towns to progress without being displaced by them.[28]

An even more ambitious effort at unification was John Dyer's "The
Fleece," a stirring tribute to "noble Albion." Dyer packs his poem with
all the stock pastoral images, extolling Britain's "blue ethereal vault,"
"verdurous lawns," "clear brooks," and "spacious flocks of sheep." Into
this picture, he has no trouble incorporating the world of power,
trade, and urbanization as he continues,

> To these thy naval streams,
> Thy frequent towns superb of busy trade,
> And ports magnific add, and stately ships
> Innumerous. But wither strays my muse?

Although the rhetorical question interjects a moment of doubt in the poem, the feeling is immediately subsumed beneath an overwhelming optimism as the poet contemplates the scene:

> Please'd like a traveller upon the strand
> Arriv'd of bright Augusta: wild he roves
> From deck to deck, thro' groves immense of masts,
> 'Mong crowds, bales, cars, the wealth of either Ind;
> Through warfs, and squares, and palaces, & domes,
> In sweet surprize; unable yet to fix
> His raptur'd mind, or scan in order'd course
> Each object singly; with discoveries new
> His native country studious to enrich.

Likewise, when he turns to the new manufacturing city of Leeds, Dyer describes it nestled in "rich fields" surrounded by "Hillock and valley," its numerous chimneys "up wafting to the clouds / The incense of thanksgiving." In a scene reminiscent of a pastoral harvest, the inhabitants appear as contented laborers who daily "issue from their cells / In bands unnumbered, eager for their work" and whose "virtuous efforts" include "haste[ning] / With warm affection to each other's aid."[29] Although Dyer merely employs the old pastoral rhetoric to describe the increased urbanization of England, the poem does effect a resolution. It suggests that rural virtues and peace obtain in the city because that milieu is a natural outgrowth of Albion's "verdurous lawns" and "clear brooks." According to "The Fleece," England has entered a halcyon age in which empire, urbanity, and rural values coalesce.

On the plane of economic theory, endeavors of reconciliation took a more practical turn. In *The Wealth of Nations* Adam Smith explained that "without the assistance of some artifices . . . the cultivation of land cannot be carried on." Smiths, masons, bricklayers, and tailors are all people "whose service the farmer has frequent occasion for." Because these tradesmen require continual assistance from one another, they must congregate in towns and cities. Thus, reasoned Smith, "the inhabitants of the town and those of the country are mutually the servants of one another." Smith added that the commerce and manufacturers of the city had aided the rural world in more seminal ways in that they "gradually introduced order and good government, and with them, the liberty and security of individuals, among the inhabitants of the country, who had before lived almost in a continual state of war with their neighbors." Even inveterate agrarians such as Arthur Young and Paolo Balsamo, professor of agriculture at the University of Palermo, argued that the city was no threat to the rural world. According to both men, the two realms existed in a happy and mutually beneficial partnership.[30]

As the century progressed, however, it became increasingly difficult to believe such claims. Part of the problem was that in Europe little effort was being made to provide urban dwellers with an environment conducive to the highly praised tranquility and virtue associated with rural life. While ritual gestures toward making cities more "natural" occurred, these were largely confined to botanical gardens in Paris and London and the creation of pleasure gardens for the wealthy, such as Vauxhall and Ranelagh in London. The majority of urban dwellers in Europe found themselves living in unsanitary, overcrowded cities, where, in the words of Jonathan Swift, open sewers teemed with "Sweepings from Butcher Stalls, Dung, Guts, and Blood, / Drown'd Puppies, stinking Sprats, all drench'd in Mud."[31] For the first time, Europeans were discovering the horrors of the industrial urban slum.

Despite the theoretical assertions of Smith and Young, moreover, the happy regional harmony between city and country was anything but a reality. Although urban-rural tensions had been building for some centuries in Europe, they reached an apex in this period. As cities grew and suburbs appeared, numerous rural dwellers found themselves displaced from land that their families had worked for generations. Many an Englishman viewed London as a huge, unmanageable monstrosity which, along with such manufacturing cities as Liverpool, Leeds, and Manchester, seemed to be sucking up the landscape. Concurrently, the enclosure laws were displacing even more farmers, virtually eliminating the independent family farm and causing writers such as Oliver Goldsmith, in his "Deserted Village," to argue that England was becoming anything but a healthy synthesis of urban and rural. On the Continent, the same tension existed. According to Moreau de St. Méry, contemporary of Young and Balsamo, many farmers were "furious because the[ir] government sold to city people the land on which they counted on establishing themselves. They hate cities, and suspect everybody of profiteering, speculation, etc." A number of these disgruntled husbandmen, he continued, were leaving Europe to settle in America.[32]

88

III

Since its discovery the New World had seemed to promise Europeans the chance for a new way of life, but only in the last half of the eighteenth century did the urban-pastoral conception of America gain currency on both sides of the Atlantic. In this period, a penchant for creating vistas of American cities developed among European artists who visited the western shore. Whether the subject was New York, Boston, or Philadelphia, a favorite device of painters and engravers such as Archibald Robertson, John Joseph Holland, and Charles Fevret de St.-Mémin was to place in the background of their work a panoramic view of the city done in soft shades. In the foreground, framing the canvas in richer, darker tones, was a bucolic scene of grazing cattle, stacks of hay, tall trees, and open fields. Often the artist included one or two rustic figures reclining, strolling, or pleasantly working in the lush verdure (see illustrations 1 and 2). The overall impression of these works is one of peace, harmony, and continuity, with the city nestling in the natural setting as though growing from it. European interest in these pastoral renditions of American cities can be gauged in part by the fact that the widely read *London Magazine* included a number of similar etchings in its "Views of Great Cities," a series which ran from 1759 to 1781. Comments accompanying these vistas spoke of cities such as Charles Town in the Carolinas and Philadelphia as urbane settlements which nonetheless retained a "natural" ease, "contentment," and picturesque appeal.[33]

In the journals of Europeans who visited America, the same kind of response appeared. In the 1790s Moreau de St. Méry found New York " a great city and powerful," which presented a "charming" view "at the entrance to the port. . . . Trees are planted along some streets" which are accentuated by "beautiful homes." Of Baltimore he explained how the bustling urban character of that city was softened by "gardens in the outskirts of the city." But "what gives Baltimore a pleasant air, peculiar to itself, is the hill which dominates it on the north. . . . The rear portion is beautified by a park. Its elevated situation; its groves of trees; the view from it . . . all these things together fill every true Frenchman with both pleasure and regret; his mind and heart alike rejoice in the vistas and sensations they inspire." According to Robert Honyman, a Scottish physician who eventually settled in Virginia, such vistas were numerous in America, where, he explained, a typical scene consists of "a pretty little town & most

1 "New York from Brooklyn Heights" (1778), by Archibald Robertson

2 "View of the City of Philadelphia" (1797), by Gilbert Fox after John Joseph Holland

beautiful fields" so that cities are lent charm by an intervening land-scape that is "level & very beautiful & . . . improved very much." Honyman also found little opposition between rural and urban in-habitants during his visit. All, he noted, are of one mind, being "fu-rious in the cause of liberty."[34]

Such responses continued well into the first half of the nineteenth century, despite the more jaundiced pictures of urban America that Dickens and Mrs. Trollope drew. When the utopian reformer Frances Wright visited America in the 1820s, she recorded how Baltimore struck her as something of a pastoral paradise. Entering the town, she wrote, "seemed like stepping into fairyland, when . . . we turned into a clean broad street, lined with balsam poplars, the fragrance of whose young leaves, glistening with raindrops, perfumed the air." Of New York she remarked, "nature has done everything for it." Unlike European cities, it exhibited "no dark alleys, whose confined and noi-some atmosphere marks the presence of a dense and suffering popu-lation." Some Europeans, though, were less interested in the presence of greenery or the absence of squalor and more in the degree of re-finement and culture in urban America. The Frenchman Levasseur, who visited America with Lafayette in 1824–25, noted that Ameri-can city dwellers "although ardently devoted to all sorts of business, are not ignorant of those studies which form the taste, and extend the resources of the mind." The difference between European and Amer-ican cities, he went on, was that in the New World "luxury and the arts, in being introduced among the population . . . have not brought with them the effeminacy and corruption which some pretend are their inseparable companions." In America, so it seemed, a society uniting the best of urban culture, natural beauty, and virtue was pos-sible.[35] No doubt such an idea helped inspire European reformers such as George Rapp, Joseph Bimeler, and Étienne Cabet to immigrate to America for the purpose of building their utopian communities.

It was in the eighteenth century, however, that the idea of America as the site of an enlightened, historical, and secular urban-pastoral so-ciety first took hold. At that time, it was not sufficient to consider the American landscape solely as the source of agrarian interests. It was a symbol denoting American difference, forever guaranteeing the uniqueness and superiority of American institutions. According to this belief, there was room for the city in the garden, a proposition which enlisted the efforts of numerous native writers. One was Hector St. John de Crèvecoeur, naturalized citizen of New York and author of the popular *Letters from an American Farmer* (1782). Despite its putative purpose of interpreting American experience in terms of a rural ideal, Crèvecoeur's *Letters* ultimately affirms an urban-pastoral development of America.

The *Letters* does not so much announce that position as dramatize it through a series of shifting perspectives. Farmer James, the narrator for the bulk of the work, represents the first of those views. An enlightened rustic, he accepts the standard assumptions of the age that people are inherently benevolent and that environment determines everything: "Men are like plants; the goodness and flavour of the fruit proceeds from the peculiar soil and exposition in which they grow." It follows, therefore, that men are best able to experience their natural goodness when they remain close to nature. And what better place for such a life than in America, where "Nature opens her broad lap to receive the perpetual accession of new-comers"?[36]

In the farmer's moral geography, which dominates the first three letters, the primary feature of America is its pastoral character; it is an ideal rural landscape, bordered on one side by the primitive frontier and on the other by urban Europe. In contrast to Europeans, who live in "a crowded society where every place is overstocked," American yeomen "are almost insulated, and the houses are at a considerable distance from each other." Above all, the abundance of land and the opportunity to work it distinguish life in America. "The instant I enter my own land," says Farmer James, "the bright idea of property, of exclusive right, of independence, exalt my mind." The soil "feeds, it clothes us," allowing husbandmen to lead self-sufficient, independent lives. But aside from material or political advantages, the farmer values most the spiritual benefits that the landscape imparts. "As we silently till the ground and muse along the odoriferous furrows of our lowlands," he proclaims, "the salubrious effluvia of the earth animate our spirits and serve to inspire us."[37] Under the peculiarly benevolent effects of native soil, it is possible for Americans to remain close to the elemental conditions which animate life. Owing to the power of the landscape, the farmer can assert confidently that he and his family will continue to lead happy, full, independent, and insulated lives.

Given the picture that emerges in the first few letters, one would expect Crèvecoeur's book to end in a crescendo of optimism with an inspired vision of America as a permanently rural "asylum," as the farmer calls it at one point. But that is not what happens at all. By the close of the *Letters* the Revolution has come, and the farmer finds his family and whole way of life threatened. The great world of power, complexity, alliances, political contentions—in a word, the city—has intruded upon the farmer's domain, and he must make a choice. However, he realizes that neither of the most obvious alternatives offers hope. If he joins his "mother country" (i.e., England), he will become an enemy to his own region, but should he follow his American countrymen, he risks losing all in the fight. He settles, therefore, on a third course; he will move to the frontier where he will attempt to create a new rural asylum.

It is unlikely, however, that Crèvecoeur means us to see this choice as a total reaffirmation of the farmer's "rural scheme." Such a reading simply does not accord with the somber, tragic tone that defines the thrust of this last letter. Even in his ritualistic gesture the farmer admits, "My fate is determined; but I have not determined it." Dominating this letter is a sense of uncontrollable power (we may call it history) bearing down on the farmer's world, making any arcadia, at best, a temporary retreat. As the farmer asks, "Whatever virtue, whatever merit and disinterestedness we may exhibit in our secluded retreats, of what avail?" On "the scale of great events," the purely pastoral world is "defenceless."[38]

Overtly, it seems, the last letter undermines the values professed earlier, and in part that is true—but only in part.[39] For in the course of the *Letters*, Crèvecoeur has provided an alternative vision which nonetheless affirms the human need to remain close to nature and the sanative potential of the American landscape. Our initial sense of that alternative develops as early as Letter 3, where the farmer formulates his answer to the question "What is an American?" Despite his emphasis on the pastoral qualities of the native scene, he must admit that when a European first arrives in America, in addition to orchards and meadows dotted here and there with family farms, he beholds fine roads, villages, and "fair cities." He even calls these cities "miracles of industry and freedom" which dazzle the observer with their "elegance."[40] What is odd about these remarks is that they are totally irrelevant to the ideography of the first three letters. There the farmer had defined the American scene as a bucolic retreat midway between the wilderness and the city. In the third letter, therefore, it is difficult to decipher what role Crèvecoeur sees the city playing in this vision of America, and having established the thematic pattern of the first three letters, Crèvecoeur was no doubt wise in eschewing an explanation there.

We can obtain at least a rudimentary understanding of Crève-coeur's position on this point, however, if we turn to his *Sketches of Eighteenth-Century America*, a posthumously published continuation of the *Letters*. Despite the American farmer's ostensible self-sufficiency, Crèvecoeur explains here that the yeoman can succeed only if he has a market for his products.

> Were not we to consume all these articles which our farms produce, were they not converted into wholesome, pleasant food, they would be lost. What should we do with our fruit, our fowls, our eggs? There is no market for these articles but in the neighbourhood of great towns.

Unlike the farmer's ebullient prose, the language here strikes a hard-headed, practical note. At one point in the *Sketches*, Crèvecoeur says quite frankly that "to live, it is necessary to go to market," and markets require "sea-port towns."[41] Crèvecoeur, that is, implies in the *Sketches* that to survive, the rural landscape must take into account the great world with its laws of supply and demand, trade, and economics.

In the first part of the *Letters*, Crèvecoeur begins to suggest the same thing in a half-articulated manner. In effect, he begins to alter the standard moral geography of pastoral writing by incorporating an urban-pastoral component. Although qualified, many of the farmer's values remain alive at the close of the *Letters*, but his exclusively arcadian vision gives way to an idea of America as an urban-rural medley. That ideal emerges fully in the *Letters* in Crèvecoeur's depiction of Nantucket.

Although constituting nearly half of the twelve letters, this section of Crèvecoeur's work generally receives little attention. As one critic has noted, most readers find the chapters on Nantucket disproportionately long and even tedious, and it is easy to see why.[42] These letters contain little of the unqualified exuberance of the farmer's resonating language. In fact, the sense of Farmer James as a character, a living being, is entirely absent from this section. The voice of these letters seems disembodied, like that of an impartial observer. But this impartial quality is what lends this section its significance. We sense here that the speaker, unlike the fictive farmer, closely resembles Crèvecoeur himself.[43]

Appropriately, Crèvecoeur adopts a more controlled tone in these letters. He admits that the soil on Nantucket is sterile and sandy and requires much effort to produce a crop. Yet he notes that "by bringing a variety of manure and by cow-penning," the inhabitants have "enriched several spots, where they raised Indian corn, potatoes, pompions, turnips, etc." If life on the island appears more demanding than it does on Farmer James's plot, it is nonetheless productive: "I believe there never were any people in their circumstance, who live so well, even to superabundance." The inhabitants, he explains, are happy in their agricultural pursuits and "would not exchange their pleasure for those of the most brilliant assemblies in Europe."[44]

Nonetheless, Crèvecoeur instructs his readers that they "must not imagine that every person on the island is either a landholder or concerned in rural operations; no, the greater part are at sea, busily employed in their different fisheries." This undertaking, which consists of a fleet of two hundred ships, requires a complex, highly organized, communal effort. As such, its operations are centralized in the only town on the island, Sherborn, a community in which the "bustle and hurry of business" make one "imagine that" it "is the capital of a very opulent and large province." This "little metropolis" of "about 530 houses" lends the society of Nantucket an urban character entirely missing from the world of Farmer James.[45]

To our modern way of thinking, Sherborn hardly may seem a great city, resembling instead a small rural town dominated by an extractive economy, but we should not project this distinction too far into the past. As Carl Bridenbaugh has explained, *town* and *city* connoted similar environments until the first few decades of the nineteenth century. Beverley, as we have seen, employed the two terms interchangeably in writing about Williamsburg and Jamestown, and Franklin would do the same in his *Autobiography*. This is not to say that colonial Americans could not distinguish a town from a city; they could and did, but their distinctions tended to be intuitive rather than quantitative. The point is that in the history of ideas, the two terms are important not for their accuracy in describing place but for the concepts to which they refer—concepts that change with time. When Crèvecoeur speaks of cities, towns, and the country, he is not thinking about population totals, precise ratios of demographic density, or complex definitions of metropolitan regions, as we do today. What concern him are the types of institutions at Sherborn. Hence, in detailing life in the town, he explains that, in addition to agriculture and fishing, the inhabitants engage in local manufacturing and trade. The latter pursuit, resulting from the fishing industry, extends the community's concerns beyond local extraction of raw goods to commercial relations with other locales. As Crèvecoeur notes, "the spirit of commerce, which is the simple art of a reciprocal supply of wants, is well understood here by everybody."[46] For Crèvecoeur, Sherborn is a "little metropolis" clearly distinct from the farmer's rural milieu.

What allows him to distinguish between Sherborn and its European counterparts is the way he integrates it into the thematic pattern of this section, making Sherborn and the rural scene coalesce:

> The town regularly ascends toward the country, and in its vicinage they have several fields and gardens yearly manured with the dung of their cows and the soil of their streets. There are a good many cherry- and peach-trees planted in their streets and in many other places.

At one point Crèvecoeur even calls the town a "pastoral one," blending commerce, industry, and arcadia in a single environment. The inhabitants evince a similar synthesis. Many attend to the business of the town and still till gardens and farms or raise sheep. Even those involved solely in the fishing industry are absorbed in the pattern because, he explains, they are farmers of the sea. Like the noble husbandman, who traces "the fragrant furrow on the plain," the fishermen at Nantucket "plough the rougher ocean," gathering from the sea the material and spiritual "riches it affords." Equally conducive to Sherborn's distinctiveness is the absence of certain institutions which are also missing from the farmer's world—institutions that Crèvecoeur associates with decadent Europe. The island possesses no aristocratic families, no kings, no ecclesiastical authorities, "nor any pageantry of state, neither ostentatious magistrates nor any individuals clothed with useless dignity." In their stead, the inhabitants of Nantucket cultivate a community spirit and plainness of manners that "have acquired the authority of laws."[47]

Particularly decisive in preserving this community "in the bonds of peace and tranquility" is the fact that "idleness and poverty, the causes of so many crimes, are unknown." The reason is that here, as in all America, "human industry has acquired a boundless field to exert itself in—a field which will not be fully cultivated in many ages."[48] Although these words are sometimes cited as the encapsulation of Crèvecoeur's faith in the relation between America and the special, superior position of the farmer, they actually express a different idea.

Significantly, Crèvecoeur includes this encomium, not while discussing the life of the farmer, but when depicting the customs at Nantucket. If the American landscape presents a boundless field, he insists, it is because it offers itself to numerous occupations, both rural and urban. As illustrated by this island community, what differentiates life in America is the opportunity to build a society where the two ways of life can exist in harmony.

In keeping with the more controlled tone of this section, however, Crèvecoeur displays no illusions about the quality of life at Nantucket. He admits that, by some standards, these people are less than affluent, but he is willing to accept that fact. "After all," he asks, "is it not better to be possessed of a single whale-boat or a few sheep pastures, to live free and independent under the mildest government, in a healthy climate, in a land of charity and benevolence, than to be wretched as so many are in Europe, possessing nothing but their industry . . . without the hopes of rising?" If affluence and luxury are absent on the island, so too are their reprehensible cousins: poverty and degradation for the majority of the laborers. Having admitted this limitation, Crèvecoeur can conclude his discussion of Nantucket by affirming that "the least imperfect [society] is undoubtedly that where the greatest good preponderates; and agreeable to this rule, I can truly say, that I never was acquainted with a less vicious or more harmless one."[49]

By privileging the community at Nantucket in this way, Crèvecoeur begins to qualify the idea expressed earlier that the farmer's exclusively rural world is the best possible realm. Furthermore, he continues that qualification in the next letter (Letter 9), simultaneously reinstating the farmer as narrator. In this epistle the index of limitation appears initially in the subject matter. The farmer does not speak of his happy rural home, the bounty of the soil, or the peculiar spiritual regeneration of husbandry. Instead he begins with a description of the city of Charles Town in the Carolinas:

> Charles Town is, in the north, what Lima is in the south; both are
> capitals of the richest provinces of their respective hemispheres; you
> may therefore conjecture that both cities must exhibit the appear-
> ances necessarily resulting from riches. Peru abounding in gold, Lima
> is filled with inhabitants who enjoy all those gradations of pleasure,
> refinement, and luxury which proceed from wealth. Carolina pro-
> duces commodities more valuable perhaps than gold . . . ; it exhibits

also on our northern stage a display of riches and luxury, inferior indeed to the former, but far superior to what are to be seen in our
northern towns.

In light of both the farmer's values expressed previously and the description of Nantucket just completed, this picture of Charles Town is
hardly flattering. Adhering to the Lockean environmentalism of the
first few letters, the farmer explains that part of the reason for the distinctive way of life in Charles Town is "the softer situations of Carolina, where mankind reap too much, do not toil enough, and are
liable to enjoy too fast the benefits of life." The people of Charles
Town, like Beverley's lethargic Virginians, simply exploit the country,
ignore nature's messages, and fail to develop a right relation with the
landscape. Engaging in "dissipation and pleasure," though the heat of
"the climate renders excesses of all kinds very dangerous," they live li-
centious but short lives. To the "scenes of misery overspread in the
country" and the "woes of their poor slaves" they are oblivious; "their
ears by habit are become deaf, their hearts are hardened." In this
"strange order of things," as Farmer James refers to it, the very laws of
nature seem abrogated—an idea which the farmer himself suggests
when he asks of Charles Town, "Oh, Nature, where art thou?"[50]

Though the farmer's disparaging picture of Charles Town is in
many ways a typical critique of cities from the perspective of a rural
advocate, we must understand it as part of the larger pattern of the
Letters. Through James's remarks Crèvecoeur denigrates Charles
Town not because it is a city but because it is a city that has failed to
effect a meaningful relationship with the valuable features of the rural
world. Separated by its corrupt, overcivilized citizens, Charles Town
becomes a blight on the American landscape, an "anti-society" as
Jean Beranger has called it, diametrically opposed to the American
model at Sherborn.[51] Clearly one purpose of this section is to provide
a contrast with Nantucket—one that sets off that society to even
greater advantage.

Just as importantly, Crèvecoeur uses his depiction of Charles Town
to undermine the farmer's position. Unlike the Nantucket letters,
which only hint at the limitations of an exclusively pastoral vision,
Letter 9 begins to encircle the exhilarating rural landscape with dark,
ominous implications. For in this letter a world of power, exploitation,
and carelessness—an urban world unredeemed by contact with nature—begins to intrude upon the farmer's sensibilities. Nothing

makes the tenor of this letter clearer than the scene of the caged black slave, in which the farmer is shocked and sickened by the sight of a kenneled human devoured by birds and insects. Letter 9 foreshadows the mood and theme of the last letter, which reveals the bucolic dream as an illusion.

In that culminating epistle Crèvecoeur brings the farmer to a similar understanding of his world. As he surveys the present maelstrom, James admits that before the war he never had considered fully the source of true felicity: "I lived on, laboured and prospered, without having ever studied on what the security of my life and the foundation of my prosperity were established." Now he realizes what he had ignored previously: the fact that man "cannot live in solitude; he must belong to some community bound by some ties, however imperfect. Men mutually support and add to the boldness and confidence of each other; the weakness of each is strengthened by the force of the whole."[52] Of course, having established the farmer's predilections and the turbulent situation, Crèvecoeur cannot allow James to act on his insight. Despite what he has learned, the farmer incorrigibly holds to his rural ideal, and his decision to escape to the frontier to recapture his rustic past serves as a final ironic commentary on the shallowness of pure pastoralism for a changing America. Yet it is clear where Crèvecoeur's allegiance lies. Like Beverley, he believes that security, peace, and abundance—values which the country was associating with a life closer to nature—require cohabitation and community. Unlike Beverley, however, Crèvecoeur weaves into the thematic pattern of his entire book the idea that pastoral America can persist only when yoked to urbanization, a process which itself can be enhanced by that synthesis. In his *Letters from an American Farmer*, Crèvecoeur places his imprimatur, not on the rural idyll of the fictive Farmer James, but on the rural-urban ideography manifested and symbolized in Nantucket.

IV

Although the reconciliation which Crèvecoeur depicts always had been the goal of the urban-pastoral ideal, not all Americans could subscribe to the idea that the country's urban culture could best be served by its closeness to rural life. Some Americans, such as Dr. Alexander Hamilton of Annapolis, were unwilling to concede that the particular value of the native scene lay in its predominantly rural character. Like other urbane Americans, Hamilton had few illusions about the rural world. He remarked in his *Itinerarium*, a record of his journey through the seaboard colonies in 1744, how he found rustics "quite wild," uncouth, and prone to "stare like sheep" when beholding a person of culture and refinement.[53] Despite this disdain for rural conditions, however, his *Itinerarium* suggests that Hamilton, like Crèvecoeur, was attracted to the urban-pastoral ideal, though in a different form—one that reveals the immense plasticity of that image in relation to native ideas about America's urban development.

When Hamilton set out on his journey and decided to record its details, he undoubtedly had no grand ideological or literary purpose in mind. Holding a degree of doctor of medicine from Edinburgh, he had come to America in 1734, settled in Annapolis, begun a practice, and six years later decided to take a journey "only for health and recreation" and "to see that part of the country" to the north. Reflecting this simple goal, most of his journal for the trip consists of random observations of life in the colonies, from Maryland to Maine. Yet clearly Hamilton already had imbibed the new empirical philosophy and the feeling for landscape that was making itself felt. Dominating the *Itinerarium* are his visual and olfactory responses to the scenes before him. Of Delaware he writes how "the people all along the road were making of hay which, being green and piled up in rucks, cast a very sweet and agreeable smell." In describing the scene at Thunder Hill and Cook's Island along the Hudson River, he explains how "this wild and solitary place, where nothing presents but huge precipices and inescapable steeps where foot of man never was, infused in my mind a kind of melancholly and filled my imagination with odd thoughts which, att the same time, had something pleasant in them."[54] Interesting here is the way nature seems to infuse itself into Hamilton's sensibilities. His response approaches the feeling which aestheticians of the age were soon to label "the sublime": the unique mixture of pleasure and dread evoked by nature's panorama.

What inspires Hamilton the most, though, are scenes which blend the beauty of the landscape with man-made developments. Consequently, he spends considerable time describing vistas of American towns and cities. Schenectady he depicts as a town of brick houses "built upon a pleasant plain" and beautifully "inclosed all round att about a mile's distance with thick pine woods." In his description of New Haven we hear unintentional echoes of the Puritans as Hamilton discloses the pleasant panorama afforded by that town. "It stands," he writes, "on a large plain, and upon all sides . . . it is inclosed with ranges of little hills as old Jerusalem was according to the topographicall descriptions of that city." Hamilton, however, takes greatest note of the major cities. Boston displays an enchanting picture of an animated city before a backdrop of "severall pleasant plains, and on the west side of the peninsula are three hills in a range." Of New York he says, "This city makes a very fine appearance for above a mile all along the river" as its "great deal of shipping" punctuates the delicate flow of the Hudson. While he finds Philadelphia less attractive than New York, he still perceives the "platform" of the city, with its regular squares, as a delightful counterpoint to the shimmering curves of the Delaware and Schuylkill rivers and remarks how "the country round the city of Philadelphia is level and pleasant, having a prospect of the larger river of Delaware and the province of East Jersey upon the other side."[55] Like the well-composed cityscapes of European artists later in the century, these verbal paintings evoke the idea that in America the city is a natural part of the landscape.

Up close, however, the towns of the colonies disclose a different impression for Hamilton. In Philadelphia, he says, "the majority of the houses [are] mean and low and much decayed, the streets in generall not paved, very dirty and obstructed with rubbish and lumber." The laying out of the city in a grid has caused it to be "altogether destitute of variety." In contrast, he finds both Boston and New York somewhat disagreeable because "the streets, in generall, are but narrow and not regularly disposed."[56] To an extent, some of these statements seem rather perplexing. On the one hand, Hamilton condemns irregularity, while on the other, he decries its absence. Since Hamilton was an urbane, cultured gentleman, we would expect him to feel most at home when thoroughly involved in the urban world, yet some of his most captious comments occur when he is moving through the streets of a Boston or New York.

Though Hamilton's reactions to urban America seem self-contradictory, his ideas become clearer if we consider his comments in light of his impressions of nature and of cities when seen from afar. These responses imply that for Hamilton American cities have not yet been shaped to take full advantage of the conditions provided by their location in the landscape. Though presenting a distant vista in which its topography blends pleasantly with furrowed plains and placid rivers, urban America lacks a corresponding internal pattern of harmony in which streets and houses display a grandeur and diversity as appealing to the eye as nature's. Hamilton, that is, implicitly espouses an aesthetic version of urban pastoralism predicated on man's ability to employ the examples of nature to give cities a comely form. Not concerned with questions of rural virtue or tranquility as desiderata of urban life, he suggests instead the need to create cities whose appearance would be as attractive and even as inspiring as nature's own.

In effect, what Hamilton desired was an urban design that would function as a visual token of the nature-civilization synthesis so central to urban pastoralism. By the 1780s and 1790s, an interest in such an aesthetic blend would become common in America. For example, Timothy Dwight, Connecticut literatus and grandson of Jonathan Edwards, would write of Boston in 1796:

> Had ten open squares been formed at the proper intersections of the
> principal streets, the largest containing ten, and the smallest five
> acres, all beautified with selected ornaments, or had some other
> plan, substantially resembling this, and directed by the nature of the
> ground, been completed, Boston would even now have been the
> most beautiful town that the world has ever seen.[57]

Six years before Dwight's statement, a similar idea had inspired the young engineer Pierre Charles L'Enfant in his design for the new national capital of the embryonic republic. In his hands, the aesthetic ideal of a pastoral city would receive full expression, inspired by a social and moral purpose.

L'Enfant's plan for Washington, D.C., was perhaps the most ambitious attempt in the eighteenth century to incorporate the urban-pastoral ideal into an actual urban design. His plan, however, embodied more than the ideas of a single man. The fledgling Congress itself was concerned that the Federal City should represent the goals of the republic and the national character. Choice of site was especially important. To promote geographical unity, the members believed, the capital must be located in a place of convenient access to all parts of the country, symbolically reflecting the newly formed Union. After numerous compromises and political machinations Congress succeeded in passing the Residence Act of 1790 that designated an undeveloped site along the Potomac River as the location for a permanent capital. Less than a year later, President Washington commissioned L'Enfant to design the new city.[58]

That L'Enfant shared with the Congress many of its goals is evident from his letters discussing plans for the Federal City. Writing to Jefferson in March 1791, he explained his desire to build the city on a "grand scale" in accordance with the expansiveness and grandeur of the American scene. A month later, in a letter to Alexander Hamilton, he expressed his belief that the new city must be quickly populated to encourage national unity and "deface that line of markation which will ever oppose the South against the East." To create a capital that would be both a symbolic and literal hub of the country, L'Enfant hoped Congress would build in the surrounding area new roads connected to the main thoroughfares of the city, linking the rural milieu to its new urban center. This synthesis was to be mirrored internally in his plan to construct a city that was both a complex of government and business and "a compleat heden [i.e., hedonistic] garden."[59] L'Enfant's design for the Federal City would make it a topographical embodiment of the urban-pastoral image of America.

Not that similar efforts had never been attempted previously on a full scale, at least on the provincial level. Even before the urban-pastoral ideal began to assume secular coloration, William Penn had conceived of the unimproved land between the Delaware and Schuylkill rivers as an appropriate site for what he called "a green country town." Penn's experience in England had convinced him that massive urbanization, which was drawing people away from the land, had produced in England rampant corruption. For Penn, London in particular epitomized "the excess and sloth of the Age." The problem, as he saw it, was that "the Country being thus neglected . . . no due Balance [is] kept between Trade and Husbandry, City and Country." As a result, urban dwellers in England were losing the contact with nature which "allows opportunity for reflection, and gives the best subject for it." Penn foresaw his colonial venture as a vehicle for reintegrating city and country and conceived of Philadelphia, *the* green country town, as the most visible embodiment of that ideal.[60]

Whether the actual plan of Philadelphia drawn by Surveyor-General Thomas Holme in 1683 accurately reflected Penn's original goals, as some historians have recently doubted, is uncertain.[61] If the design did deviate from the initial objective, however, Penn clearly sanctioned Holme's work. Not only did he include a copy of the layout in his 1683 letter to the Free Society of Traders in London; he also lauded the plan's judicious appropriation of space, which provided each inhabitant with "room enough for House, Garden, and small Orchard, to the great Content and Satisfaction of all here concerned." Holme's design constituted an object lesson in incorporating pastoral elements into the urban scene. The grid plan of the city was suited precisely to the natural landscape, the intersecting streets running smoothly over the flat, level land between the two rivers. Besides the large lots reserved for each house, Holme had set aside five spacious squares of open land, one at the center of the grid and one in each of its quadrants, as bucolic oases for recreation and communal gatherings. To the north, "Liberty Lands" added by Penn for grazing and more extensive farming served as a greenbelt connecting the city to the surrounding rural environment.[62]

Even Penn's design, however, pales in comparison to the ambitious scheme for the Federal City, as L'Enfant himself recognized. "To change a wilderness into a city," he wrote to Jefferson in 1792, "to that degree of perfection necessary to receive the seat of Government of a vast empire . . . is an undertaking vast as it is novel." Few native residents, however, were better suited than L'Enfant to direct such a project. The son of a French landscape painter, he had been a student at the Royal Academy of Painting and Sculpture, receiving thorough training in the single art of landscape. Profoundly affected by the growing interest in the natural scene, he was also influenced by André Le Nôtre's design of the Tuileries and Versailles, the latter of which he had studied closely during his father's residence as court painter.[63] Through such training, augmented by his work as a military engineer under Washington, L'Enfant possessed an expertise in accommodating the products of art to geography, and in his selection of a precise site for the capital he put that ability to use.

After carefully surveying the land along the Potomac, L'Enfant decided on the area where Washington, D.C., now stands, partly because it afforded a "really beautiful . . . prospect," as he informed Jefferson, but also because it "present[ed] a situation most advantageous to run streets and prolong them on grand and far-distant points of view." The numerous springs and creeks in the area he saw as natural sources for the ponds and fountains he was planning to incorporate in his design. His enthusiasm for the site appears fully in a letter to Hamilton in which L'Enfant exclaimed, "no position in America can be more susceptible of grand improvement than that between the eastern branch of the Potomac and Georgetown" rivers. Of course, the belief that the special conditions of the native landscape somehow betokened urban greatness had existed for some time. In the background of L'Enfant's remarks we hear echoes of Strachey on Kecoughtan and Penn on the Delaware Peninsula. "Of all the places I have seen in the World," Penn wrote of that strip of land, "I remember not one better . . . appointed for a Town." But in the 1790s such an idea was enhanced by post-Revolutionary exuberance and so took on a credibility it never had before. American spokesmen of this period, as Cecelia Tichi has shown, celebrated the Revolution as the start of a new golden age in which environmental reform would lead to the fulfillment of the American destiny.[64] And what more important environmental reform existed than the building of the new national capital?

To L'Enfant, however, remaking the landscape did not mean imposing random forms. Believing that the "grand and truly beautiful [are] only to be met with when nature contributes with art and diversifies the object," he sought to integrate his design with the natural surroundings. Convinced that the standard grid pattern "would absolutely annihilate every [one] of the advantages" which the terrain presented, he combined elements of the grid with a radial street pattern to accentuate the gently rolling landscape. Taking their character from the open expanse of ground, the main avenues were to be 160 feet wide with 30 feet of gravel walk on each side, both being immense dimensions for the time. To enhance the air of natural openness, rows of trees were to trim the main thoroughfares.[65]

Not just with wide streets and arborous borders did L'Enfant attempt to create an aura of generosity and naturalness in his plan. Spacious gardens lined main thoroughfares such as Grand Avenue so that these leading streets, as L'Enfant explained in his "Observations" accompanying the plan, would pass "over the most favorable ground for prospect and convenience." To lend the presidential house the charm and "agreeableness of a country seat"—to make it a rural retreat in the city—he surrounded the manor with a sumptuous park, 1,800 feet by three-quarters of a mile. Every lot within the city received enough land "for spacious houses and gardens," while along the border of the capital a hundred lots were reserved "for the habitation of whole families of laboring people with vegetable gardens and fields for rearing of catil."[66] These latter provisions reveal L'Enfant's concern not only with the *haute culture* of the city but with the quality of life there as well.

No doubt that concern was partially responsible for L'Enfant's scheme for populating the city. Realizing that the capital would not be a true community until adequately peopled, he proposed that groups of individuals from the various states settle in sixteen independent units, eventually "branching out" and connecting with one another. L'Enfant saw the streets, gardens, rows of trees, and public buildings as a skeleton to be fleshed out by subsequent development. Repeatedly expressing his ideas in organic metaphors and natural imagery, he described the sixteen settlements as "roots of distinct establishments" which would "rise and range like trees in a young orchard." The streets and avenues themselves, he wrote, would facilitate growth and stability by "serv[ing] as does the main artery in the animal body, which diffuses life through the smaller vessels, and improves vigor, and activity throughout the whole frame."[67]

Notable in L'Enfant's plan is the way its synthesis of pastoral and urban elements and its provision for progressive change amid stability stand as mute testimony to the values of the age. That symbolic purpose even seems to have been part of L'Enfant's goal. Though interested in the quality of life in the capital, he was especially concerned that the city function as a token "worthy of its name." Above all, he wrote, the "mode of taking possession of, and improving, the whole district . . . must leave to posterity a grand idea of the patriotic interest which promoted it."[68] For L'Enfant, the national capital represented a literal and visionary symbol of American development—an original hieroglyphic, the characters of which were to be reinterpreted and reused in cities of the future.

To a degree, L'Enfant's hopes were realized. Though he worked on the city for only a year before being dismissed over an altercation with the commissioners of the project, subsequent planners followed his design closely enough so Washington, D.C., still retains many of the essential features in the original plan. Besides inspiring urban development elsewhere, L'Enfant's bold design exerted substantial influence on the forms of newly developing cities such as Indianapolis and Buffalo. In 1797, Seth Pease laid out the plan for Cleveland according to L'Enfant's synthesis of rectilinear and radial street patterns, and Augustus Woodward put the same model to use in his "honeycomb" design for Detroit in 1802. Shaping the contours of a score of smaller communities as well, the plan for Washington, D.C., became a fountainhead of pride and hope for the development of urban America.[69]

Of course, not everyone admired or appreciated the new capital. To some observers, the grandness of the plan, so indebted to forms first used to embellish the palaces of tyrannical regimes in Europe, seemed at odds with the ideals of the American republic. Then too, the slow growth of the city's population precipitated occasional criticism of the capital as a collection of tree stumps and undeveloped building sites. Such complaints, however, were more than balanced by approbation of a design which so clearly embodied the belief that the embryonic republic signaled the start of a new golden age. At this time Americans saw urban development converging with geographical uniqueness to contribute, in the phrase of the era, to "the rising glory of America."

Equally important was the manner by which this image of America helped assuage self-doubt. Although native spokesmen routinely denounced Europe as an overcivilized, effete society lacking the resilience and vitality of its transatlantic offspring, few could deny that in the arts, manufacturing, refinement, and history, Europe was far richer. Yet in this quarter the ideal of urban-rural synthesis did some of its most effective work. By identifying the local scene as a healthy blend of city and country—the best of nature and the best of civilization—Americans found that they need not renounce the distinctive features of enchorial geography to possess the refinements of Europe. Under the banner of urban pastoralism, Americans could claim they possessed both. Accordingly, one writer of the period announced that "the *industrious village*, the *busy city*, the *crowded port*—all these are the gifts of liberty" nurtured by the "verdant meadows, enameled pastures," and "yellow harvests" of the demigod "PLENTY."[70]

In the last quarter of the century such sentiments spread rapidly and powerfully, appearing in the work of even staunch Jeffersonians such as Freneau. In his *Rising Glory of America*, written with Hugh Brackenridge, Freneau proclaims that "visions of the rustic reign," though important in America, "would scarce employ the varying mind of man," since "Each seeks employ, and each a different way: / Strip Commerce of her sail, and men once more / Would be converted into savages."[71] To be truly civilized, man must develop a society that harmonizes agriculture and commerce, the latter of which Freneau identifies as an urban activity. Happily, such a society exists in America. Where once had been a wilderness of "rude inhabitants," the foreign visitor now "descry's our spacious towns, / He hails the prospect of the land and views / A new, a fair, a fertile world arise."[72] Reflecting the native zeitgeist, Freneau employs natural images here to equate American cities with geological fecundity and to suggest that agricultural and urban development follow from and enhance one another.

Freneau also projects the same equation into the future. With the

vatic exuberance of an "Isaiah," a "Jeremy," and an "Amos," he foresees the nourishing waters of the Ohio converting the unimproved
land into "many a town / Of note," while the "Potowmack, navigable
stream," vies with the Thames, Tiber, and Rhine by yielding "an
hundred towns." In Freneau's vision, the native geography will produce a natural paradise dotted with "cities and men" in a spontaneous
transformation recalling the millennial promise. But Freneau does
not rest with implication. The last lines of the poem evince the affinity between the enlightened, patriotic version of urban pastoralism in
America and its biblical antecedents. When the land has become one
vast *rus in urbe*, Freneau proclaims,

> A New Jerusalem sent down from heav'n
> Shall grace our happy earth, perhaps this land,
> Whose virgin bosom shall then receive, tho' late,
> Myriads of saints with their almighty king,
> To live and reign on earth a thousand years
> Thence call'd Millennium. Paradise anew
> Shall flourish, by no second Adam lost.[73]

According to Freneau's epic, the ultimate reconciliation of city and
country, which had so long eluded humankind, beckons on the horizon of America's future.

A similar idea, though without the explicit millennial gloss, appears in David Humphrey's "Future State of the Western Territory."
Like Freneau, Humphreys envisions the period when "the wilderness
shall blossom as the rose" and the West shall "like Eden bloom." With
this deft allusion to Isaiah, he announces nothing short of an idealized
urban middle landscape in America.

> Then cities rise, and spiry towns increase,
> With gilded domes, and ev'ry art of peace.
> Then Cultivation shall extend his pow'r,
> Rear the green blade, and nurse the tender flow'r;
> Make the fair villa, in full splendors smile,
> And robe with verdure all the genial soil.[74]

That Humphreys, who espoused the aristocratic leanings of the Hartford Wits, could be a trenchant poetic and political enemy of Freneau
and still hold the same vision suggests just how puissant the idea was.
It could cut across what were otherwise unbreachable ideological lines

to reinforce the belief in American uniqueness. Both Humphreys' and Freneau's poems reflect the intense national pride and confidence of this period. Any doubts about the compatibility of "robed verdure" and "golden" cities are swept away by the image of reconciliation borne aloft in a rising tide of native optimism.

The trope of reconciliation, however, did not exist only in poetry, essays, or paintings. What is remarkable is the way it materialized in plans for urban development and in the actual shape American cities were taking. Formative in the projects of L'Enfant and Pease, the idea even infused itself into the thinking of that arch-agrarian, Jefferson, who, despite his aversion to cities, was intimately involved in the plans for the national capital and strongly supported L'Enfant's design. Jefferson's attraction to urban pastoralism emerges most noticeably in an 1805 letter to C. F. Comte de Volney in which Jefferson explained that Americans must begin "building our cities on a more open plan" to ensure moral and physical health in those environments. To effect that purpose, he proposed a city plan based on a checkerboard pattern in which every other square would remain free of buildings. Because "every square of houses will be surrounded by four open squares" in this ingenious design, "the atmosphere of such a town would be like that of the country" while still remaining urbane. "I have accordingly proposed," he continued in the same letter, "that the enlargements of the city of New Orleans, which must immediately take place, shall be on this plan." Less than twenty years later, Dr. William Lattimore advocated the same design as the basis for Jackson, Mississippi, because "having trees of the forest or artificial groves" within the town would promote "comfort, convenience and greater security against fire, as well as a fairer promise of health." By the close of the eighteenth century Boston, New York, and Philadelphia had either an open common or a public pleasure ground reserved for the recreation of their populace. Citizens in Newport, Philadelphia, and Boston undertook "beautification" projects for laying out public walks with elms, and inhabitants of Charles Town became noted for their cultivation of formal gardens.[75] Coupled with the verbal and pictorial presentations of urban America, these activities reveal the important role of urban pastoralism in the American self-image in this period.

Though the idea, however, had numerous supporters by the last two decades of the century, it had not yet reached the stage where it could function fully as a mythic embodiment of the American urban ethos.

Something was missing—something that could personalize the belief that America offered unique opportunities for inaugurating a new type of urban society. For myth is more than weltanschauung; it requires a universe and a hero. In embracing the ideal of urban-pastoral synthesis, Americans had constructed the universe—the moral geography—yet there was no urban counterpart to the noble husbandman to seize the imagination. The problem was, what kind of hero could embody the values of the ideal in a way commensurate with the promise of the native landscape? Put another way, the question involved the identity of the nation itself: Was the American character capable of combining the virtues of democratic pastoralism with a progressive, energetic, and communal urbanity? In the same year that Washington chose L'Enfant to design the Federal City, Benjamin Franklin, approaching death, was adding the final strokes to a self-portrait that would provide answers to those questions.

V

Although a complete English version of Franklin's *Autobiography* did not appear until 1868, the book bears the imprint of the time, or more appropriately the times, in which it was composed. Quintessentially a work of the eighteenth century, the memoirs reflect the American need to define its national in terms of its urban character. While physical nature plays only a minor role in the book, the *Autobiography* may be the fullest American expression of urban pastoralism before 1820 because it validates the ideal in a uniquely significant way. Instead of teeming gardens fused with urban forms, the memoirs present a hero and a milieu which unite rural and urban values through a social pattern of individual and communal fulfillment.

This is not to suggest that Franklin composed his memoirs guided throughout by an overarching mythopoeic design. The opening section, written in 1771, is directed to his son, and while commentators repeatedly have discounted this address as a rhetorical gesture, Franklin reasserted in a letter to Mathew Carey fifteen years later that private familial instruction had been his original purpose. By contrast, the remaining three sections, written at different times and in varying styles, were "intended for the Publick" as Franklin himself explains in their pages. Despite the memoirs' ostensible fragmentation, however, the concern Franklin displayed throughout his life for the image he projected—a concern expressed overtly in the *Autobiography*—makes it highly unlikely that he viewed his self-portrait as a patchwork of variform narratives. We know that before his death he revised the sections, possibly with an eye toward thematic unity, and his role in the decision to publish the *Autobiography* in its unfinished form suggests that he conceived it as a complete work.[76]

The best evidence for the homologous mythic unity of the *Autobiography*, however, is the text itself. Its structure constitutes a pattern of sequential expansion which affixes a cultural significance to the character Franklin creates. While Robert Sayre has pointed out that the autobiographical form inherently gives its subject a cultural dimension, numerous students of the memoirs have noted that the character who emerges from its pages preeminently embodies the values and position of Americans at the time. That Franklin himself conceived much of the *Autobiography* in similar terms is indicated by his decision to include at the beginning of section 2 a letter from Benjamin Vaughan in which the latter asserted the *Autobiography* could well encapsulate "the internal circumstances of your country." "All that has happened to you," Vaughan maintained, "is also connected with the detail of the manners and situation of *a rising* people."[77] This archetypal Franklin, however, does not reside solely in the last three "public" sections introduced by this letter. Beneath its overt purpose, section 1 also contributes to Franklin's creation of a mythic urban hero whose growth is intrinsically related to the native environment and whose ever-widening potential makes the very open-endedness of the *Autobiography* part of the mythopoeic pattern.

To present himself as an exemplary embodiment of American urban ideals, Franklin devotes much of the first section to fashioning a moral landscape that incorporates Lockean presuppositions about the effects of environment on character. Finding his early life in Boston tense and restrictive, he decided at nineteen to leave his native city, as he tells us, to "assert my Freedom" from the tyranny of apprenticeship under his brother, James. This movement toward freedom figures more than a retreat from servitude. Much of the life defining the Boston he left behind had proved to be oppressive, according to Franklin. In recalling his Boston past, he conveys the impression of a society burdened by an artificially inflated economy and onerous laws resulting in the temporary imprisonment of his brother and an injuction against the printing of his paper. Boston appears as a repressive environment choking off individual opportunity—an image which Franklin extends to his family. Telling how financial restraints had prevented his father from assuming leadership in political and church affairs, he presents Josiah as a man constrained by environmental factors beyond his control.[78] Franklin even suggests that such a situation obtained in his own relations with the family. Thwarted by his father in his desire to go to sea, subject to beatings and other improprieties from his brother, he presents the Boston of his youth as a place precluding freedom and promoting frustration.

Far from incorporating the urban-pastoral promise of America, Boston resembles more the London described later in section 1. Having worked there for a time as a pressman, Franklin delineates this Old World city as a restrictive society where he "just rubb'd on from hand to mouth" and where, while working at Watt's Printing House, he was harassed by his co-workers, who were repeatedly "mixing my Sorts, transposing my Pages, [and] breaking my Matter" because he refused to pay an extra sum for the compositors' beer, which he never drank. Like Boston, London offered few opportunities. Unable to prosper, Franklin had to enter a "new business" as a tradesman, a career which abruptly terminated when his mentor died. The similarity between London and Boston also extends to the way each threatens virtue, in that the only moral "errata" Franklin ascribes to himself occurred in these two cities. To free himself of his Boston apprenticeship, he had taken advantage of a private agreement with his brother—an action, he realizes, which "was not fair in me to take" and so constituted "one of the first Errata of my Life." In London, likewise, he found himself wasting his money, attempting "Familiarities, (another Erratum)" with a young woman living at his hostelry, and forgetting his commitments at home.[79] Through such an association, the Boston of section 1, like Crèvecoeur's Charles Town, emerges as an alien manifestation, an aberrant extension of Europe in conflict with the dominant values of the *Autobiography* and the democratic promise of America. In the memoirs' moral geography, Boston becomes the corrupt city which Franklin must escape.

In recounting his decision to leave, however, Franklin makes clear that he does not repudiate the civilization he has left behind. Conveying a certain fondness for his Boston heritage, he describes his father with admiration as a man of "sound Understanding, and solid Judgment," and proudly gives the history of his family's immigration to America. Franklin willingly accepts certain elements of his old city because they comport with the values of the *Autobiography* in a way that envelopes his life within a native paradigm. Just as his family, like thousands of other Americans, had moved to the New World "to enjoy their Mode of Religion with Freedom," Franklin departs from Boston out of a similar desire for independence. His voyage to the embryonic Philadelphia of 1723 thus parallels an archetypal pattern of the culture: the American journey to new cities in a fresh landscape.[80]

As Franklin recounts that journey, he expands his moral geography to encompass other mythic elements of America's historical terrain. Before he can reach Philadelphia he must undergo, as did the first wave of colonists, a series of privations at the hands of raw nature: a squall off Long Island which "tore our rotten Sails to pieces," a feverish night in the scuttle of his ship, thirty hours on shipboard "without Victuals, or any Drink but a Bottle of filthy Rum," and a thorough soaking from a rainstorm during a fifty-mile hike from Amboy to Burlington. After devoting almost five pages to these events, Franklin then describes his appearance upon entering Philadelphia on a Sunday morning in what is by now one of the most famous passages in American writing:

> I was in my Working Dress, my best Cloaths being to come round by Sea. I was dirty from my Journey; my Pockets were stuff'd out with Shirts and Stockings; I knew no Soul nor where to look for Lodging.

What is significant about this description, as Franklin himself notes, is the figure he cuts. Subject to the effects of the wilderness, he has been purged of most of the elements of his past. His possessions consist only of the few articles of clothing stuffed in his pockets and a Dutch dollar. Thrown upon his own resources—"I knew no Soul nor where to look for Lodging"—he is entirely self-reliant.[81]

The figure which Franklin makes here bears a striking resemblance to many characters of American writing but especially to the simple yeoman of eighteenth-century pastoralism. Like that noble rustic, the Franklin of this episode seems to be a tabula rasa, a new man divested of those elements of his European past irrelevant to his "New Country," as he calls Philadelphia. In both cases the cardinal metaphor of value becomes the promise of fresh beginnings made possible by westward expansion, an activity which, Franklin once wrote, was "making this Side of our Globe reflect a brighter Light."[82] In the *Autobiography*, Philadelphia assumes the role of the middle landscape, offering, as a city of the West, a new light of hope to the individual.

The connection between Philadelphia and the pastoral ideal extends beyond the former's location. The ambiance of the city itself resembles that of the farmer's cultivated milieu. As Franklin presents it, Philadelphia seems to possess an almost natural fecundity and rural flavor. Bread, to his surprise, is plentiful and inexpensive, while wants seem few—Franklin is "refresh'd" by a roll and "a Draught of the River Water," an elemental meal. The inhabitants are friendly, as evidenced by the young Quaker who conducts him to suitable and "reputable" lodgings. Even the atmosphere seems to promote benev-olence, as the indigent Franklin gives two of his newly purchased rolls to a woman and her child. Despite his shabby appearance upon en-tering the city, young Ben is immediately accepted in the company of other simple, but "clean dress'd, People," joining them in "the great Meeting House of the Quakers near the Market." "I sat down among them," he explains, "and after looking round a while and hearing nothing said, being very drowzy thro' Labour and want of Rest the preceding Night, I fell fast asleep, and continu'd so till the Meeting broke up, when one was kind enough to rouse me." In Philadelphia Franklin does not encounter a frantic pace or a competitive spirit. His rough exterior somehow blends smoothly with that of the other in-habitants, who readily welcome him with kindness. Far from engag-ing in immediate exertion, he finds the city a place of refreshment and rest, as though it were a somnolent country village. This Sunday tran-quility prevails even the next day, glossing Franklin's account of his efforts to find work. Relating his dealings with the two printers of the town, Keimer and Bradford, Franklin explains how he "endeavour'd to put his [Keimer's] Press . . . into Order fit to be work'd with; and promising to come and print off his Elegy as soon as he should have got it ready, I return'd to Bradford's who gave me a little Job to do for the present, and there I lodged and dieted."[83] The movement back and forth between various jobs is rendered in a placid cadence, punctuated by a domestic image of ease and relaxation.

This calm atmosphere pervades the entire *Autobiography*, giving the work, as several commentators have noted, a surprisingly relaxed tone even with all the activity involved.[84] The effect results largely be-cause Franklin records achievements, especially his business suc-cesses, without going into the emotional struggles behind them. The ideal of serenity, at the time associated increasingly with country life, becomes in Franklin's pages an important characteristic of the devel-oping urban milieu. By such a strategy Philadelphia emerges as a city-scape of idyllic pliability and congeniality, promoting a life of "constant Felicity."

In accommodating himself to this new milieu, of course, Franklin must not only compete with the other printers but face corruption in the form of Keimer's duplicity. Yet we never get the sense that this competition is straining or that Keimer's scheming poses a danger because Franklin presents the old printer as a comic figure whose failure quickly dispatches him from the scene. What prevents that failure from dampening the hopeful mood of the memoirs is the way Franklin attributes responsibility for Keimer's demise, not to social conditions, but to Keimer's incompetence. Since he lacked industry, "kept his Shop miserably, sold often without profit for ready Money," and failed to keep accounts, Keimer created his own misfortune.[85] If we feel little remorse at his fate, it is because he appears as a ridiculous, low character whose narrowness and greed are out of place in the developing world of Philadelphia.

For Philadelphia is a place of opportunity, offering possibilities commensurate with the edenic myth of the fresh start. Whereas in Boston Franklin was nothing more than an unappreciated apprentice, he is now a man of skill who can sell his services openly in the town. Part of the reason he can do so is that the low quality of work done by the other printers makes Franklin's expertise a unique commodity, but that complementarity between the individual and his environment is precisely the point. Just as Philadelphia provides opportunity because, like the unimproved landscape, it needs amelioration, Franklin willingly works to make the most of the chance. Possessing initiative, industry, and instinctive wisdom, he belongs in the same way that the good farmer belongs to his land. In both instances the environment animates the central figure who uses his talents to achieve success and independence. Franklin's quest for progressive development becomes possible by a return to a simpler, bucolic past represented in the young city of Philadelphia, where individual efforts to improve self and society have an impact.

This beneficial relationship between the individual and his environment constitutes a central motif of the *Autobiography* because of Franklin's ability to depict himself as a man eminently suited to his surroundings, an inspirational figure at once larger than life and common enough to encourage imitation. It has been said that Franklin, throughout his life, not only sought to cultivate an image of himself as an exemplary American but actually embodied a range of cultural values that made him representative. Peter Gay has called him "the savage as philosopher," a man who epitomized "the virtues of nature and the triumphs of civility," and that duality clearly obtains in the *Autobiography*.[86] A pioneer willing to explore new areas in science, politics, and morals, Franklin possesses an adaptability, a boldness, a self-reliance, and a natural sagacity that anticipate the traits later decades would associate with the frontier hero. Yet the rugged, uncouth backwoodsman is probably too extreme a figure to identify with Franklin because the latter's naturalness is always domesticated with a morality as seemingly simple as it is durable, while being attuned to a milieu marked by substantial refinement. Instead of the urbanite wearing buckskin, the Franklin of the memoirs is more the city dweller clothed in homespun, who combines learning, sophistication, and a business acumen with the virtues of the noble husbandman.

The opportunistic environment of Philadelphia is closely tied to Franklin's virtuous temperament as interrelated factors in both his business and civic accomplishments. Because of the work required in this young western city, Franklin learns to cultivate his moral character. "In order to secure my Credit and Character as a Tradesman," he explains, "I took care not only to be in *Reality* Industrious and frugal, but to avoid all *Appearances* of the Contrary. I drest plainly; I was seen at no Places of idle Diversion." While such virtue carries with it material benefits in that, "being esteem'd an industrious thriving young Man," Franklin receives more business, the relationship between the material and the moral is reciprocal. If virtue abets economic gain, economic independence is a means of "securing Virtue, it being more difficult for a Man in Want to act always honestly, as . . . *it is hard for an empty Sack to stand upright.*"[87] Through his own example, Franklin suggests that one can retain those values associated with rural life even while participating in the economic world of the city.

The pastoral elements of Franklin's character are perhaps most visible in the section of the memoirs devoted to his "bold and arduous Project of arriving at moral Perfection." In his study of the yeoman dream in America, Rex Burns has explained how in the eighteenth century the ideal husbandman was associated with several major traits: competence, morality, independence, and industry. Notable in Franklin's project is the way it encompasses those very qualities. While his methodically tenacious approach to the plan displays competence, the virtues themselves define a moral life of temperance, sincerity, justice, and tranquility. "*Frugality and Industry*" in turn become the means of "freeing me from my remaining Debt, and producing Affluence and Independence." Franklin even alludes to the similarity between his moral goals and those traits conventionally ascribed to the virtuous farmer by couching his plan in an agricultural metaphor. By devoting "a Week's strict Attention to each of the Virtues," he explains,

> I could go thro' a Course compleat in Thirteen Weeks, and four Courses in a Year. And like him who having a Garden to weed, does not attempt to eradicate all the bad Herbs at once, which would exceed his Reach and his Strength, but works on one of his Beds at a time, and having accomplished the first proceeds to a Second; so I should have, (I hoped) the encouraging Pleasure of seeing on my Pages the Progress I made in Virtue.

Although Franklin never gains moral perfection, that failure does not deny value to his program because, he asserts, "I was by the Endeavour a better and a happier Man than I otherwise should have been, if I had not attempted it." The very attempt possesses significance as a yeomanly effort of virtuous labor with social import.[88]

Indeed, Franklin identifies an inclination toward virtue as the basis for both individual development and communal participation. While it is partially true that his precepts, as Norman Fiering has argued, are directed toward personal growth and character building, almost all of them possess public implications as well. "Silence" entails "Speak[ing] not but what may benefit others or yourself"; "Frugality" means "Mak[ing] no Expence but to do good to others or yourself"; "Sincerity" requires "Us[ing] no hurtful Deceit"; "Justice" demands "Wrong[ing] none"; and "Chastity" precludes "us[ing] Venery . . . for . . . the Injury of your own or another's Peace or Reputation." Even the private virtues of temperance, order, and resolution take on social coloration in that silence, as Franklin explains, "tends to procure that coolness and Clearness of Head" that allow one to practice order and resolution, which in turn lead to the frugality and industry that procure affluence and independence.[89] Personal moral growth and independence thus become the means for turning outward to promote the well-being and advancement of society.

In the last two sections of the memoirs Franklin displays the beneficial results of such a philosophy in what stands as a vade mecum for urban life. By keeping his wants to a minimum, in the pattern of the virtuous farmer, he is able to prosper in this trade, become independent, and hence "turn my Thoughts a little to public Affairs." In 1736 he becomes clerk of the General Assembly and the year after is appointed postmaster general of Pennsylvania. Two years later he initiates action to form the province's first fire company, and in 1744 he helps found the American Philosophical Society. By the late 1740s and early 1750s he is devoting his attention to establishing an academy "for a compleat Education of Youth," later to become the University of Pennsylvania. Sometime in the late 1750s, while serving as a member of the Pennsylvania Assembly, he proposes bills for paving and lighting the streets of Philadelphia. And the accomplishments go on. Franklin, meanwhile, becomes a figure of mounting prestige, enjoying, as he says, a "Degree of Reputation among the Learned" and the confidence and esteem of the citizenry.[90] Sections 3 and 4 of the memoirs become a compendium inculcating the message that personal fulfillment and public good are one. The conflict between self and other, which Freud would identify as the Gordian knot of society, Franklin simply unravels in reciprocating coils of individual and social progress wound around the eighteenth-century ideal of enlightened self-interest.

What is remarkable in the *Autobiography* is Franklin's ability to present a harmonious balance in character while conveying a sense of growth and change. As a youth, the Franklin of the memoirs is unsophisticated, simple, and hard-working—almost rustic—yet commercially minded and aware of what success requires. In his practice of virtue and his trade, he elevates both himself and the community. By the second half of the book, the older Franklin is aware, worldwise, at times subtle, yet he has managed to achieve independence through industry, frugality, and diligence—an independence which has freed him to contribute to society at large. In both phases, Franklin the character manages to mediate between sophistication and simplicity, to balance and harmonize self and others by satisfying the demands of both the individual and the group. Through such development, the author of the *Autobiography* incorporates within a representative figure the reconciliation of stability and progressive change which has been an important feature of post-Enlightenment urban pastoralism. Possessing just enough flux to be interesting, Franklin stands as a factual yet ideal hero of an urban middle landscape. His world is a careful blend of myth and reality, directed by the resilient Franklin and appealing as much for what it omits as for what it includes.

By the close of the *Autobiography*, as it turns out, that world in-

cludes quite a bit. Repudiating Boston earlier, Franklin now symbolically embraces it. He mends the rift with his dying brother, assuming
guardianship of James's son, and becomes intellectually indebted to
the city of his birth, learning about electricity from Archibald Spen-
cer. We see Franklin cultivating intercolonial friendships and even
promoting the Albany Plan for unification of the colonies, all the
while extending his influence to cosmopolitan proportions. Traveling
at the close from Philadelphia to New York and finally to London, he
becomes the envoy of the colonial message: the right of local sover-
eignty free of autocratic meddling. The last section of the *Autobiography*, that is, functions as a symbolic, unfinished journey pointing to
an ever-widening scope for the American promise—a journey which
the post-Revolutionary reader, drawing on his knowledge of Franklin's
subsequent international activities and the success of the early republic, must complete.

By its very open-endedness, the *Autobiography* identifies itself as a
document commensurate with the optimism about America's destiny
so prevalent at the time. Confident about the American future, native
writers such as Freneau were claiming that "the Old World taught by
you, / Shall blush to own her barbarous laws, / Shall learn instruction
from the New." Similar sentiments were echoed by those viewing
America from the other side of the Atlantic, as Thomas Pownall's
Memorial Addressed to the Sovereigns of America reveals. Asserting that
America was "the means in the hands of Providence, of extending the
civilization of human society," Pownall went on to argue that by taking
up their "character within themselves, and hold[ing] out its operations and effect to the Old World," Americans "will become a Nation
to whom all Nations will come." The difference between these generalized statements and the *Autobiography* is that Franklin's book connects this belief to the urban-pastoral conception of America. In the
process, Franklin reaffirms the universalist component originally
present in the biblical version of that idea. At the center of the new
world, however, he does not place the New Jerusalem. Instead he positions a historical urban hero who helps make Philadelphia, as Franklin once called it, "the Center of the Continent Colonies." If "the
Salvation of English Liberty depended," as Franklin claimed in 1775,
"on the Perseverance and Virtue of America," the memoirs offer a
model for maintaining that virtue in the native urban scene.[91]

The *Autobiography*, like Beverley's *History* and L'Enfant's plan for
the Federal City, embodies an urban-pastoral vision extending beyond

the idea of improving cities by infusing them with domesticated nature or rural tranquility. All three project forms of the ideal inherently connected to visions of America as a special place. But unlike Beverley, who concentrated on the material and moral benefits of a partnership between town building and agriculture, or L'Enfant, who foresaw a capital whose shapely marriage with the natural terrain could symbolize the national dream, Franklin provides an exemplum of pastoral urbanity manifested in the social atmosphere of a city and the character of its citizens. Presenting a version of urban pastoralism centered on a symbolic hero, Franklin's book stands as the culmination of a century which believed that in America a new type of city was possible, combining the best of rural and urban and inhabited by individuals drawing on native talents and inspired by the promise of the open landscape and fresh beginnings. Together with the other pronouncements and plans examined here, the *Autobiography* opened the way for a new century in which Americans would embrace with even greater enthusiasm the pastoral conception of their urban future.

IV

Landscape as Cityscape
Urbanization and the Western Garden

Although belief in American distinctiveness had been developing since the age of settlement in the seventeenth century, that idea became central to native mythology in the sixty years before the Civil War. Separation from Europe was the rallying cry, as spokesmen for the American ethos identified their country's destiny, not as a continuation of history, but as a pathway to origins. Addressing young America in 1844, Emerson affirmed that the new republic was "the country of the Future" precisely because "it is a country of beginnings, of projects, of designs, of expectations." It seemed that the nation had awakened from the burdens of the past to face a fresh horizon. According to Robert Mills, a prominent architect in this period, America had "entered a new era in the history of the world." "Our vast country is before us," continued Mills, "and our motto [is] Excelsior." Such remarks were echoed repeatedly in the popular magazines of the period. One writer in *Putnam's*, for example, paid tribute to the "startling and momentous" facts of the age, though he did not cite the distinctive character of the landscape or the success of democracy. Instead, he explained with amazement, what distinguished America at this time, and what constituted "the great phenomenon of the Age," was "the growth of great cities."[1]

What sparked this claim was the tremendous increase in American urbanization from 1790 to 1850. At the opening of this period 5 percent of the population lived in urban areas; by 1850 that figure was approaching 20 percent. The 24 incorporated places of 2,500 or more had become 236. Instead of 5 cities exceeding 10,000, demographers now tallied 60 cities above that total, with 6 having populations over 100,000. Under the influence of developing industrialization, the

Northeast experienced the most substantial growth. Its four leading cities—Baltimore, Boston, Philadelphia, and New York, including Brooklyn—claimed a combined 1.3 million inhabitants, swelling the urban population to over 30 percent of the region's total. In the forty years before 1860, population increases in northeastern cities, when compared with the region's overall growth, had proceeded at a faster rate than they would at any other time in the century.[2]

Though Americans long had cherished urban development as a sign of increased prosperity and success, most were surprised at the dramatic growth of their cities in the first half of the nineteenth century. For some, however, that development carried dark implications. At a time when the romantic fondness for nature was strengthening the Jeffersonian ideal of a green republic, a number of artists and intellectuals feared that such unprecedented urbanization threatened America's position as nature's nation. Because cities developed in part through increased migration from rural areas, these individuals argued that unchecked urbanization drained off the vitality of the country and, in the process, endangered democracy, which they continued to believe flourished best in a rural environment. Such was the message of a number of liberal clergymen including Amory Mayo and Edwin Chapin, whose full-length works on urban life addressed the question of city-country relations in America. Asserting that "our hope of a Christian Democracy is in the country life of the nation," Mayo, a Massachusetts Unitarian, warned that "just now, commerce is flaunting her sudden successes and intolerable follies of luxury in the eyes of the country, inflaming young men with the aspiration to exchange the honors of health and the independence at home for slavery and effeminacy in the town . . . and the exhausting pleasures of a city career." Chapin, a Universalist minister from New York and founder of a home for the indigent, put forth a similar admonition, lamenting that "young men" of today, "brought up in the pure air and among the hills, will not stay upon the bosom of nature." Instead, "they quit the fields, where they might make the grass grow, and increase the abundance of corn, to lean over counters, to stifle at writing desks, and, too often, to throw themselves away in the tide of dissipation."[3]

While some felt that increased urbanization augured ill for the pastoral ideal of America, reactions to the upsurge included more hopeful assessments. Building on ideas from the previous century, urban apologists maintained that increased growth was part of the natural pattern for producing a healthy balance between city and country.

Confident of native conditions, they asserted that the nation's urban development was consonant with rural values and with the themes of American uniqueness and nature's ascendency.

I

Although a number of strategies were developed for affirming the nexus of landscape and cityscape, one of the most common was to depict a particular city as arising, like agriculture, from natural laws and the distinctive features of the native terrain. This strategy repeatedly appeared in periodicals such as *Hunt's Merchants' Magazine*, the *Atlantic Monthly*, *DeBow's Review*, and the *North American Review*, which served as organs for commercial and urban interests. One article in the *Atlantic* defended New York as the "American Metropolis" by claiming that that city, located amidst "the richest grazing, grain, and orchard land in the Atlantic States," had arisen by a principle "as fixed as that defining the course of matter in the line of least resistance." Depicting the Atlantic states as one large, organic body, the article asserted that the region's agricultural products "ran down to the managing, disbursing, and balancing hand of New York as naturally as the thoughts of man run down to the hand which must embody them."[4]

Often technological advance, rural values, and urban growth were combined at this time in a vision of unprecedented progress and harmony. An 1831 article entitled "Thoughts on the Moral and Other Indirect Influences of Rail-Roads" predicted a period in which regions would grow closer as the railroad reduced travel time. Sectional feelings—including rural-urban antagonism—would disappear, and the native ethos would "be merged in national oneness." Reaching out the friendly arm of iron rails, eastern cities would help the nation become one vast *rus in urbe*, allowing Americans to "possess a large share of the knowledge, refinement, and polish of a city, united to the virtue and purity of the country." By the 1850s some Americans were unwilling to stop at mere forecast. In his report *The Trade and Commerce of . . . North America* (1853), Israel D. Andrews, professor of political science and natural philosophy at Marietta College, proclaimed that the Erie Canal had promoted "the growth of the city of New York in population, wealth, and commerce," which in turn was "infusing life and vigor into the whole" of America. Eliminating distinctions between country and city, the canal "had secured and maintained to the

United States the characteristics of a homogeneous people." Because
of it, America was experiencing a union of the agricultural interior
and the cities of the East—an urban-pastoral linkage spanning half
the continent.[5]

In this period paeans to agriculture and rural life repeatedly were
coupled with praise of urbanization, particularly when the union became part of a tribute to democracy's advance. Thus another writer in
the *Atlantic Monthly* announced that "as cities have been the nurses
of democratic institutions and ideas, democratic nations, for very obvious reasons, tend to produce them." Convinced that cities "are the
natural fruits of a democracy" (note the organic metaphor), he went
on to state that "with no people are great cities so important, or likely
to be so increasingly populous, as with a great agricultural and commercial nation like our own, covered with a free and equal population."[6] With a deftness approaching legerdemain, this advocate of
urbanization easily reconciled cities with the Jeffersonian ideal of
democratic pastoralism.

If the twin demigods of progress and democracy were invoked to affirm the synthesis of rural and urban, the distinctive features of native
geography and institutions were cited as guarantees that American
cities never would resemble those of Europe. Amory Mayo took this
approach while addressing the changing character of his native New
York. "*An American city*," he explained, "*is essentially a different thing
from an European capital.*" Whereas "the old cities abroad are . . . the
centres of imperial influence; a court, a palace, a royal army, with the
peculiar results of such institutions," an "American municipality,"
lacking these autocratic trappings, is always "representative." "Its
money is the accumulation of the country's industry; its commerce is
the exchange of the products of the prairie . . . ; and its institutions
of philanthropy and religion are supported by . . . men and means
from the sects that spread over entire States." As a result, "an American city is only a convenient hotel, where a free country people come
up to tarry and do business, with old recollections of nature," and
where "the foreigner halts at his landing and, if able and enterprising,
pushes on to the 'Far West.'"[7] According to Mayo, the fluidity of
American life, made possible by democracy and especially the opportunity of open land, would prevent American cities from becoming
overcrowded collections of oligarchies and impoverished workers, as
European cities were.

While Americans such as Mayo argued that the landscape made all the difference, others said that, in effect, it did not matter. Surprisingly, this period, which otherwise continued to express faith in the sanative influence of life close to nature, witnessed a set of arguments that American cities offered more opportunities than did the country for developing characteristics traditionally associated with rural life: physical and moral health. The same essay which asserted that American cities were "the fruits of a democracy" also proclaimed that, contrary to the "old notion," statistics on urban life "have proved the city, as compared with the country, the more healthy, the more moral, and the more religious place." The author's reasoning was simple. Because farm life is arduous, "more constitutions are broken down in the hardening process than survive." Isolation and the lack of intellectual stimulation in rural areas "lower the tone of humanity, drive [rustics] to sensual pleasures and secret vices, and nourish a miserable pack of mean and degrading immoralities." An analogous though less vociferous argument formed the basis of Edwin Chapin's two major works on urban America: *Moral Aspects of City Life* (1853) and *Humanity in the City* (1854). While "innocence may strive best in the sweet air of the country," explained Chapin, what is "strongest and noblest in our nature is illustrated in the city," because "the city reveals the moral ends of being." Chapin supported this claim by subscribing to a liberal version of the fortunate fall: Virtues such as charity develop only because there are "dark ways to be trodden by its bright feet, and . . . suffering and sadness to require its aid." For Chapin the innocence of the country was mere puffery. True morality came only in the city where "the close contact that excites the worst passions of humanity also elicits its sympathies."[8]

What is interesting is that several of these defenses appear in works, such as Chapin's and Mayo's, which also express uneasiness over increased urbanization. This mixture of hope and fear suggests that at this time deep ambivalence existed over the direction urban development, primarily in the East, was taking—and with good reason. By the 1840s and 1850s the older cities along the Atlantic seaboard were assuming rather ominous shapes. As early as the second decade of the century, slum neighborhoods had begun to develop in Boston's North End and in the Five Points district of New York as unskilled laborers abandoned worn-out farms, moved to the city, and underbid one another for employment. The first major wave of European immigration in this period only magnified the dilemmas of insufficient housing and poverty which began to confront older cities. In the 1840s alone, over

1.5 million immigrants arrived in New York, many passing on to other towns and to the West but many more remaining, huddled together in noxious, overcrowded neighborhoods on the Lower East Side. By 1864, when the population of New York reached 800,000, almost 70 percent of the residents lived in the 15,000 tenements in the poorer neighborhoods of the city. Nor did the advent of industrialism provide an answer to these problems. Although new manufacturing produced some jobs, it was unable to absorb the full number of laborers crowding into New York, Boston, Philadelphia, and Baltimore and so check growing unemployment and penury. By 1835, almshouses in these four cities contained over 10,000 indigents, half of them foreign born. Adding to the predicament, urban crime and mob violence, developing largely from the discontent which overcrowding and poverty caused, increased as criminal districts and gangs of terrorizing thugs, phenomena previously confined to Europe, appeared in northeastern cities. According to Samuel Eliot, mayor of Boston in the late 1830s, a growing "spirit of violence" characterized urban life in Boston, New York, and other seaboard towns.[9]

Degenerating sanitary conditions in the larger eastern cities compounded the problems. In 1844 the editor of the *New World* wrote that New York's streets were so "abominably filthy" that "they are too foul to serve as the styes for the hogs which perambulate them." Nor was this picture an exaggeration. In an 1865 report, the Council of Hygiene of the Citizens Association of New York recorded with horror that municipal officials regularly allowed garbage to collect to depths of two or three feet before hauling it away. Though such unhealthful conditions existed most prominently in New York, inadequate sanitation plagued residents of Boston, Philadelphia, Baltimore, New Orleans, and Washington, D.C. Moreover, developing industrial activity began to produce a deleterious atmosphere in these rapidly growing cities. One journalist warned that "slaughter houses and manufactories of offensive stuffs" in Philadelphia, Boston, and New York were converting neighborhoods into "pestilential enclosures."[10]

While physical squalor and density were disturbing in themselves, more unsettling were the moral implications they carried. Such conditions betokened in the minds of many an expanding breach with the image of America as a land of virtue and lush green landscapes. As crime and poverty spread, contemporary observers increasingly feared that American cities were becoming morally flaccid—a debasing development, they warned, not limited to life among the lower orders. Ministers and other purveyors of American values repeatedly complained that upper- and middle-class residents had become overly fond of luxury and display, signaling a departure from the simple values of the past. Though such animadversions were conventional, in this period overcivilization seemed especially menacing to the urban-pastoral ideal as the sign of a sinister class consciousness threatening democracy. According to Edwin Chapin, the tendency of a certain "class of people" in the city "to set themselves apart as exclusive—as holding an inherent and divine patent of nobility" was both nefarious and unnatural since it was "inconsistent not only with the mutual dependence ordained by nature, but with our [democratic] theory of man." Reflecting a common response, Chapin believed that, far from evincing a happy balance of nature and civilization, American cities were moving away from nature and the egalitarian principles it "ordained."[11]

Despite claims to the contrary, New York, Boston, and other seaboard towns were displaying the same appalling conditions found in European cities, and some Americans were saying as much. In an 1847 entry in his diary, Philip Hone, former mayor of New York, recorded his profound fear that "our good city of New York has already arrived at the state of society to be found in the large cities of Europe . . . where the two extremes of costly luxury" and "squalid misery and hopeless destitution" are "presented in daily and hourly contrast." Even the manufacturing towns of Massachusetts such as Lowell and Waltham, which had been designed specifically to prevent those abuses common to European factory cities, received similar criticism. In 1849 Gilman Kimball, director of the Lowell Hospital, surveyed the conditions of that city, which had grown to 35,000, and concluded, "The same evils that so glaringly and deplorably affect the sanitary conditions of the manufacturing towns of Europe, are gradually making their appearance in our own." For a growing number of Americans, it seemed that Europe's grim history was enveloping the urban East and that in the future America would have to cast its vision elsewhere. Of course, the next logical step was predictable. For nearly a century Americans had directed their hopes toward the lush, undeveloped landscape, and in the first half of the nineteenth century many looked there again. As one writer for *Putnam's* put it, "The East is our past. . . . But Atlantis is still in the West."[12]

II

Although faith in the West as a repository of new opportunities had been building since the late 1700s, this tentative expectation developed into an unquestioned conviction by the fourth decade of the nineteenth century. Coupling it to the idea of manifest destiny, indigenous writers and spokesmen identified development of the continental interior as the key to America's future. *"The West,"* Emerson noted, "is the leading topic" of the day and for good reason. Here lay an immense stretch of land offering possibilities surpassing even those encountered by the first settlers of the Atlantic regions. Repeatedly writers pointed to the Mississippi and Ohio valleys as regions of immensely fertile soil, unlimited natural plentitude, and uncluttered space. As one article in the *Western Monthly Review*, a Cincinnati journal, announced in 1827, "no [other] country . . . can be found, which contains so great a proportion of cultivatable and habitable land, compared with the whole of its surface." According to this image, the natural greenness of the West prefigured an agricultural paradise where the pastoral ideal finally would be achieved. By 1850 the idea had become so thoroughly established that C. W. Dana's widely read *Garden of the World*, which appeared seven years later, was simply invoking a commonplace with its title.[13]

Yet this theory, like the eighteenth-century pastoral version of America at large, was qualified from the very beginning by urban expectations and activities. For one thing, town building had spearheaded development of the Mississippi and Ohio valleys. Long before any significant farming had occurred in these regions, Pittsburgh, St. Louis, Louisville, and Cincinnati had been built as depots providing the services necessary for inland expansion. Though these outposts were little more than forts at first, in the 1830s and 1840s they grew into substantial cities under the influence of the expanding railroad and canal systems. By 1850 Cincinnati was the sixth largest city in America with 115,000 people, while Pittsburgh, St. Louis, and Louisville had populations approaching or surpassing 50,000. Improved transportation had given rise to other inland cities such as Buffalo, Chicago, Cleveland, Detroit, and Milwaukee with the result that the western region contained a dozen cities with populations greater than 17,000. Nor did this trend go undetected. Besides the published census figures, reports by travelers in the West informed Americans of tramontane urban growth. In the words of one reporter, reflecting the excited response to such feverish activity, the stranger who visited the West "views here with wonder, the rapidity with which cities spring up in the forest; and with which barbarism retreats before the approach of art and civilization."[14]

While the phenomenon of urban growth qualified the image of an exclusively agrarian West, the theories of progress and civilization, which maintained that agriculture constituted only a preliminary stage of progress, to be supplanted eventually by thriving commercial and manufacturing cities, challenged that image on an ideological level. As these theories became widely accepted in the first half of the nineteenth century ("The assumptions of Condorcet," wrote John Greenleaf Whittier in 1845, find "echoes in all lands"), native writers proclaimed that civilization's advance became possible only through urban activity and turned to the past to validate this proposition. "All history," asserted one advocate in *Putnam's*, "bears uniform testimony that no nation or tribe ever passed from any condition which history or philosophy calls 'uncivilized,' 'savage,' or 'barbarous,' to a civilized character, except by . . . and through the agency of great cities." Consequently, when Americans directed their attention to western development, they often incorporated in their responses a vision of advancing civilization predicated on urban growth. Of course, such a vision proved problematic because, by asserting that civilization would triumph in the West only with substantial urbanization, it directly controverted the idea of the region's preeminence as an agricultural heartland.[15]

Urban development and the theory of civilization posed for Americans at this time the same dilemma that Europeans had encountered in the eighteenth century: finding a satisfactory solution to the conflicting claims of the primacy of agriculture and the inexorable march of civilization. While their answers were no more final than those of their European predecessors, western promoters did manage to produce arguments circumventing the paradox. Drawing on the very image of the West as a place where nature offered unique opportunities and abundance, they proceeded to make room for the city in the garden.

A leading practitioner of this strategy was Jesup Scott, a former businessman and lawyer in Connecticut and South Carolina, who moved to Ohio in 1831. Serving for a time as editor of the *Toledo Blade* while investing in prime city land, Scott became by 1860 one of the most-quoted authorities on urban development in the West. Although propounding his theories most fully in the articles he wrote in the 1840s and 1850s for *DeBow's Review* and *Hunt's Merchants' Magazine*, Scott became interested in western urbanization as early as 1832.[16] From studying demographic data, he realized that western cities were growing much faster than the region as a whole and that their rate of increase outstripped that of even the older cities of the East. One of the first to recognize the implications of these trends, he concluded that the continental interior was destined for urban greatness. But he also knew that such a bold prediction would seem farfetched to Americans who argued that the immense tracts of land would deter concentration in cities as individuals fanned out to settle the open landscape. Accordingly, when he began to publish his predictions, Scott assumed a defensive posture. In a series of articles entitled "Internal Trade," which appeared in the ephemeral *Western Monthly Magazine* in the late 1830s, he admitted that many people believed the Mississippi-Ohio Valley was destined to be "fixed . . . to an almost exclusive pursuit of agriculture" because in the past, "foreign commerce . . . constituted the only source of wealth; and . . . large cities could grow up no where but on the salt sea." Having made that concession, however, Scott proceeded to overturn it by arguing that such assumptions failed to consider the complex relationship among agriculture, trade and manufacturing, and urbanization. Drawing on the arguments of Adam Smith and the physiocrats and the record of the past, he asserted that "most of the countries distinguished for manufactures have first laid the foundations in a highly improved agriculture," which provided a surplus of goods stimulating "internal industry and trade." These activities, in turn, constituted the prime "agency in building up great cities." Considering these facts, explained Scott, think what would happen in the Mississippi Valley, which possessed "a fertility of soil not equalled by the old world." "Growing within its boundaries nearly all the productions of all the climes of the earth," the interior of the continent shortly would yield an abundance requiring "some convenient central point" for processing and distribution. Soon the region's vast mineral deposits also would be unearthed, further stimulating central areas of production, while its network of rivers and natural harbors would provide the means of transportation facilitating trade. As a result of this deterministic triad, Scott proclaimed, great cities would develop.[17] Precisely those features of the terrain which others said would make the West an agricultural paradise, Scott identified as conditions promoting city growth.

Scott, however, did not stop at predicting the rise of a few great cities. Through further demographic study, he refined his arguments in the 1840s and boldly claimed that in a hundred years the area between the Appalachians and Rockies would be predominately urban, containing a population six times that of the Atlantic states. At the base of his argument lay the conviction that population must increase because "the resources of our exuberantly rich soil" would continue to attract inhabitants, while the unmatched healthfulness of the climate would speed natural increase. Since the soil was so rich and since "our agriculture would be so improved" in fifty years, less than one-third of the people, he predicted, would have to "reside in the country as cultivators . . . to furnish food and raw materials for manufacture for the whole population." The other two-thirds, or 180 million people by his calculations, would be "left for towns."[18] Thus, an urban West was inevitable. Although Scott continued to elaborate this idea in his subsequent writings, it continued to rest on his single, major premise: that western geography must and would yield an urban pattern.

A parallel but more esoteric premise served as the basis of the developmental predictions put forth by William Gilpin, one of the most strident proponents of western supremacy. A personal friend of Andrew Jackson, Gilpin, like Scott, began his career of western advocacy through journalism. But Gilpin knew the West more thoroughly than did Scott. He accompanied John Charles Frémont on the trail to Oregon in the 1840s, served as a major in the First Missouri Volunteers, and eventually was appointed the first governor of the Colorado Territory. Perhaps this extensive contact with the undeniable grandeur of the West accounts for the bardic and almost mystic quality that Henry Nash Smith has pointed to in Gilpin's prose.[19] Certainly there is no denying the vatic enthusiasm of his writing, which helps explain the popularity of his works. Although a number of his articles appeared during the 1850s, Gilpin made his reputation as a leading spokesman for the West with the publication of *The Central Gold Region* (1860), a work he later revised and reissued in 1874 as *The Mission of the North American People.*

In *The Central Gold Region* Gilpin employs the standard image of the West as "the PASTORAL GARDEN of the world" where "nature has bountifully blended all her choicest gifts to locate the rural quintessence of America and of the world." To this traditional theory Gilpin adds a new argument. Borrowing from the work of Alexander von Humboldt, a German geographer and explorer whose writings circulated widely in America, Gilpin asserts that the West is ordained for greatness because of its position on the globe. According to Gilpin, an "isothermal zodiac or belt of equal warmth" circles the earth between the twenty-fifth and fifty-fifth parallels. Along this zodiac, which runs directly through the United States, Gilpin explains, all the major empires of history—Chinese, Indian, Persian, Grecian, Roman, Spanish, and British—had arisen, marking the progress of the race. History is thus a "journal" of "geographical progress" recording civilization's advance "by an inevitable instinct of nature, since creation's dawn." This advance, accordingly, will culminate in the settlement of the last unoccupied region within the zone, the American West, where, by the imperative of nature, "The American Republic is . . . *predestined* to expand and fit itself to the continent."[20]

Though Gilpin's argument constitutes little more than a quasi-scientific elaboration of the Renaissance belief that empire follows the course of the setting sun, what places his assertions directly in the context of post-Enlightenment thought is their emphasis on the deterministic quality of physical nature. Progress has resulted within the zone because it contains the greatest deposits of resources and the healthiest climate. Hence, the American West is especially suited to fulfill man's destiny. Because the Mississippi Valley consists of an unbroken, immensely fertile basin—in contrast to the divided topography of Europe and Asia, which has kept civilizations apart and at war—the West provides a unique opportunity for creating a harmonious and unified civilization. For Gilpin the "holy question" of America's union and its well-being "lies in the bosom of *nature*."[21]

Despite his emphasis on the West as "the rural quintessence of America" and his own strong Jeffersonian inclinations, however, Gilpin did not foresee an exclusively pastoral future for the continental interior. Given his emphasis on empire, in fact, he hardly could have been satisfied with such a limited vision. For Gilpin believed that "when society has assumed its largest form and attained the highest level of civilization," only then "it is defined to be an *empire.*" Adhering to the theory that civilization reaches an apex through urban development and asserting that such development was immanent in geography, he predicted that the Mississippi basis would give rise to cities "such as antiquity built at the head of the Mediterranean and named Jerusalem, Tyre, Alexandria and Constantinople"—cities which would possess "the geographical position, and the existing elements with which any rival will contend in vain."[22] Confident of the uniquely benevolent quality of the western landscape, Gilpin was certain that the garden and the city could exist in harmony.

Although Gilpin and Scott produced the most elaborate arguments for an intrinsic relationship between nature and cities in the interior, they hardly were the first to employ this line of reasoning. Many promoters of an urban-pastoral West enlisted geographical determinism, though in a less intricate and arcane manner, to proclaim an organic relation between landscape and urban development. As early as 1815, Daniel Drake, a Cincinnati physician and local historian, published his *Natural and Statistical View; or, Picture of Cincinnati,* in which he argued that "many of the villages which have sprung up within 30 years, on the banks of the Ohio and Mississippi, are destined, before the termination of the present century, to attain the rank of populous and magnificent cities." Well circulated and even translated abroad, Drake's *View* based its assertions on a faith in the copious resources along the Mississippi-Ohio river system. Its quantity of water, "the diversities of aspect, and inexhaustible fertility, of the region which it irrigates—the boundless and perennial forests, which in the east, and in the north, overshadow its sources—the numerous beds of coal and iron which enrich its banks" inexorably foreshadow urban growth, since they are the "principal inducements for immigration" to the region.[23] Anticipating Scott and Gilpin, Drake drew a direct line between beneficent nature and inevitable development of cities in the West.

Although Drake identified Pittsburgh, Cincinnati, and Louisville as the places possessing the greatest potential to become the loci of this ideal association, he predictably asserted that his native "CINCINNATI IS TO BE THE FUTURE METROPOLIS OF THE OHIO" River Valley because it possessed the healthiest, most extensive site and the richest hinterland. Of course, while Drake extolled the virtues of Cincinnati, others used the same arguments to defend localities he slighted. One writer for the *Pittsburgh Mercury* claimed that of the three cities Pittsburgh would achieve ascendency because of the fertility of its surrounding region, the pleasantness and elegance of its site, and its geographical position in relation to trade routes. Likewise, Ben Casseday, in his 1852 *History of Louisville,* argued that the fecundity and immense quantity of the surrounding land and the town's advantageous location on the Ohio River would make Louisville "the Great City of the West."[24] The important point to note about these encomiums is not their focus on different cities at the expense of others but the assumptions which they share. Each predicates urban development on the pastoral image of the West, linking the growth of towns to geographical advantages and natural abundance. In each, city and garden constitute distinct yet interconnected components of the evolving landscape.

When spokesmen for this version of urban pastoralism directed their attention farther west, they tended to employ the same theory. Citing the immense tracts of arable land in its vicinity and its central location on the Mississippi and Missouri rivers, one writer for *Hunt's* proclaimed that "St. Louis is ordained by the decrees of physical nature to become the great inland metropolis of this continent." Similarly William Bross, newspaper editor and later lieutenant governor of Illinois, argued in 1852 that Chicago, built amidst "boundless prairies and groves" yielding unlimited products, is "destined to become the great commercial centre of the Northwest, and among the first, if not *the first,* city in the Mississippi Valley." In his *Annals of the City of Kansas* (1859), Charles C. Spalding, a local booster and self-styled historian, announced that because Kansas City is located on the bourn of "great fertile valleys" and rich deposits of coal and lead, "it is *her destiny* to become the extreme western and commercial emporium of mountain, prairie, and river commerce."[25]

It is unnecessary, however, to make an exhausting list of these paeans to the future development of western cities. Every city had its boosters, every booster had his favorite city, and they all shared a common vocabulary and rationale which everyone understood. When Timothy Flint, in his widely read *Geography and History of the Western States* (1828), asserted that Indianapolis would become "one of the largest towns between Cincinnati and the Mississippi" by dint of its position "in the centre of one of the most extensive and fertile bodies of land in the western world," it was the obviousness and simplicity of his pronouncement that gave it compelling power.[26] By assuring their readers that the cultivation of nature and the development of cities were part of one process, such pronouncements effectively minimized any tension implicit in the two ideologies informing those activities.

Part of the efficacy of such statements lay in the fact that they were drawing on a well-established tradition: the belief that a happy balance of rural and urban was immanent in the very nature of the native landscape. Yet as America moved into mid-century, the credibility of such a belief, when applied to older eastern cities, grew increasingly tenuous. If the East seemed to be abandoning its legacy, the West, according to the rationale of the day, would be the true heir to the urban-pastoral promise. Amidst this shifting valuation the old strategies were reapplied in a fresh context, as western spokesmen developed their own version of the moral opposition intrinsic to urban pastoralism, substituting for the Euro-American dichotomy a distinction between West and East. Hence we find Daniel Drake predicting that the West would not duplicate the fate of eastern cities. Certain that nature made all the difference, he claimed that a healthier, more moral society would grow in the Mississippi-Ohio basin. Particularly decisive for determining the quality of life in this region, both urban and rural, was the utter newness and isolation of "the green and untutored states of the West."

> Debarred, by their locality, from an inordinate participation in foreign luxuries, and consequently . . . secluded from foreign intercourse, and thereby rendered patriotic . . . the inhabitants of this region are obviously destined to an unrivaled excellence in agriculture, manufactures and internal commerce; in literature and the arts; in public virtue, and in national strength.

Providing a refuge from the corruptions of Europe and the urban East, western geography would yield an ideal harmony of the best of the rural and urban worlds. In a similar vein, William Gilpin prophesied that, when the western garden was fully planted and cities had risen in its furrows, a better civilization, cultivated by the hoe of democracy, would result, "inaugurat[ing] for mankind a code of political practice, which shall bring the science of government into accord with the divine code of morals and religion."[27] For Drake, Gilpin, and other promoters of the West, that region would achieve what the East had not. Central to this "creed" was a vision of rolling farms and commercial cities existing side by side in a benevolent synthesis.

The iconography of this period graphically illustrates this vision of the West even as it mirrors the gradual alteration occurring in attitudes toward the East. When popular artists and engravers early in the century began to produce views of cities such as New York, Philadelphia, and Washington, D.C., they frequently borrowed the techniques Europeans had employed in the late eighteenth century to depict urban America. Repeatedly these native renditions place the city in a frame of soft pastoral scenes with grazing cattle and lush foliage dominating the foreground. But by the 1840s and 1850s artists virtually abandoned such an approach when pictorializing Eastern cities, emphasizing instead their thickly clustered buildings, architectural forms, and rectilinear street patterns (compare illustrations 3 and 4). Instead of disappearing, however, the old technique remained

3 "Baltimore Taken Near Whetstone Point" (1830), by W. J. Bennett

4 "New York . . . from the Latting Observatory" (1855), by W. Wellstood after B. F. Smith

5 "Cleveland" (1850), by J. Mueller

6 "Louisville, Kentucky" (1853), by Wellstood and Peters after J. W. Hill

a favorite device for depicting such western cities as St. Louis, Cincinnati, Cleveland, and Louisville (illustrations 5 and 6). If American artists found it increasingly difficult to affirm the connection between landscape and cityscape in the East, no such compunction restrained their tendency to view western urbanization as eminently compatible with the pastoral image of the region.

Not all Americans, of course, acceded to a vision of an urban-pastoral West. Many continued to conceive of the continental interior in exclusively bucolic terms, either because of agrarian loyalties or because of doubts that the region ever could produce substantial cities. Nonetheless, as Charles Glaab has noted, works promoting an urban West probably existed in greater numbers than any other writing about the region, and many of these pieces based their claims on the inevitable effects of landscape upon cityscape. This pattern appeared even in some of the most ebullient depictions of the West as an agricultural paradise. C. W. Dana, for example, in his *Garden of the World* concluded each chapter on the various states and territories of the interior with radiant accounts of urban progress in these areas. In particular Dana singled out St. Louis as an inevitable "mart of wealth and commerce scarcely inferior to any in the United States," since it rested in "the geographical centre" of the fertile Mississippi Valley.[28] For Dana and other western advocates, the very edenic plentitude of the trans-Allegheny region demanded urban growth and destined urban greatness.

Although many of these pronouncements and predictions focused on the economic and commercial value of nature as a stimulus to cities and so seemed to display little concern with the moral implications intrinsic to urban pastoralism, even this emphasis on the landscape as commodity carried moral connotations. Implicit in statements by Scott, Bross, Spalding, Dana, and others of similar inclination was a belief that western urbanization constituted a moral activity in accordance with the features of the terrain and, by extension, nature's pattern. A remark by William Carr Lane, first mayor of St. Louis, can be taken as representative of this way of thinking. Writing in 1823, Lane averred that "the progressive rise of our city is morally certain, the causes of its prosperity are inscribed upon the very face of the earth, and are as permanent as the foundations of the soil and the sources of the Mississippi."[29] Behind such an assertion lay an unshakable, even mystical faith, shared by most promoters of an urbanized West, in the power of landscape to produce a thriving, happy relationship between nature and civilization, country and city, to the immense benefit of the inhabitants.

As western cities developed, this rationale was acknowledged and employed with greater boldness. No longer content with prediction, spokesmen for an urbanized version of the western garden argued that, owing to nature's plentitude, great cities already were developing. In 1854, Jesup Scott maintained that Toledo, Chicago, Cleveland, Detroit, Buffalo, and Milwaukee had become "rapidly growing cities" because of their "manifest advantages in position, climate, and ample resources . . . all provided by nature." Three years earlier an article in the St. Louis-based *Western Journal and Civilian* made the same claim for Pittsburgh, Cincinnati, Louisville, and St. Louis. In effect, such statements declared that a congenial partnership of landscape and city lay not merely in the future but in the present, too. Nor was this relationship unilateral. A number of writers in this period noted that, while nature stimulated city growth, urbanization and its accompanying features were helping domesticate nature by bringing out its hidden powers. Summarizing the development of Chicago in 1855, William Bross announced that "the commerce, the manufactures and the improvements of our city . . . have promoted . . . the interests of . . . our great and glorious Northwest . . . in changing our broad prairies into fruitful fields, and in bordering our beautiful groves with ample farm houses—the homes of comfort, plenty, intelligence, virtue and peace." According to such an assessment, town and country acted in a moral consortium to push back the wilderness and create an ideal urban middle landscape of verdant fields and prospering cities.[30]

This benign union, according to pronouncements at this time, was being replicated on the municipal level as well. Descriptions of western cities by both promoters and eastern visitors repeatedly pointed to the ample, spacious layout of these towns, their large open blocks, and the high visibility of nature within them. In St. Louis, C. W. Dana found "wide and airy" streets punctuated with houses "surrounded by ornamental yards and gardens," while John Peyton, a Virginia lawyer who visited the Great Lakes region in the 1840s, explained that Chicago deservedly was called the "Garden City" because the gardens which the inhabitants tended were both numerous and "enormous." Charles Hoffman, a New York lawyer and man of letters, noted with pleasure that in Cincinnati one discovers "gilded spires gleaming among gardens and shrubbery" interwoven with "spacious avenues terminating always in the green acclivities which bound the city." Commonly, descriptions pointed to the picturesque charm of these towns nestled, in Timothy Flint's words, in the "bosom [of] the beautiful surrounding nature." As one of many examples, a "Beautiful Description of Cincinnati," printed in the *Western Monthly Review and Literary Journal*, explained that from a summit terminating that city's major thoroughfare, the "view is magnificent. Below is the town in a superb amphitheatre, hollowed out of as glorious a collection of verdant hills as Nature has piled together anywhere. Breaking this circuit you see here and there a winding vale of exceeding softness and beauty. To complete the picture, you see the smooth and lovely Ohio rolling through these wild hills and woodlands, and lingering in many a graceful sweep through the city, as if reluctant to leave such admirable scenes."[31] By invoking the pathetic fallacy, this description suggests a quasi-religious affinity between nature's principles and man's accomplishments as if the two agents shared a common "consciousness." There hardly could be a more vivid, though admittedly saccharine, example of the urban-pastoral ideal operating in this age.

Yet some writers realized that an urban West, even a green one, might alarm those who continued to associate virtue and democracy with rural life. Taking that proclivity into account, urban promoters were careful to praise the morality of western cities. Another piece in the *Western Monthly Review and Literary Journal* assured its readers that Chicago "is settled with a community highly intelligent, enterprising and moral," while a writer for *Hunt's* remarked that the "numerous associations for the promotion of religious, moral, and charitable objects" and the advancement of "the cause of temperance" in Pittsburgh clearly indicate that "an extensive moral influence pervades the community." Ben Casseday, the Louisville historian, even claimed that his native city "is singularly free from absolute vice of all sorts." The reason, he explained, was that "the restlessness, the turmoil and the eagerness in the pursuit of wealth" characterizing eastern cities "in Louisville . . . does not appear." Instead, "business is pursued quietly and without ostentation; no efforts are made by any to convince others of their success; no factitious means are employed to display the results of labor, no hurry or restlessness or confusion attends even the largest and most prosperous houses. Trade . . . is not allowed to blind its votaries to every other pursuit of life." Free from the artificiality, contentiousness, and indulgence in luxury plaguing urban life in the East, citizens of Louisville can lead a virtuous existence "which proceeds rather from natural instinct than from knowledge of the rules of etiquette."[32] From such descriptions, despite their obvious exaggeration, it seemed that western cities offered a peaceful, roomy, nearly bucolic life in marked contrast to that of the East. According to these sanguine statements, America was embarking on an urban-pastoral quest embracing the entire continent west of the Alleghenies.

To be sure, descriptions of western cities as peaceful and pastoral were not the only ones tendered, nor were they the most common. Usually promoters and visitors focused on exactly the opposite feature of these cities: their bustle and activity. Yet even such pictures could be incorporated into the idea of the West as a land of spiritual inspiration, since activity, as one writer in *Hunt's* put it, displayed the "public spirit" of "an energetic and driving community"—a sign of vitality, hope, and fresh beginnings according fully with the regenerative image of the West. From this perspective, western urbanites, inspired by the open landscape, actively engaged in trade, manufacturing, the arts, and the sciences to form the vanguard of democratic civilization as it "converted the wilderness into the peaceful homes of men."[33]

In the period before the Civil War, many Americans shared a belief that the West was developing into a beautiful balance of cityscape and landscape in both the regional and municipal spheres. No one, however, could identify the time at which that balance might tip and make western cities like those of the East. Nor could anyone explain how that balance would be maintained in the face of civilization's inexorable march. What is remarkable, in fact, is that such questions rarely if ever were asked, even after slums and overcrowded neighborhoods began to supplant the open squares and gardens in Pittsburgh, St. Louis, Cincinnati, Chicago, and other major trading marts. So powerful was the image of an urban-pastoral West that tributes to it continued well into the latter part of the century, masking urban problems and contributing to municipal complacency. Perhaps Americans, assuming that the open landscape was the last hope for a new type of urban society, refused to believe that the West was duplicating the fate of the East. If so, we have at least a partial explanation for remarks such as those made by Sara Lippincott, one of the first female newspaper correspondents in the United States. In 1873, recording her reactions to Chicago during a visit to the West, Lippincott noted that "with all the distinctive characteristics of a great city, it has preserved in a wonderful degree the provincial virtues of generous hospitality, cordiality, and neighborly kindness. A lady from the East lately said of it, very charmingly, 'It is New York with the heart left in.' "[34]

V

Organic Cities
Nineteenth-Century Urban Reform

When the editor of Cincinnati's *Liberty Hall* urged his readers in 1851 to turn "every morning to the west, instead of worshipping toward the east," he was taking a position which many Americans shared in the first half of the nineteenth century.[1] If eastern cities seemed to stand for all that was reprehensible and dangerous, the developing western towns could symbolize a truly virtuous future for urban America. A significant number of Americans, however, hardly were ready to abandon the urban East. Believing that the entire continent lay heir to the urban-pastoral legacy, they advocated that eastern cities be remade physically and socially to bring them in line with the image of the green republic. While western promoters were making room for the city in the garden—the *urbe in rus*—defenders of the East inverted this rationale to argue for a restoration of the *rus in urbe*.

Advocates of this position employed a variety of media for promoting their goal, from the actual reshaping of cityscapes and the establishment of benevolent societies, to calls for moral and social reform explicitly rendered in tracts and monographs and implicitly inculcated through the dramatizations of didactic fiction. Among the ranks were popular novelists such as Catharine Sedgwick and Maria Cummins and some of the leading intellectuals of the day, including Horace Bushnell, Theodore Parker, Horace Mann, and Ralph Waldo Emerson. Emerson, in fact, was one of the few major writers to embrace the ideal, but he did so by advocating urban revision as re-vision. For he believed that "the amelioration of outward circumstances will be the effect, but never can be the means of mental & moral improvement."[2] Yet if Emerson stressed working from the inside outward, he nonetheless shared with conventional reformers a central conviction. Beneath their diverse efforts lay the belief that urban life could be made more meaningful by reestablishing the connection among nature, rusticity, and the city.

I

Though America rarely had been without a reform movement of some sort since Cotton Mather and other Puritan divines devised the jeremiad to denounce the moral turpitude of New England, in the antebellum period this impulse was augmented by the widespread belief in progress and the development of perfectionist utopianism often linked to evangelical Christianity. Many of these reformers, looking to Jefferson as their inspirational paterfamilias, held that the values of Jeffersonian pastoralism could serve as a guide for solving the social and physical problems in eastern cities. What disturbed some Americans, however, was that such retrenchment, particularly as it related to the physical shape of cities, was necessary in the first place. Adhering to the faith in a unique geography, one writer in the *Atlantic* argued that "there is some excuse for the overcrowding and irregular character of Old World cities. They grew and were not builded." In America, however, "where land is sold at one dollar and twenty-five cents the acre by the square mile," open space and parks should be the rule.[3]

Since the seventeenth century Americans had expressed a desire to include gardens and grazing lands as part of their cities, but in the early nineteenth century efforts in that direction were redoubled. Although romantic thought helped inspire this renewed interest, equally decisive was a growing, quasi-scientific belief that light, fresh air, and greenery could help reduce disease in cities by dispelling harmful "vapors" that caused sickness. Leading the efforts to restore nature to cities were Andrew Jackson Downing, the father of landscape gardening in America, and such liberal clergymen as William Ellery Channing and Horace Bushnell, both of whom had an interest in urban "greenness" that encompassed social patterns and the physical shape of cities. Bushnell was especially interested in urban design. In an essay entitled "City Plans," he wrote that the health and beauty of a city "depends, to a considerable degree, on the right arrangement and due multiplication of vacant spaces" as "so many breathing places" for the inhabitants. "The providing and right location of a sufficient park, or parks," he continued, "is a matter of still greater consequence." Bushnell's interest in "vacant spaces" can be gauged in part by his own work in laying out a park for his native Hartford and his call for a professional elite of urban planners.[4]

Such tentative calls for parks and playgrounds soon received support. In Philadelphia, where the open squares of Holme's plan had degenerated into garbage dumps and cemeteries, city officials passed ordinances for restoring the squares to their original purpose and providing funds for their maintenance. In 1850, Millard Fillmore commissioned Andrew Jackson Downing to design a mall for Washington, D.C., along Pennsylvania Avenue, a project Downing undertook by planning a formal park with gardens, shrubbery, and gracefully curving walks. Downing's plan is especially noteworthy because it so clearly embodied the belief that natural forms, carefully ordered and integrated with the city, could enhance the urban topography by providing a contrast that also complemented. As he explained in his notes accompanying the plan, "The straight lines and broad Avenues of the streets of Washington would be pleasantly relieved and contrasted by the beauty of curved lines and natural groups of trees" in the public grounds, which in turn would "form the most perfect background or setting to the City, concealing many of its defects and heightening all its beauties." Downing even hoped that the mall-park, when completed, could have far-reaching effects on the shape of urban America by "becom[ing] a Public School of Instruction in everything that relates to the tasteful arrangement of parks and grounds" in the city.[5]

Even more ambitious plans for creating an urban park were under way in New York City. To a number of New Yorkers the need for a centralized park seemed especially acute. Although the Commission of Streets and Parks had laid out a new plan for Manhattan in 1811, providing seven open squares and a parade ground totaling 450 acres, by 1838 commercial encroachments had reduced these areas to a cribbed 120 acres. To the north, the area abutting the network of streets, though remaining open, consisted of swamplands and scrub terrain used for grazing goats and dumping refuse. Among the first to call for a new park was William Cullen Bryant, who was discussing the idea with friends as early as 1838. By 1844 he began promoting the concept in a series of editorials in the *Evening Post*, and in 1848 Downing joined the campaign through editorials and letters in his own magazine, the *Horticulturist*.[6]

Although the idea drew substantial support, advocates faced an uphill struggle. Ironically, some New Yorkers objected to a park on the grounds that American conditions precluded its necessity. As one detractor explained, while parks may be indispensable in dense European cities, "our circumstances are very different: surrounded by broad waters on all sides, open to the sea breezes, we need no artificial breathing places." A similar remonstrance appeared in the *Journal of Commerce*, which claimed that the verdant countryside on the northern part of Manhattan provided convenient and ample opportunity for communion with nature.[7] By arguing that landscape already exerted a beneficial influence on the city, these objections reveal that the urban-pastoral ideal could be invoked at times for contradictory purposes.

In the end, however, support for the park won out, especially when Ambrose Kingsland, running on a park platform, was elected mayor of New York. In the same year that the state authorized the city to acquire lands for a central park, Kingsland sent a letter to the Common Council of New York City explaining that the park would be especially useful to the city's well-being by providing an alternative to "thousands who pass the day of rest among the idle and dissolute, in porter-houses, or in places more objectionable." What is interesting in Kingsland's message is his belief that the park would possess value beyond its capacity to promote physical health. For Kingsland and other advocates of open spaces and parks, their benefit carried moral implications as well. As the *American Journal of Science and the Arts* asserted, "plac[ing] in a town or city, a spot with spreading trees, and pleasant walks between" would allow "the feelings of that people . . . [to] flow in a kinder and smoother channel; there would be more cheerfulness and more happiness than there would otherwise have been." By offering opportunity for recreation and amusement, parks were to provide a release for the wellsprings of love and friendship and so lead to a tranquil and more contented society. Such a belief lay at the center of a number of works on urban development in this period. In an oration before the New York Geographical Society in the early 1850s, Henry Tappan, minister, philosopher, and first president of the University of Michigan, told his audience that "the multitudes of a city crave excitement and amusement. Provide them with beautiful public gardens and places of culture, and they will generally be content." But "leave them without cultivation," he warned, and they will become barbaric.[8]

People such as Tappan and Kingsland were saying, oddly enough, that by incorporating nature in the city, Americans would be improving society by making it more civilized. Though somewhat curious, this idea was part of a larger shift in thinking in some quarters regarding the values associated with the alternate poles of country and city. We should recall that before the nineteenth century the city traditionally had been identified with stability and social order while the countryside symbolized freedom and individualism. As older American cities increased in size and urban society became more pluralistic and mobile, however, many Americans, particularly in the East, began to transpose these values. Although harbingers of this transformation had existed in Western thought for several centuries, the tendency to equate rusticity with stability and to identify urban life as unrestrained and indulgent gained momentum in the antebellum period as increases in urban crime and violence suggested a breakdown in the order which supposedly characterized cities. According to Edwin Chapin:

> [N]o one needs to be told that there are savages in New York, as well as in the islands of the sea. Savages, not in gloomy forests, but under the strength of gas-light, and the eyes of policemen; with war-whoops and clubs very much the same, and garments as fantastic, and souls as brutal, as any of their kindred at the antipodes.[9]

Chapin's remark was part of a growing concern among Easterners in the first half of the nineteenth century that their cities were becoming "barbaric" and "savage"—epithets equating urban conditions with the howling wilderness.

Others were troubled by what they saw as an increasing transience in urban life, a fear revealed, for example, in an 1841 work entitled *The Moral Influence, Dangers and Duties, Connected with Great Cities.* In the city, the author lamented, "your acquaintances come and go,—are here to-day, and off to-morrow, and you have hardly time, or opportunity, to form deep attachments. The increasing hurry, and perpetual pressure for time, prevent our forming those deep attachments which we do in country life." The febrile urban pace, according to some, was leading to a fragmentation of city life and, more unsettling, a disruption of communal spirit ostensibly still flourishing in the rural village. The transcendental reformer Theodore Parker identified the cause of this disintegration in the inclination "to value money more than men." For Parker, this trend produced a self-aggrandizing individualism which was destroying social responsibility and com-

munal integrity in urban life. Edwin Chapin shared this belief, warning that "in the city . . . the most prominent figure, the figure that
might be significantly inscribed on the stores, and the houses, and
even the churches is number *one*. . . . And here is the foundation of
. . . every den of infamy, every haunt of profligacy and crime in the
city." In the opinion of laymen and clerics, the city did not lack freedom but offered so much that it was threatening the order of civilization. Far from being a unique feature of postbellum anti-urbanism,
as Morton and Lucia White have claimed, the belief that eastern cities were not overcivilized but undercivilized already was prominent
before the Civil War.[10]

Identifying such an attitude as anti-urban, however, constitutes a
gross oversimplification. Most critics of eastern society in antebellum
America were not engaging in any simpleminded rejection of the city.
As we have seen, ministers such as Chapin and Mayo defended urban
life as vociferously as they denigrated it. To understand their diatribes
we must realize that they were part of a larger body of social criticism
which was the secular legacy of the Puritan jeremiad. From this perspective, protests against the city correctly can be identified, not as
anti-urban statements, but as objections to what were seen as aber-
rations in cities. Like the jeremiads, they advocated a return, not to
a nonurban past, but to a purer urban society now neglected. This
need to recapture a more natural urban past formed the gist of Bushnell's argument that the "error" of the day was "the tendency of all our
modern speculation . . . to an extreme individualism." For Bushnell,
all society was or should be "organic—the church, the state, the
school, the family"—with individuals tied to the whole social body.[11]
Such an emphasis fully accorded with his interest in providing open
spaces in cities and his call for an urban-planning profession. All
three were intended to fertilize the ground for a more organic, and
hence more civilized, urban life.

Many shared Bushnell's concern with organicism and agreed with
him on the four areas which could be the seedbeds of urban reform:
the church, the government, the school, and the family. For the
clergy, the church was especially important as a means to reorganize
society and eliminate its abuses—a belief which led to the rise of the
social gospel in this period. "The great work of the Pulpit," wrote
Chapin in 1856, "is the work of legitimate reform, in which, by a natural law, the genuine seeds of the past are retained and developed in
the vesicles of the future. . . . The preacher, especially in the city,

must be a true reformer." The triad of values which Chapin identified—returning to a simpler past, reawakening religious spirit, and following natural law—became the basis of the social gospel in the city. With a nostalgic eye on the rural village, ministers such as Chapin, Channing, Bushnell, and Mayo believed that a rebirth of Christian sensibility would return community to urban America. For the majority of these liberal clergymen, Christian spirit and natural law were in fact identical in that, as Chapin explained, "whatever is injurious, capricious, insincere—in one word, essentially unnatural—is immoral and irreligious."[12]

This emphasis on natural patterns appeared in many urban-reform programs before the Civil War. A desire for naturalness underscored the urban temperance movements, which held that alcohol, the cause of idleness and poverty, was the bane of a healthy, organic community. A similar emphasis played a part in efforts to establish a suitable home life for indigent, fatherless urban families through benevolent societies and houses of refuge, such as New York's Five Points Mission. These halfway houses and the numerous asylums founded in Boston, Philadelphia, New York, and other eastern cities constituted, as Thomas Bender has observed, "an effort to impose an idealized version of the orderly and peaceful eighteenth-century village onto the disorderly nineteenth-century city."[13] For reformers, the pastoral ideal became the basis of plans to create civilized cities by making them more natural.

Adhering to this habit of thought, some reformers proposed schemes which were, at best, chimerical. In the same work in which he expressed a fear that cities were draining the countryside of its vitality, Amory Mayo advocated rural immigration as a solution to the artificiality and fragmentation of urban life. Apparently forgetting that cities already had experienced such immigration in large doses, Mayo asserted that a massive influx of rural inhabitants, "reared amid the inspiring influences of nature and taught in the best school of youthful discipline, . . . would pour into our depraved and debilitated cities the life blood of a higher civilization." To achieve the same end, Horace Greeley outlined a plan exactly the opposite of Mayo's. Believing that contention and poverty in eastern cities occurred because "the greater number are constantly crowded with surplus laborers . . . underbidding each other," Greeley identified "the Monopoly of land" in America as the underlying culprit which drove people off the farms and into cities. For a solution, he proposed that laws be "so changed that no man were permitted, in this boasted land of equal rights, to hold as his own more than a half square mile of arable land." Such laws, by encouraging people to stay on the farm, would reduce urban density, eliminate the labor surplus, and produce healthier, more stable, and thus more civilized cities. By restoring the Jeffersonian ideal of the independent yeoman, America could rectify its urban problems.[14] For Greeley, remaking the city required remaking the country; the fate of the two were intertwined. Despite their antithetical plans, Mayo and Greeley thus shared a confidence in the landscape as a panacea for urban woes.

Other reformers held the same belief, although few proposed such extravagant designs. For Theodore Parker, as we have seen, the major problem in America was the mercenary attitude pervading urban industrialism, which threatened the Jeffersonian ideal. Instead of leading to a higher standard of living for all, industrialism increased the wealth of the powerful and created greater class antagonism. While such a "priestly, monarchic, nobilitary, or despotic" society might be expected in a country where resources were scarce or the climate bad, wrote Parker, in America, with its abundance of land and materials, it was unconscionable. To obviate this growing urban oligarchy, Parker sought a more equitable distribution of goods. Though not advocating a communal sharing of property, his radical democratic stance did impel him toward a vision of an urban society which would incorporate the ideals of the supposedly egalitarian, bountiful world of Jefferson's rural republic. One way to achieve such a society, Parker believed, was to have municipal authorities tax wealthy individuals and use the money to provide inexpensive, adequate housing for the poor in cities. Asserting that the "duty of the State [was] to watch over the culture of its children," Parker anticipated what would become a common and paradoxical aspect of modern urban-pastoral reform: a belief that returning to a simpler society necessitated more elaborate and complex institutional and governmental activity.[15]

The perfectionist reformer Horace Mann also singled out "poverty" and "profusion" (what Thorstein Veblen later would call "conspicuous consumption" among the wealthy) as the most enervating problems facing eastern cities. But Mann did not believe that changing a few laws would provide a solution. Instead, he felt that urban Americans were improperly educated and so were unaware that "we are moving toward those extremes of opulence and penury, each of which unhumanizes the mind." Mann's solution was formal education for the masses. Diffusive education in democratic values, social responsibility, and human integrity, he believed, would help wipe out class lines and so reduce urban conflict and disintegration.[16] Like Parker, Mann sought a modified urban version of the classless, peaceful world presented since antiquity in pastoral poetry and millennialist visions of a new earth.

Although the institutional reform that has become a hallmark of urban America first came into prominence in the opening half of the nineteenth century, a number of reformers sought to reconstruct urban life on a more elementary level. If cities lacked order, virtue, and community, they argued, restoring these required a revitalization of the most basic unit of society: the family. Behind this emphasis lay the inherited belief that the family was a divine ordinance, "forecast," in Chapin's words, "in the peculiarities of our very nature." As a gift of nature and nature's God, the family served as "the foundation of all society" and "the germ and ideal of the state." As Bushnell explained, a healthy, stable society required a healthy citizenry, and nothing produced good citizens more than the "organic *working* of a family."[17]

Contributing to this emphasis on home life was a growing tendency to link the indulgence and fragmentation of urban life to a breakdown of the family. In metropolitan America, Amory Mayo lamented, "we have no American home." Instead, "we have gilded metropolitan hotels" and "boarding of all sorts, from genteel to ungenteel. . . . Our houses hardly rest on solid ground." Indeed, concurred Chapin, "in a city . . . the idea of a homestead is almost obsolete," primarily because of "the perpetual change" and "the rapid tide of business" characterizing urban life. Such remarks were echoed everywhere: in religious tracts, in the leading periodicals, in sentimental fiction, and even in comments by foreign observers. When Marie Fontenay de Grandfort toured America in the 1850s, she remarked that New Yorkers seemed oblivious to "the pleasure of the family circle."[18]

Partly a response to such a belief—and partly a cause for it—was the penchant of American writers and spokesmen in this period to identify the ideal home with a rural setting. Though such an identification was not new (in the eighteenth century Freneau, among others, described the noble rustic as one who "seeks the humble dome, / And centers all his pleasures in his home"), the increased separation of working and domestic spheres under industrialization, and the growing mobility of urban life, which reduced the influence of the extended family, encouraged this way of thinking. It appears, for example, in the writings of Mayo, Bushnell, and Chapin, the latter arguing that "the central idea of home is *stability*, and this has much less chance to be realized in the city than in the country." Charles Loring Brace, a leading lay reformer and founder of the Children's Aid Society, subscribed to this conviction by instituting a program for placing slum orphans in rural homes.[19] The model of rural domesticity, furthermore, became a central theme in sentimental fiction, such as Sarah Hale's *Traits of American Life* and *Sketches of American Character*, A. J. Graves's *Girlhood and Womanhood*, Catharine Sedgwick's *Married or Single?* and *Clarence*, Emma Southwood's *The Mother-in-Law*, and Martha Read's *Monima*. In Read's novel, for instance, the heroine and her father escape Philadelphia to a country retreat, where the full benefit of wholesome family life can teach Monima virtue and religious sensibility.[20] Widely read and extremely influential in molding middle-class opinion, these works encouraged Americans to associate the ideal household with rural conditions and natural surroundings. Although Mark Twain later would satirize the meretriciousness of this idea through his depiction of the violent Grangerfords in *Huckleberry Finn*, little qualification accompanied its initial development. As a result, a cult of rural domesticity became firmly established by mid-century.[21]

According to this cult image, it seemed as if maintaining an orderly, natural family life required leaving the city or remaining in the country. However, because the books propagating the image were written for a predominantly urban audience, which simply could not pack up and desert the city, they inculcated a more subtle idea: that urban Americans, by strengthening the family, could duplicate an element of rural life that would help stablize the town. A revitalized family, according to this theory, would be a link to a more natural, civilizing order. This was the message of both Chapin and Mayo, who urged Americans to "recreate this sphere of life" by cultivating "simplicity" and "unaffected refinement" as alternatives to the hurly-burly and artificiality of the city. Didactic novels such as Maria Cummins' *The Lamplighter* and Sedgwick's *Clarence*, self-help guides on family life, and magazines such as *Godey's Lady's Book* (edited, significantly enough, by Sarah Hale) defined the ideal urban home as a pastoral enclosure where virtue, love, companionship, and a saving constancy would prevail. Advocates of urban domesticity identified home and family as a self-contained social unit insulated from the corruptions and distortions of the city at large.[22] As such, the home would serve as an idyllic asylum, nourishing the natural goodness of its members and administering an antidote to the dislocation of urban existence.

Although few could agree on how to recapture a rural home in the city, many reformers proposed solutions. Mayo believed that the potential rested with American women, who could "lay the foundation of home" in the city by marrying for love and not for position and by conducting their households according to a "practical" economy and "a natural style of behavior and manners." Chapin felt that a reconstituted family life would result only when urban Americans forsook their "fashionable treatment of home, which leads people to abandon it almost every night in pursuit of pleasure." Making the home the center of life, he explained, would allow city dwellers to rekindle the "instinct which associates the most genuine happiness" with that domestic "enclosure of affection" and so reduce the transience and unfeeling barbarity of the city. Others asserted that proper child rearing was the answer. Books on child nurture, such as Lydia Sigourney's *Letters to Mothers* (1838), stressed the importance of simple foods and recreation and urged mothers to develop their children's natural goodness. Instead of employing a stern restraint, mothers could raise more humane citizens by cultivating their children's intuitive and emotional inclinations. As Bushnell explained in broaching the subject, children should be "refined . . . without any ambition to copy the mannerisms of refinement; refined by the fining of their intelligence and feeling." Here, then, is an encapsulation of domestic urban pastoralism. In the ideal urban home, which encourages a healthy balance of thought and feeling, the child imbibes the best of high civilization without being corrupted by its extravagances. Still others held that remaking the physical home was the answer to a better family life in the city. The new domestic architecture that arose in this period stressed the importance of a separate parlor for socializing, a secluded nursery, and individual bedrooms for family members. This emphasis on individuation and separation contributed to the idea of the home as a rural retreat in the city.[23]

The irony in all this activity is that reformers, by promoting the home as an urban enclave, inadvertently may have encouraged Americans to withdraw from active participation in society at large, thus contributing to communal fragmentation and inhibiting efforts to reduce crime and poverty in eastern cities. Yet reformers in this period seemed to recognize this danger even if they were unable to eradicate it. Chapin warned his readers, "You cannot shut yourself within comfortable walls, and say—'Here is the limit of my obligations, and here I will do as I please.' " In a similar manner, Mayo solicited the city dweller not only to "make your home a paradise" but also to "stir up your neighbors to pure and pleasant enjoyments, and identify your name with the growth of a community in Republican grace." Such calls did not go unheeded. Many middle-class women sought to expand the influence of the home by working in benevolent societies, organizing clubs for social reform, and filling the ranks of the temperance armies. Some proponents of women's suffrage even argued that enfranchisement, by extending the domestic sphere, would lead urban politics back to a Jeffersonian purity.[24]

Although not all urban reforms in the period before the Civil War possessed a nostalgic, pastoral cast, many reformers at this time, in the words of Daniel Levine, "longed for a society closer to the natural order" and sought to restore to cities the values of the old Jeffersonian republic.[25] This retrospective tendency created in urban reform a look-both-ways attitude, as Americans gazed at their urban future through the lens of their rural past. By reconstituting their cities according to the image of the green republic, they believed that they would secure a more natural, harmonious, and civilized social order. Even today this belief has not lost its hold on the imaginations of Americans.

II

In his house in Concord, Ralph Waldo Emerson listened to the clang and jangle of urban promotion and reform and grew increasingly dissatisfied. Though he could write several essays on reform and even occasionally slip into the idiom of western promotion, Emerson felt, as he explained in a letter to Thomas Carlyle, that Americans had gone a "little wild" in their projects to make new communities and remake old ones. The problem was that while cities were growing at an unprecedented pace, the majority of Americans, he believed, still lived in "Lilliput." In his countrymen he found a "fussy, self-asserting, buzzing" which lacked a clear direction, lacked proper motives and even conviction: "We want principles which shall give the greatest strength to our social union, and the greatest efficacy to social action." Though seeing this problem everywhere in America, he found it especially prominent in the native response to cities. For Emerson recognized a deep uneasiness in his fellow citizens—a latent fear that an inherent difference between the natural and the urban did exist, despite all their assertions to the contrary. "We talk of deviations from natural life," he explained in his second "Nature" essay, "as if artificial life were not so natural." Yet, "if we consider how much we are nature's, we need not be superstitious about towns, as if that terrific or benefic force did not find us there also, and fashion cities. Nature, who made the mason, made the house."[26]

Emerson's ability to embrace the city in this way no doubt seems curious in light of his transcendental emphasis on the inspirational value of the countryside, the woods, and the forest. We think of Emerson as the speaker in the first *Nature* essay, declaring that "country-life possesses, for a powerful mind," a substantial "advantage . . . over the artificial and curtailed life of cities" because "in the tranquil landscape . . . man beholds somewhat as beautiful as his own nature." The characteristic Emerson is the author of "The Young American," urging his countrymen to embrace "whatever events in progress shall go to disgust men with cities and infuse into them the passion for country life and country pleasure." Yet such statements form only a part of Emerson's ideas about urbanization. Just as central are affirmations like the following:

> I see the vast advantages of this country, spanning the breadth of the temperate zone. I see the immense material prosperity,—towns on towns, states on states, and wealth piled in the massive architecture of cities. . . . [W]hen I look over this constellation of cities which animate and illustrate the land, and see . . . how much each virtuous and gifted person, whom all men consider, lives affectionately with scores of excellent people . . . I see what cubic values America has.

We should recall that the moment of insight Emerson records in *Nature* occurs not in a rural retreat, but while he crosses a town common at twilight. The image of Emerson as a rural advocate simply cannot account for such facts and pronouncements nor for the numerous discussions in his letters about profits from his lecture tours and financial investments—hardly the concerns expected from a man committed to withdrawing into nature.[27]

As Michael Cowan has reminded us, Emerson spent half his life in cities and recognized the ineluctable need to come to terms with the urban world in meaningful, not dismissive, ways. In his study of Emerson and urban metaphor, Cowan has demonstrated that "Emerson's evaluation of actual urban civilization was productively complex and shrewdly optimistic" because he realized that urban materials could provide the artist with useful tropes for larger, abstract concerns. Yet while Emerson, as Cowan contends, did perceive cities as "literary vehicles by which he could relate the external and the internal, the actual and the ideal," Emerson also was very much concerned with the social conditions of America and of its cities.[28] Maintaining that the true "test of civilization" consisted in "drawing the most benefit out of cities"—benefits that could enrich the inner and outer being—Emerson came to believe that what behooved both himself and the nation was not to choose between literature and life, abstract and concrete, city and country, but to discover a way to unite rural and urban for spiritual and social advancement.

Although Emerson valued the countryside for the solitude it afforded as a path to self-awareness, he nonetheless was attracted to urban society because, as he explained, in itself "solitude is impracticable" and even "against nature" in that it is a "half view." While asserting that "solitude & the country, books, & openness, will feed you," he also thought that "man must be clothed with society, or we shall feel a certain bareness and poverty." Urging his fellow Americans to "go into the city" for "your humanity" and for "strength & hope & vision for the day," Emerson by 1850 had come to believe that the complete individual must not reject society but fully participate in it.[29] Although he continued to value the solitude of the open landscape, he held that, as alternatives, "solitude is naught & society is naught"; a union of the two could provide the only means for a full character. "The balance must be kept," he recorded in his journal as early as 1841; "the social & the solitary humour, man & opportunity" must "coexist." For Emerson, the needs of the individual and the needs of society were part of one dynamic process, which, properly synchronized, could lead to an exalted individualism and the advent of a beatific community.[30] His vision of synchronicity was another version of the urban-pastoral impulse, given transcendental coloration.

What is remarkable is the way Emerson's own choice of residence points to a desire to bring together his fondness for isolation and community, nature and the city. Though Sherman Paul certainly is correct in saying that Emerson moved to Concord to bring himself closer to nature, Emerson explained that he had moved to his "*ancestral* village," not only because "it was the quietest of farming towns," but because it lay "on the directest line of road from Boston to Montreal." A devotee of "Boston Common, Boston Atheneum, Lowell Institute, [and] Railroads" by his own admission, he sought to remain close to his native city—and with good reason. Though delighted with farming and gardening, Emerson did not adhere to a simpleminded faith that a rural existence was inherently ennobling. On the contrary, he wrote, "the planter . . . is seldom cheered by any idea of the true dignity of his ministry. He sees his bushel and his cart, and nothing beyond." Anticipating the writer in the *Atlantic* who claimed that life among the furrows was enervating, Emerson wrote in 1845 that all experience shows that "hard labor on the farm untunes the mind, [and] unfits [it] for the intellectual exercises which are the delight of the best men." This conclusion, he recognized, had implications for his own position. As he explained two years later in a letter to Carlyle while discussing his efforts to "lay out a patch of orchard near my house," the "works of the garden and orchard . . . will eat up days & weeks, and a brave scholar should shun it like gambling, & take refuge in cities & hotels from these pernicious enchantments."[31] Though written somewhat in jest, these words suggest that for a man of urbanity, as Emerson was, rural life or even life in Concord village was insufficient in itself. The city was necessary to counterbalance the effects of the farm.

Besides reflecting his own preferences, Emerson's attitude toward country and city had its source in his philosophy of intellect. His well-known distinction between two ways of knowing, which he identified as Understanding (the lower, empirical mode that "adds, combines, measures") and Reason (the higher, intuitive mode that transcends Understanding by finding affinities and order in larger patterns) incorporated a geo-epistemology that identified each faculty with a particular locality. "The city delights the understanding," he wrote, because both are "made up of finites: short, sharp, mathematical lines, all calculable." "The country," on the other hand, with its "unbroken horizon" is "the School of the Reason."[32] Because he praised reason over understanding, which he called "a sort of shop clerk . . . for petty ends," students of Emerson have made much of this distinction as an index to his preference for the country. However, Emerson's moral psychology cannot be reduced to such a simple dichotomy. Though emphasizing the need to develop reason because he believed that Americans lived too often on the lower plane, he never intended to dismiss understanding. As he explained in his essay "Memory" (1857), "we can help ourselves to the *modus* of mental processes only by coarse material experiences," which the understanding imbibes. Since reason could operate only through the accumulation of data, stored in the memory, reason and understanding had to work in partnership. "Every true man," Emerson asserted, "has a majestic understanding, which is in its right place the servant of reason," providing it with materials and anchoring it to the world. If a person "be defective at either extreme of the scale," he believed, "his philosophy will seem low and utilitarian, or it will appear too vague and indefinite for the uses of life."[33] Although reason was more conducive to insight, understanding was nonetheless necessary—as was its training ground, the city. Instead of rejecting the utilitarian and the urban, Emerson advocated the need to reconcile urbanity with a commitment to nature, striking a balance between seemingly opposite values in an evocative series of analogous pairs: reason and understanding, solitude and society, self and community, nature and civilization, country and city.

But if we occasionally forget Emerson's emphasis on balance and his urbanity, no doubt because he often deemphasized the latter, we need to remember also that in his published writings he spoke primarily to an urban audience. When he called for a life closer to nature, he was not naively arguing that people should quit great cities, though at times he seemed to suggest that. "Is it not pedantry," he asked rhetorically, "to insist that every man should be a farmer as much as that he should be a lexicographer?" Instead of urging a literal withdrawal, Emerson employed his call as a rhetorical device to encourage urban dwellers to reach down and discover the organic principles of their own being. Believing that "we are predominated herein . . . by an upper wisdom" and always stressing the primacy of ideas, he held that from any spot on the globe one could cultivate a spiritual, moral relationship with first principles. In doing so, the individual would take delight "in every show of night or day, or field or forest or sea or city," since all visible creation, including the city, was "the terminus or the circumference of the invisible world," the divine mind, or in Emerson's terminology, the Oversoul. Emerson could embrace urban life because he believed that the city and nature were inextricably linked as "points in this curve of the great circle." The human task was to discover a perspective that would allow insight into that organic relationship.[34]

According to Emerson, this need was especially pressing in America where the geographical features—"the nobility of this land" and "its tranquilizing, sanative influence"—provided a unique opportunity for "just relations with men and things." Yet Emerson felt that his countrymen were squandering this chance. "My own quarrel with America," he confided in 1850, is "that the geography is sublime, but the men are not." Misdirecting their efforts, Americans had attempted to make their cities more organic by incorporating physical nature or advocating purer manners, but such efforts addressed themselves only to the surface of existence. And herein lay the inadequacies of reform as Emerson's contemporaries practiced it. "The Reformers affirm the inward life," he observed, "but they do not trust it, but use outward and vulgar means." Emphasizing the material, institutional, and external at the expense of the internal, reformers had sought "to raise man by improving his circumstances" and had failed to recognize that "society gains nothing whilst a man, not himself renovated, attempts to renovate things around him." If America seemed to lack unity and lie "broken and in heaps," if cities seemed to be separating from nature, if ideals and actualities seemed to be growing asunder, it was "because man is disunited with himself." But the true reformer helps mend this spiritual rift by becoming "a mediator between the spiritual and the actual world."[35] He points men to a true understanding of the relation among the self, the products of his action, and the universal pattern by helping to sharpen the inward and outward eyes.

Indeed, sight was the most important sense to Emerson, not only because it was the keenest, but because it symbolized true insight and inspiration. Believing that the fate of American cities ultimately depended on how they were perceived, he found in reformist and promotional efforts substantial indications that Americans lacked a proper vision. Using Lilliputian eyes to gaze at their cities, too many of his countrymen suffered from a mental myopia, viewing particular urban phenomena and whole cities from a limited perspective. Cognizant that the facts of urban life, viewed as "detached," inevitably appeared "ugly," Emerson urged his fellow citizens to adopt the proper "point of view" toward cities: a panoramic perspective that would enable them to experience urbanization as part of nature's plan. From that perspective, "the light of higher laws" would shine through the city, revealing it as part of the "one design [which] unites and animates the farthest pinnacle and the lowest trench."[36]

Of course, Emerson did not think that such a perspective readily came to the mind's eye. Acutely aware of the disjointed and unsettling ways of urban experience and ever conscious of man's own duality, he nonetheless believed that this unified vision lay at every man's disposal, with the aid of language. Asserting that words are signs of physical facts which in turn symbolize spiritual facts, Emerson esteemed language as an especially powerful tool for creating perspective. For this reason he admonished "wise men [to] pierce this rotten diction and fasten words again to visible things," since only by being fixed to things could language lead to spiritual truths. This duty lay, above all, with the poet-scholar who, in rearranging the possibilities of language, "re-attaches things to nature and the Whole."[37] By revealing affinities and correspondences hidden from most people, he serves as the medium between first principles and the bulk of humanity. If the insight he provides exists only momentarily in life, at least the idea of unity resides permanently in his text.

To assume that Emerson distinguished between art and life in terms of a permanent correspondence, however, would be to draw a false distinction in his metaphysic. For Emerson, language did not constitute a separate world in which an illusion of correspondence is momentarily available to the reader. Rather, that correspondence always exists, though people may be unaware of it. The text or artistic product does not create unity but discloses it and possesses value insofar as it successfully does so. When Emerson wrote, "Let the river roll which way it will, cities will rise on its banks," he was employing language to reveal the place of urbanization in nature's organic pattern.[38] Such an image was no mere poetic construct for Emerson; it symbolized the order of reality and the workings of the world.

In confronting cities, therefore, Emerson believed that the poet-scholar should reveal the spiritual significance of urban phenomena by divulging their intrinsic relation to nature's pattern. As the true reformer, he must "build a bridge from the streets of cities to the Atlantis" and so prepare the way for a truly organic urban life.[39] Unveiling the affinity among first principles, nature, and cities, the poet-scholar can assert and exemplify society's ability to do the same. His efforts constitute both a prelude to and microcosm of society's task as a whole.

Following his own lead, Emerson provided just such an example of urban-pastoral re-vision in his 1861 lecture "Boston." The beginning of the address seeks to establish Boston's position in the American landscape by uniting the city's history to natural phenomena. Describing the effects of climate on the city's life, Emerson explains that "according to quality and according to temperature, it must have effect on manners," and so it does in Boston. Although the atmosphere is not luxurious, all the better, since "wisdom is not found with those who dwell at their ease." Like Beverley and Crèvecoeur, Emerson believes that a pampering climate does not promote a "stirring" society conducive to "youth and health." Happily, he asserts, Boston's does: "the power of labor which belongs to the English race fell here into a climate which befriended it." Because of the hardy atmosphere, there is a "stimulus in our native air" which causes "people [to] think well and construct well" and so develop all their faculties. As a result, Bostonians have been compelled to vigorous activity. Though "not at all accustomed to the rough task of discoverers," the first settlers had to master external nature, but they did not do so by exploiting it "for pleasure and for show." Accepting the "divine ordinance that man is for use," as is nature when carefully husbanded, "they knew, as God knew, that command of Nature comes by obedience to Nature." "Unlock[ing] the treasures of the world" slowly and carefully "by honest keys of labor and skill," they built their city in accordance with the dictates of God and nature.[40]

Having located an organic nexus between the city and nature through climate, Emerson continues by identifying the relationship between Boston and its topography. "In our beautiful bay, with its broad and deep waters . . . ; with its islands hospitably shining in the sun; . . . with its shores trending steadily from the two arms which the capes of Massachusetts stretch out to sea," the landscape has provided optimum conditions for a city. Hence, the distinctive features of Boston, and its every existence, have depended on natural configurations. "How easy it is, after the city is built, to see where it ought to stand," he points out.

In these remarks, Emerson takes a tack found in much of the urban-pastoral promotional literature of the West: identifying environmental conditions as the impetus to a city's rise and greatness. Yet what distinguishes this essay is the way it goes beyond this strategy to expand the relationship between geography and urbanity. In discussing Boston's climate, for example, Emerson says that "the desire for glory and honor is powerfully generated by the air of that place, in the men of every profession." The air impels the inhabitants toward noble pursuits, in part because the "air" consists of the activities of professional men who set the urban pace. By expanding the meaning of *climate* to include the social atmosphere of Boston, Emerson suggests parallels between urban activity and nature's ways. Like a divining rod, his language points beneath the surface to draw out hidden affinities and relationships. Accordingly, when he explains, "Who lives one year in Boston ranges through all the climates of the globe," he refers to both the weather and the cosmopolitanism of the city, which "unites itself by natural affinity to the highest minds of the world; nourishes itself on Plato and Dante, Michael Angelo and Milton; on whatever is pure and sublime in art."[41]

Boston's cosmopolitan attitude, moreover, looks both east and west, to the best of Europe and to the developing American scene. Since the city's dawn, Bostonians have been engaged in improving the landscape. Not only did the first settlers of Massachusetts, directed by Boston, domesticate the wilderness so that "Nature has never again indulged in . . . exasperations," but the 1647 statute of education, framed by the General Court in Boston, established universal elementary instruction in New England, so that now, in rural districts, "lectures are read and debates sustained which prove a college for the young rustic." The effects have been far-reaching. Because of Boston's lead, today "New England supplies annually a large detachment of preachers and schoolmasters and private tutors to the interior of the South and West." This link to the interior, however, incorporates more than education. Massachusetts, growing from its Boston center, has been "sending out colonies . . . [to the] South and West, until it has infused all the Union with its blood." Boston's "climate," therefore, is commensurate with the American "climate." Providing "planters of towns, fellers of the forest," and "farmers to till and harvest corn for the world," Emerson proclaims, "our little city thrives and enlarges, striking deep roots, and sending out boughs and buds, and propagating itself like a banyan over the continent." Confident of Boston's growth, as expressed in this organic metaphor, Emerson is convinced that its expansion accords with nature's principles. Just as "Nature is good" so, he asserts, is Boston "a good city."[42]

Emerson here makes creative use of a conventional strategy in defining the organicism of cities. Declining to emphasize the economic and material union of Boston and the landscape—the device usually used by western promoters and other defenders of the urban East—he focuses instead on the people themselves, prefiguring the more complex use Whitman will make of humanity in the city. Emerson suggests that the human presence in the city creates an organic unity within itself and with the landscape because the galvanic activities and aspirations of individuals have exfoliated into a national community. For Emerson, the true organic significance of Boston lies in the values and traits of its inhabitants, especially their "real independence, productive power and northern acuteness of mind,—which is in nature hostile to oppression."[43]

The independent spirit of Bostonians is particularly important because it links the city to the prevalent feature of America: democracy. "Emancipation," Emerson explains, using the term in its broadest sense to mean political freedom, takes root in "our freedom of intellection," which has been a trait of Boston since its settlement. The first Puritans brought with them "the culture of the intellect" and a "saucy independence" which, though "confined" in England, received full "swing and play" in their "new country." In this interplay of environment and spirit, an atmosphere of dissent, the basis of democracy, developed, with the result that "Boston never [has] wanted a good principle of rebellion in it, from the planting until now." Finding that rebelliousness in the Puritans' "Petitions to the King, and the[ir] platforms for churches," Emerson identifies it as "the essence of the Massachusetts Bill of Rights and of the American Declaration of Independence." Thus, he proclaims, the dominant formula of his own day—the democratic ideal which allows every American to say, "I'm as good as you be"—"was at the bottom of Plymouth Rock and of Boston Stone."[44]

Although such a "democratizing" of the Puritans seems, from our perspective, to distort history, Emerson seeks here to rewrite the past in a different way for his contemporaries. For Emerson alters the myth of the Revolution as a rural rebellion by expanding it to include the city. If Massachusetts farmers led the rebellion, he is saying, their dissent was founded on the principles of "Plymouth Rock" and "Boston Stone"—principles that expanded with the growth of America. Having infused the Union with their blood, Bostonians have carried with them an invigorating spirit of rebellion and adventure that courses through the national body. Because of it he can assert unequivocally that "Boston commands attention as the town which was appointed in the destiny of nations to lead the civilization of North America."

Although Boston's development and its influence on the native scene are momentous in themselves, their true consequence lies in their symbolic implications. For Boston exists ultimately for Emerson as a synecdoche for American development in general and urban expansion in particular. Its growth and its alliance with the continent mirror that of other "great cities" in America, including New York, New Orleans, and new cities of the West, all of which are bound to the landscape through "influences" which "you cannot compute." Under their hand, "America is growing like a cloud, towns on towns, states on states," and "gardens fit for human abode where all elements" are "right for the health, power and virtue of man."[45]

In his lecture on Boston, Emerson heeds his own advice that American writers must "convert the vivid energies acting at this hour in New York and Chicago and San Francisco, into universal symbols."[46] His prose discovers beneath the physical and cultural facts of Boston a central spiritual fact: the organic, unified design for American development. In employing language as he does, Emerson supplies in "Boston" a model for other American poets. By following his example, they can reveal the correspondence among landscape, cityscape, and first principles and so provide their countrymen with an ennobling perspective on urban America. While such a perspective cannot alter the physical and social shape of cities, it can lead to an appreciation of them as organic components of a national and natural pattern.

Yet Emerson did not think that the entire process ended there, since vision was finally for him a preliminary stage of enlightenment leading to concentrated, prudential action. Possessing a strongly practical turn of mind to balance his emphasis on the transcendent and nonutilitarian ("every thought is practical at last," he wrote in 1853), Emerson was keenly aware that urban reforms were desirable and even necessary, particularly in trade and commerce, which were "vitiated by derelictions and abuses." Because insight must lead to efforts which would conform urban life to its immanent, organic pattern, he believed that the poet-scholar should not only provide a proper perspective on the city but also "prepare the minds of his countrymen for the novel schemes of the Reformer" so as to make his countrymen reformers themselves. "The true romance which the world exists to realize," Emerson explained in "Experience," "will be the transformation of genius into practical power." "What is man born for," he asked, "but to be a Reformer?"[47]

Given his fondness for the pluralism of American culture, however, how did Emerson expect people to agree upon modes of reform—or even that a particular reform was necessary—without degenerating into the party making he so deplored? That Emerson was aware of the danger is evident in his remarks in "Lecture on the Times" (1841) in which he denounced factionalism in America. "The two omnipresent parties of History, the party of the Past and the party of the Future," he warned, "divide society to-day as of old." But he also believed, as he explained in the same lecture, that party making was receding in his own day, since

> The revolutions that impend over society are not now from ambition and rapacity, from impatience of one or another form of government, but from new modes of thinking, which shall recompense society after a new order. . . . There was never so great a thought laboring in the breasts of men as now. It almost seems as if what was afore-time spoken fabulously and hieroglyphically, was now spoken plainly.[48]

Because of intellectuals, poets, and scholars like himself, who are revealing underlying truths, Americans shortly will synchronize their activities to conform with universal principles.

In his thinking on this matter, Emerson shared a common assumption of intellectuals and reformers of his age. As John Thomas has explained, most believed that individuals could trust a properly directed conscience because it was "the repository of divine truths." In doing so they provided a model for others who, in turn, inevitably would reach similar conclusions. "Individual conscience thus creates social conscience and a collective will to right action." According to this ideology, correctly informed thought becomes a consensus, allowing people to direct their actions to one shared goal. For Americans concerned with urban conditions, that end consisted of creating a truly urban-pastoral society. In a similar conviction lay the basis of Emerson's faith. Confident of the essential unity of humankind and convinced that "actions will be harmonious, however unlike they seem," if "they be each honest and natural in their hour," he was certain that diverse efforts to create organic cities would interconnect as points on the vast spiral of progress. By making their cities more organic, Americans would be "conspiring with the designs of the Spirit," to construct "a new and more excellent social state than history has recorded."[49]

III

Believing that urban reform and development in the direction of nature must be a social goal with moral and spiritual implications,

Emerson sought to lead his countrymen to a similar recognition. Among those who shared his goal was Frederick Law Olmsted, the progenitor of landscape architecture in the United States and a man whose work in urban park planning would profoundly affect subsequent efforts to make American cities more natural.

Although the extent of influence is uncertain, Emerson's ideas clearly had an impact on Olmsted's conception of himself and his profession. As a youth the latter had attended a number of the transcendentalist's lectures, and by the time he was twenty-two he was energetically urging his Hartford friends to read *Nature: Addresses and Lectures*. Later, in his *Mount Royal* (1881), Olmsted echoed Emerson's distinction between reason and understanding in asserting that natural scenery affects not only the empirical faculties but also "the highest functions of the system, . . . tending, more than any single form of medication, to establish sound minds." Defining the landscape architect as an artist who reveals the "beauty and designing powers" of nature "to cultivate the intellectual" in man, Olmsted shared Emerson's belief that art, as a way to ennoble humanity, constituted a social activity.[50]

Yet Olmsted's idea of the sanative potential of nature and the social commitment of art did not result from sudden inspiration. While his encounter with Emersonianism did affect him, his rural experiences as a boy already had conditioned his fondness for nature. In what he later termed his youthful "tours in search of the picturesque" and in his vagabond ramblings at an early age in the fields and woods around Hartford, Olmsted imbibed a romantic love for cultivated nature and rural life which formed the basis of his belief that analogous conditions could regenerate the human spirit in the city. His readings in Emerson as well as in Lowell, Ruskin, and "other real prophets," as he called them, mostly reinforced his predispositions by instilling "the needed respect for my constitutional tastes and inclinations to poetic refinement in the cultivation of them that afterwards determined my profession."[51]

Though Olmsted's initial inclinations lay entirely with agriculture, by the late 1840s he was expanding his interests beyond farming in the direction of urban life. One factor precipitating this shift may have been his growing friendship with Horace Bushnell and Charles Loring Brace, both of whom exemplified a strong dedication to urban reform. More important perhaps, his visits to the South in 1853 and 1854 and to the utopian community near Red Bank, New Jersey, helped reinforce his growing conviction that agricultural life in itself lacked cultural fullness. As a result, he was coming to believe, along with a number of Americans at the time, that "our country has entered upon a stage of progress in which its welfare is to depend on the convenience, safety, order, and economy of life in its great cities." While Olmsted never abandoned his interests in rural life, from the mid-1850s on he felt that for himself as well as for America "no broad question of country life in comparison with city life is involved; it is confessedly a question of delicate adjustment."[52]

Unfortunately, few American cities, in Olmsted's opinion, provided such an adjustment. In particular, he cited the noxious air and overcrowding in metropolitan areas as the major "source[s] of morbid conditions of the body and mind, manifesting themselves in nervous feebleness . . . and various functional derangements" found among urban dwellers. While he felt that the commercial areas of cities may necessitate such "conditions of corruption and of irritation," he argued that "commerce does not require the same conditions to be maintained in all parts of a town." Like other defenders of open spaces, Olmsted believed that public parks and recreational greens provided an answer to these problems. Planting public gardens and establishing a system of parks throughout cities would not only alleviate injurious conditions but also make the urban world more humane and civilized by promoting "harmonious cooperation of men in a community." Having written at the age of twenty-four that he wanted to "help to advance the condition of Society, and hasten the preparation for the Millennium," Olmsted translated this desire into a secular vision of progress toward more natural, open cities. Creating an urban-pastoral America was to be the goal of the landscape architect as artist, and Olmsted charted his career as a voyage toward that goal. Appropriately, his first effort, the plan for New York's Central Park, was entitled "Greensward."[53]

In submitting his plan for Central Park, Olmsted hoped that its design would be the first step in restoring to New York a proper balance of nature and civilization. For the "hundreds of thousands of tired workers, who have no opportunity to spend their summers in the country" and so experience the therapeutic effects of nature, Olmsted wrote, the park would provide a "constant suggestion to the imagination of an unlimited range of rural conditions." As such, the park was to provide not just an exemption from the noise, bustle, and stress of urban life, but an environment "remedial of the [debilitating] influences of urban conditions." Most important to Olmsted, the park, as a permanent asylum for the tired and overtaxed in the city, would be a check against the future when "New York will be built up" and no trace of nature would remain "with the single exception of the few acres contained in the Park."[54] In the midst of a changing city, Olmsted believed the park could remain unchanged—a pastoral enclave removed, in effect, from history; a progressive construct constraining "excessive" progress.

To achieve these goals, Olmsted designed the park as an ideal middle landscape of "tranquil, open, pastoral scenes," as he called them. Besides a tree-lined mall and several playing fields, the park possessed man-made ponds for skating in the winter and boating in the summer. All traces of the original rocky and broken surface disappeared beneath sinuous trails winding among picturesque collections of trees and shrubs. In an ideal marriage of art and nature, gently curving roads led through a series of opening and closing vistas, giving the visitor the impression that he was in a world set apart. Olmsted was careful to perpetuate this impression by planting a line of trees around the periphery to conceal the houses on the opposite sides of the streets. To eliminate the disruption of traffic cutting through the park, the major cross-roads were sunken below ground level, further encouraging the sense of an idyllic asylum. "A great object of all that is done in a park, of *all* the art of a park," Olmsted retrospectively explained in 1872, was "to influence the mind of men through their imagination."[55]

This emphasis on the park as a catalyst for higher sensibilities was consonant with Olmsted's definition of the landscape architect as artist and his Emersonian faith in nature as an inspirational force. He hoped that under nature's guiding hand, an agreeable suggestion might be "conveyed[,] to the imagination[,] of freedom" and so relieve New Yorkers of the sense of constraint they felt in the city. By the same token, however, Olmsted hoped that the pastoral landscape would have "a manifestly civilizing effect" by encouraging "community and the intimate relationship and constant intercourse and interdependence between families." Regarding the latter, he held that the park would provide circumstances favorable to "the association of children, of mothers, of lovers, or those who may be lovers, [and] stimulate and keep alive the more tender sympathies." Concerning the former, he believed that the mixture of social classes meeting in the park would produce neighborliness and an enduring order in the urban milieu by reducing social discontent and placating "the rough element of the city." Calling his plan a "democratic development of the highest significance," he expected it to yield an amicable relation between rich and poor in the tradition of democratic pastoralism.[56]

Although Olmsted stressed democracy and innovations in park planning, his ideas, significantly enough, reveal the basic conservatism underlying urban-pastoral reform. By seeking to reduce social discontent without correcting its manifold causes, Olmsted attempted simply to smooth over lower-class disgruntlement in New York beneath a veneer of tokenism. As Geoffrey Blodgett has pointed out, the park was to be a means for procuring a good, genteel society in which "hierarchy, deference, and skilled leadership might impose tranquility on a contentious, egalitarian people." As a result, Olmsted "underestimated the aggressive thrust of American pluralism" and so conceived a rather rigid image of a healthy urban society.[57] Of course, the same can be said of most urban-pastoral ideas, and this shortcoming is precisely what Hawthorne would dramatize in his fiction. However conservative or liberal Olmsted's ideas may have been, therefore, he clearly shared several assumptions characterizing the urban pastoralism of his age: that a sound community and sturdy family life are best promoted when cities contain a distinct pastoral element; that nature encourages people's inherent goodness and social inclinations; that a return to a more organic environment can promote, paradoxically, both greater constructive freedom and beneficial restraint in urban society; and that the needs of a pluralistic urban population can be permanently met by a particular version of the garden city.

Despite the shortcomings of Olmsted's vision (as revealed in the present conditions of Central Park and New York), it is important to stress that his ideas were particular manifestations of a way of thinking, both intellectual and popular, which persisted well into the final decades of the 1800s. In fact, Olmsted's career can be seen as a symbolic bridge spanning the two halves of a century which displayed an unflagging commitment to the urban-pastoral ideal. While Olmsted went on to design over thirty-five parks in cities around the country and to plan numerous "green communities" such as Riverside, Illinois, the early success of Central Park, more than any other factor, helped turn the tentative efforts in park planning before the Civil War into a national park-planning movement after 1870. Parks and park departments were established in Boston, Brooklyn, Baltimore, Louisville, Chicago, Milwaukee, Minneapolis, Kansas City, San Francisco, and nearly every other major American city. As one English observer, the earl of Meath, remarked in 1890, "a veritable rage for park making seems to have seized the American public."[58]

The importance of the urban park lay in more than its physical beauties or the psychological balm it offered in providing urban dwellers with easy access to natural landscapes. It also served as a new token in continuing efforts to promote and define the special characteristics of American cities. In his 1888 book on Chicago's parks and boulevards, publisher J. P. Craig asserted that Chicago was "among the great cities of the world" in large part because it married a thriving, advanced urban culture with a "Park System [that] is not only among the most beautiful, but the most extensive." Such park books became a staple of the publishing trade in the 1880s and 1890s, enforcing their written message with photographs that visually testified to the advantages of urban parks. As Peter Hales has shown in his study of American photography of the city in the nineteenth century, parks became an increasingly prominent subject in the urban iconography of the time, as photographers sought to reassure their local and national audiences "that America's cities had succeeded in bringing nature and nurture into confluence."[59]

Meanwhile, the urban-pastoral impulse found an outlet in a relatively new direction: the suburb. Although a few suburbs had existed before the Civil War, by the late 1870s, owing to improved transportation, the number had swelled to the point where Chicago alone claimed over a hundred, with an aggregate population of 50,000. But if technological developments facilitated extensive suburbanism, what suburbs offered made them most appealing. As the anonymous author of a pamphlet entitled *North Chicago* (1873) explained:

> The controversy which is sometimes brought, as to which offers the greater advantage, the country or the city, finds a happy answer in the suburban idea which says, both—the combination of the two—the city brought to the country. This is a practical and valuable reply. The city has its advantages and conveniences, the country has its charm and health; the union of the two . . . gives to man all he could ask for in this respect.

A more explicit testimony to the hold of urban pastoralism on popular values scarcely could be found. Yet intellectuals espoused a similar faith in the ability of suburbs to provide an ideal mixture of country and city. In his *Growth of Cities* (1899), Adna F. Weber, the period's most capable demographer, asserted that "the 'rise of the suburbs' . . . furnishes a hope that the evils of city life" would be "in a large part removed." Paying tribute to the secular version of the American millennium, grounded in a conviction of native uniqueness, he concluded his study by announcing that suburbanism "will realize . . . 'a complete interpretation of city and country, a complete fusion . . . of the advantages of both, and as no country in the world has ever seen.' "[60]

Not only in park planning and suburban development did the urban-pastoral impulse make itself felt. It also infused its idealism into the urban reform of the Progressive Era, particularly in the emphasis on improving community in the city. A leading proponent of this idea, Robert Park believed that the major task facing America was "the problem of achieving in the freedom of the city a social order and a social control equivalent to that which grew up naturally in the family, the clan, and the tribe." As a result, Park urged Americans to reestablish in the city social patterns which he found in nonurban and preurban societies. A similar goal prompted Jane Addams to found Hull House in Chicago as a communal gathering place which would encourage the type of face-to-face relationships she knew as a young girl growing up in rural Cedarville. Even Henry George, as we have seen, composed his controversial plan for a single tax with an eye toward promoting a salubrious balance of country and city. *Progress and Poverty* looked forward to a time in America when "all the enormous advantages, material and mental, of a dense population, would be united [with] the freedom and equality that can now only be found in new and sparsely settled districts." Although George's radical plan was severely criticized, many Americans at the time desired the same goal: the union of country and city, nature and civilization, freedom and community that characterizes urban pastoralism.[61]

The second half of the nineteenth century thus saw the desire to combine city and country take shape in new manifestations that relocated the ideal on the fringes of existing cities or couched it in municipal improvement plans coordinated by a growing professional class of reformers. Yet these phenomena, far from marking a significant shift in the history of urban pastoralism, embodied a difference in form rather than in substance. Beneath them lay the same central assumptions that had nourished American conceptions of the good city in the generations before the Civil War. Like their ancestors, proponents of the ideal in the last three decades of the nineteenth century remained convinced that the healthy society would combine the best of rural and urban and that such a combination was inscribed in the legacy of America.

That ideal, of course, had played a prominent role in American ideas from the very beginning. Evolving from the millennialist expectations of a New Jerusalem, it had inspired a variety of plans, pronouncements, and visions in the eighteenth and nineteenth centuries, claiming credence even from such a votary of nature as Emerson and from the most ardent agrarian, Jefferson. Indeed, the unmitigated power of urban pastoralism can be located in its seeming ability to reconcile conflicting ideologies: a belief in the necessity of urban expansion and a trust in the myth of the garden; a faith in progressive development and a commitment to an unchanging order. Quite simply, there was no questioning of the ideal by those Americans who continued to assume that the native scene would bring forth a perdurably balanced society. To reveal the limitations of urban pastoralism required a different point of view.

VI

Urban Pastoralism and Literary Dissent

From "Brooklyn Ferry" to *The American Scene*

Although the urban-pastoral ideal was only one of several ways Americans responded to their cities, its attraction made it a staple of native thought and writing, including imaginative literature, as the country moved into an era of increased urbanization in the nineteenth century. But as America's first significant literary generation came to maturity in the three decades after 1830, its members brought a new perspective to the discussion. While popular novels and poems continued to affirm the integrated image of urban felicity, the works of our best writers who confronted the ideal began to treat it in a more complicated and sophisticated manner. The literary response to urban pastoralism in the nineteenth century and after thus constitutes a unique countervoice in the history of America's ideas about synthesizing nature and the city.

Exactly why writers such as Hawthorne, Whitman, Dreiser, and James were able to penetrate the vision and respond to it with greater insight is difficult to say. Perhaps part of the answer is that literature of the first rank, as F. O. Matthiessen once affirmed, possesses an intrinsic ability not only to reflect the culture but also to illuminate it. In this sense it differs from the general flow of thought and feeling found in society. Because such an answer, however, begs the question, a more satisfactory explanation may lie in the very mode our most gifted novelists and poets have chosen. For if the distinguishing characteristic of American writing, as several literary critics have claimed, is its strong romantic bent, and if, as Michael Bell has posited, the romance has developed in a society which has tended to equate that mode with "insanity and subversion," America'a leading artists have found themselves inherently at odds with a culture of which they have been nonetheless a part. As rebellious romancers, freed from the constraints of simplistic, didactic writing, which strives for direct, utilitarian confirmation of standard social values, they have been able to step back from the nation's unqualified commitment to urban pastoralism and examine the psychological implications of the ideal. As a result, their work has absorbed the currents flowing through our history and rechanneled them into cross-currents of disruptive thought.[1]

However, since sophisticated literary productions incorporating the ideal comprise a diversity which cannot be subsumed under the heading of romance, even this explanation lacks complete cogency. No generalization, finally, can explain why in every case America's most compelling writers have responded as they have to urban pastoralism, but the fact is that, either through their keener incisiveness, sensitivity, or historical imagination or through their social alienation or through a combination of these and other factors, our major artists have enveloped the ideal in a richness and complexity clarifying both its significance and inadequacies. Among the earliest to do so were Whitman and Hawthorne. Making the ideal an important thematic component in a number of their works, these two writers created divergent patterns of qualification that exemplify the major strains of artistic urban pastoralism: the internalized and the ironic.

I

Logically if not chronologically we may begin with Whitman, who celebrated the city in his poetry with an élan surpassing that of any other major American poet in the nineteenth century. As Whitman himself vowed in "Starting from Paumanok," the opening poem of the 1860 edition of *Leaves of Grass*, "I will trail the whole geography of the globe and salute courteously every city large and small."[2] Whitman's dedication to this purpose is evident in the number of poems in the *Leaves* which use the city as a major or minor symbol, setting, motif, or figure: "Song of Myself," "Once I Pass'd through a Populous City," "I Dream'd in a Dream," "Crossing Brooklyn Ferry," "City of Ships," "Song of the Open Road," and at least a score more. Whitman embraces the city so thoroughly, in fact, that he seems at times to do so at the expense of nature and the country.

In "Give Me the Splendid Silent Sun," for example, Whitman begins by declaiming his fondness for nature's abundance:

Give me juicy autumnal fruit ripe and red from the orchard,
Give me a field where the unmow'd grass grows,
Give me an arbor, give me the trellis'd grape,
Give me fresh corn and wheat, give me serene-moving animals
    teaching content,

. . . .

Give me to warble spontaneous songs recluse by myself, for my own
    ears only.

(2–5, 9)

In the second canto, however, he suddenly switches his allegiance and sings, "Keep your splendid silent sun," and "your woods O Nature" (20–21). Now he calls for

faces and street—give me these phantoms incessant and endless
    along the trottoirs!
Give me interminable eyes—give me women—give me comrades and
    lovers by the thousand!
Let me see new ones every day—let me hold new ones by the hand
    every day!
Give me such shows—give me the streets of Manhattan!

. . . .

O such for me! O an intense life, full to repletion and varied!

. . . .

Manhattan crowds, with their turbulent musical chorus!
Manhattan faces and eyes forever for me.

(24–27, 32, 39–40)

In "Splendid Silent Sun" Whitman seems to reject the rural world for the urban and to draw the traditional distinction between the two realms, suggesting that a choice must be made. Though conventionally read this way, the poem is more complex in that Whitman offers the distinction only to take it away.[3] Beneath the surface opposition, the poem actually links the two scenes as mirror images. In each half the rhythmic paralleling of phrasing, with the repetition of "give me," the unifying presence of song, and the poet's call for female companionship suggest that nature and the city are complementary realms of similar experience. What does the most effective work in drawing the two cantos and environments together is the kinship of plentitude found in both. The rich autumnal fruit, luscious unmowed grass, and bulging grapes match appositionally the "endless" faces and streets and the replete and varied movements in the city. As the poem progresses, the surface tension slowly gives way to harmony, and the seeming choice, Whitman implies, is unnecessary and even irrelevant.

Through Whitman's subtle artistry, "Give Me the Splendid Silent Sun" becomes another expression of the urban-pastoral ideal, yet we sense that even in such a short and minor poem the ideal is somehow different from most nonliterary versions. We are conscious most of all of the highly aesthetic quality of its reconciliation. As we read, we become expressly aware of the poet at work employing imagery, phrasing—in a word, language—to achieve this synthesis. The technique is similar to the one Whitman uses in most of his poems which incorporate the city as a central element. In "Song of Myself" the opposition of society and nature in the early cantos is dissolved because Whitman subsequently naturalizes the city by imaginatively dismantling it. No longer a city, it becomes a selection of urban sights and sounds gently interlaced, as in canto 15, with "western turkey-shooting" and "the plougher [who] ploughs, the mower [who] mows" (283, 316). Elsewhere in the poem, city and country become one by a series of imaginative leaps, as Whitman moves from a meditation on the significance of grass in canto 6, to a delectation of "the blab of the pave" and "the heavy omnibus, the driver with his interrogating thumb" in canto 8 (154–55), to a fanciful participation in a rural harvest in canto 9. Only by such noetic restructuring does Whitman create the "timeless . . . half-urban, half-pastoral world of primeval novelty" that Richard Chase has found in "Song of Myself."[4] If Whitman presents a world where self and other, man and nature, city and country are melded, he does so by a conjoining which is ultimately artistic. Overleaping sociopolitical interests, he announces organic cities that exist by virtue of linguistic manipulation and so inhere in language alone.

The first fact to note about Whitman's pastoral cities, therefore, is that they are not mimetic. As he himself explained in *Democratic Vistas*, he was not interested in "useless attempt[s] to repeat the material creation, by daguerreotyping the exact likeness by mortal mental means." For one thing, a striking difference exists between his poetic treatment of cities and his discursive prose comments about American urban life. In *Democratic Vistas*, for example, he lamented:

The great cities reek with respectable as much as non-respectable robbery and scoundrelism. In fashionable life, flippancy, tepid amours, weak infidelism, small aims, or no aims at all, only to kill time. In business, (this all-devouring modern word, business,) the one sole object is, by all means, pecuniary gain. . . .

Confess that to severe eyes, using the moral microscope upon humanity, a sort of dry and flat Sahara appears, these cities, crowded with petty grotesques, malformations, phantoms, . . . shallow notions of beauty, with a range of manners, or rather lack of manners, (considering the advantages enjoy'd,) probably the meanest to be seen in the world."[5]

Whitman was quite aware of the difference between the actual condition of American cities and the urban world he depicted in his poems. When we read his admission that "I have myself little or no hope from what is technically called 'Society' in our American cities," we realize that we are far from the buoyant affirmations of urban life in "Give Me the Splendid Silent Sun" or "Song of Myself."[6]

Having recognized this nonmimetic quality of his poetic cities, however, some critics have argued that Whitman presents an urban world which ought to be or will be.[7] Such a view of his urban poetry would make him either a progressive prophet like William Gilpin or a social programmer in the mold of Frederick Olmsted or Horace Mann. Whitman, however, was neither of these. Though at times he arrogated to himself a prophetic role, such instances are balanced by his denial on other occasions that he was doing anything more than "advanc[ing] a moment" toward the future "only to wheel and hurry back in the darkness."[8] Of course, Whitman was no stranger to contradiction, exuberantly claiming it as his métier in "Song of Myself." Yet what often appear as contradictory statements in his poetry can be understood as dovetailing pronouncements if we recognize that Whitman was not a votary of progress in the conventional sense of a movement from worse to better to best. His poems project not social betterment but artistic accomplishment which they both anticipate and fulfill.

Whitman's emphasis on poetic fulfillment and his disavowal of progress undermine any interpretation of his poetry as an effort to encourage urban reform or to provide a model for social betterment. The urban pastoralism of "Song of Myself" and "Give Me the Splendid Silent Sun," blatantly poetic and totally unpracticable on the social plane, reveals that Whitman carefully was attempting to avoid the "error," as he called it in *Specimen Days*, "of prescribing a specific [solution] for indispensable evils."[9] What makes the point even more graphically is the fact that, unlike reformers, Whitman identifies in his poetry no fallen city which needs to be redeemed. While prostitutes, drunkards, and the seamy side of urban life appear, they are celebrated with an equanimity illustrating Whitman's position on reform as he presented it in "Song of Myself": "Evil propels me and reform of evil propels me, I stand indifferent, / My gait is no faultfinder's or rejecter's gait" (465–66).

This is not to argue that the reformer was never a part of Whitman's personality. In his early career, before the first edition of *Leaves of Grass*, he was a didactic, reform-oriented writer, and much of the renovation he advocated coincided with the culture's general interest in developing organic cities. Repeatedly urging the officials of Brooklyn to create more parks, he was also a strident advocate of temperance and wrote his only novel, *Franklin Evans* (1842), to promote the cause. Nonetheless, the complex series of events between 1850 and 1855—including perhaps a growing alienation from organized social, political, and economic activity—made Whitman increasingly skeptical of social programming and reform. In particular, he seriously doubted that reform could be accomplished in cities by altering their physical and social structures.[10] Redefining for himself the relationship between man and the environment, self and other, thought and thing, Whitman reached a conclusion he would share with several other major American romantic artists: that ideal and actuality could meet only in theory, only in the imagination. By 1855 he had decided that the poet must be a leader in actualizing that imaginative nexus by becoming "the regent of a separate sphere, and the master of a complete poetic world of his own."[11] This creation of a separate, subjective poetic world is precisely the primary purpose of *Leaves of Grass* in general and his poetic treatment of the city in particular. Like other Americans, Whitman searched for an urban home in virgin territory, but he did so by directing his quest to a landscape of thought, to places yet unmapped in imagination.

When Whitman incorporated the city in his poems, therefore, he made it a projection of himself, or more correctly his "aesthetic personality," as he referred to his persona, who shapes urban materials into an amalgam of city and nature. Its union is his own mystical being, not imposed on the physical city, but formed within the poem and embodied in the city of the poem. In that process Whitman's poetic "I" becomes a poetic eye observing a city created by the act of perception. His world is not a depiction of urban reality as it is or will be or should be but an imaginative realization of ideal as ideal.

We can watch him engage in this process through a sequence of poems in the *Children of Adam* and *Calamus* groups, not in the order in which they were written, but in the pattern in which Whitman arranged them in the later editions of *Leaves of Grass*. In that pattern "Once I Pass'd through a Populous City," "For You O Democracy," and "I Dream'd in a Dream" depict the poet gradually absorbing and transforming urban material while slowly building an organic city of the mind. Despite a growing success as the series progresses, however, the noetic urban idyll of these short poems remains germinal. Constituting a preliminary stage, the sequence gives way to "Crossing Brooklyn Ferry," where Whitman fully constructs his literary version of the pastoral city.

"Brooklyn Ferry" commences, appropriately enough, with a salute to nature, followed immediately by a strategic invocation of urban imagery. As the poet sees the "Flood-tide," the "Clouds of the west," and the shining countenance of the sun "face to face" so, too, does he stare into the faces of "Crowds of men and women" who ride and will ride on this ferry journey with him (1–3). His anthropomorphism of natural phenomena links the urban crowd to nature in a union buttressed by the poet's all-embracing glance, which takes in both and holds them together in "meditations."

This opening coalescence becomes the central image of the poem, as Whitman reinforces and builds upon it in canto 2. Aboard the ferry, almost a part of its daily run, the poet takes in the entire scene around him, enclosing both nature and the city. The "run of the flood-tide" surging below him carries his vision along, directing it to sights of "the shipping of Manhattan," the contours of "the heights of Brooklyn," and the islands dotting the bay. Two of nature's prime elements, earth and water, thus seem inextricably fused with the activities of the city. The union continues in the progression from canto 2 to canto 3, as the rhythmic course of the water and sweeping arc of the sea gulls parallel the swinging motion of the activities along Manhattan's wharf and Brooklyn's streets.

> The sailors at work in the rigging or out astride the spars,
> The round masts, the swinging motion of the hulls, the slender serpentine pennants,

The large and small steamers in motion, the pilots in their pilot-
houses.

(39–41)

It is as if the actions of humanity and the city at large grow from and
depend upon the pulsating flow of the water. The coordination is so
complete it includes even "the fires from the foundry chimneys burning high and glaringly into the night" (47). Far from introducing the
foundries as alien and forbidding objects, as some commentators
claim, Whitman carefully matches the imagery at the beginning and
end of the canto to create a continuity.[12] Like the sun lighting up parts
of the sea gulls' bodies in yellow while leaving the rest in "strong
shadow," the foundry chimneys create a chiaroscuro of "yellow light"
and shade in the city streets. As the sun of canto 1 is "high," so too
are the foundry lights high, complementing the sun by illuminating
the city at night. Of course, Whitman can limn his harmonious picture only by ignoring, as Edwin Miller points out, the problems of industrialization.[13] But those problems are irrelevant to Whitman. He
is not writing about social actualities but is composing a poetic world,
and in that composition nature and city appear in perfect amity, all
part of one "simple, compact, well-join'd scheme" (7).

The scheme, however, encompasses more than a synthesis of nature
and the city. Present as well is the union of individual and community
harmonizing with nature. Whitman dramatizes this linkage by crea-
tively relating himself, as the poem's speaker, to what he sees, and
what he discovers when he looks at nature is himself. Reflected in the
"sunlit water," his countenance becomes a second sun with "fine cen-
trifugal spokes of light round the shape of [his] head" (33). Yet, while
the poet becomes coextensive with nature, he also acts as "one of a
living crowd," seeing what others see (23). Intrinsically united to the
community by virtue of his humanity and by shared perceptions, the
poet can validate the linkage of community and nature by presenting
both in the same manner. His face-to-face meeting with the flood tide
and clouds parallels his encounter with the urban inhabitants when
he says, "What is more subtle than this which ties me to the woman
or man that looks in my face? / Which fuses me into you now, and
pours my meaning into you?" (96–97). By canto 8, the world of the
poem has become an idyllic realm of felicity, placidity, and brotherhood enclosing the city, the poet, and nature. It is nothing short of
the urban-pastoral ideal in its most ambitious form.

Given that fact, however, Whitman manages to keep his version of the organic city from resembling a daguerreotype or a model for an actual society to come by using the same device which allows the sense of union to obtain: the presence of the poet engaged in the imaginative act. The synthesis exists only because the poet perceives it as he fashions it. The clouds, the waters, the foundries, and the crowds may be "real" in that they are drawn from the materials the poet has stored in memory, but they are transformed into ideas and feelings transcending the actualities of urban life. Whitman invokes city and nature only to coopt and refashion them into an imaginative aggregate alive in words alone.

Our sense of the imaginative quality of the urban-pastoral environment in "Brooklyn Ferry" emerges as early as canto 1, when Whitman says that the vistas and fellowship he will recount are "more in my meditations, than you might suppose" (5). (It is significant that the city is made radiant, not by a connection with nature directly, but by contact with the poet as symbol maker.) With these words, we have entered a world of the mind—a mystical meditation in which time is so fluid it is, in effect, obliterated, making the scene immutable. The world is not Manhattan and Brooklyn of 1856 but a mythical urban middle landscape existing outside time and space by dint of the poet's power as time melder.

This characteristic of the poet is important because it designates a role Whitman ordinarily reserves for himself in his more overtly dream poems, such as "Proud Music of the Storm" and "The Sleepers," the latter a symbolic mediation of death, the unconscious, and the creative principle. "Crossing Brooklyn Ferry" also stands as a kind of dream poem, in which the speaker can leap out of his body to defeat normal limitations of the senses.[14] Significantly, the poet mentions his body only once, in the past tense, as though he has undergone a figurative death (62–64), for only by passing into the realm of death and the creative unconscious (a ferry ride with Charon on the "river of old") can he act as a time melder. If the experience of "Brooklyn Ferry" resembles that of "The Sleepers," it is no surprise, since the two share common dreamlike features—the obliteration of time, a passage from light to darkness, the disembodied movements of the speaker— that produce an invigorating experience in which the mind, free from the restraints of waking consciousness, can renew itself in creative expression. In that experience in "Brooklyn Ferry," the poet successfully projects himself through time and space to create the serene, almost abstract pastoral city around him.

The atmosphere of the poem especially contributes to that ethereal effect. Despite the apparent motion and life depicted, the environment of "Brooklyn Ferry" is hauntingly dreamlike and spectral. What we have is not a world alive and moving but only the assertion of motion and life; the people of the poem seem little more than notations of trades or character traits: sailors, pilots, indolent young men. They are never fleshed out as individuals, as indeed they cannot be, since incarnation would not accord with the dream atmosphere. Moreover, the most pronounced "movements" of city and nature actually resemble moments of suspended animation, as in canto 3 when the poet proclaims:

> I too . . .
> Watched the Twelfth-month sea-gulls, saw them high in the air floating with motionless wings, oscillating their bodies,
> Saw how the glistening yellow lit up parts of their bodies and left the rest in strong shadow,
> Saw the slow-wheeling circles and the gradual edging toward the south.
>
> (27–30)

And again, later in the same canto:

> Look'd toward the lower bay to notice the vessels arriving,
> Saw their approach, saw aboard those that were near me,
> Saw the white sails of schooners and sloops, saw the ships at anchor,
> The sailors at work in the rigging or out astride the spars,
> The round masts, the swinging motion of the hulls, the slender serpentine pennants,
> The large and small steamers in motion, the pilots in their pilothouses,
> . . . .
> The stretch afar growing dimmer and dimmer, the grey walls of the granite storehouses by the docks.
>
> (36–45)

In all of this the only action words, the only legitimate verbs, are *look'd* and *saw*—words which refer to the action of the poet as creative perceiver. The other "action" words are participles and gerunds, which do not describe motion so much as indicate a continuous state of being. In such a picture, time appears to be frozen, and history becomes a panoramic conception of the moment. Space takes on a rarified texture, and people resemble shadowy, diaphanous images. Like the figures in Keats's "Grecian Urn," the inhabitants of Whitman's imaginative city reside in an arrested world of the eternal present, where there is no past, no future, no history, and so no motion. It is an unabashedly poetic environment, insulated from change and inviolable.

Because it is unassailable, the city of the poem can include the "dark patches" of urban life which Whitman catalogues in canto 6: "the old knot of contrariety," the lying, stealing, lusting, and more, all of which the poet too has experienced. By incorporating the doubtful, evil, and profane in his ideal city of imagination, Whitman invalidates the question of what elements of domesticated nature and civilization should be included in the urban-pastoral ideal and so avoids the disruptions and contradictions plaguing literal reform efforts. Such questions need not concern the poet desiring to absorb and "reproduce all," as Whitman once said, "in my own forms." While such poetic reproduction enables him to domesticate the craven, malignant, and wayward and so exorcise their evil as evil, the exorcism is unequivocally imaginative and so incapable of serving as a pattern for urban life. It constitutes a personal version of recrudescence, available to others but only as an inward experience engendered by reading the poem.

Not only does this covert opposition between the inward, imaginative city and the outward city distinguish Whitman's treatment of urban pastoralism from that in the general culture; it also points to a difference between Whitman's and Emerson's responses to the ideal. While Whitman follows the latter's advice to assimilate cities and machines in poetry—to make universal symbols of New York, San Francisco, and Chicago—he does so more purely than the "master," as he once referred to Emerson.

The primary reason for their dissimilar handling of urban pastoralism inheres in the disparity between Whitman's and Emerson's conceptions of what poetry and the poet's task consisted of. That Whitman was cognizant of this difference is apparent from his remarks in *Notes Left Over* (1882): "At times it has been doubtful to me if Emerson really knows or feels what Poetry is at its highest." He continued, "Emerson, in my opinion, is not most eminent as poet or artist . . . [but] as critic or diagnoser."[15] However inadequate this characterization of Emerson may be, it does tell a partial truth. As we have seen, Emerson believed in the correspondence between ideal and actual and so felt that first principles, already latent in the material and social world, could be brought into a full relation with that world. The poet, therefore, must fasten words again to things to reveal that correspondence and so prepare the minds of his readers for the schemes of reformers. This, in effect, is what Emerson does in his essays and poems. Whitman, however, works in an opposite manner. Skeptical of the human ability to decipher ultimate meanings from nature and believing that "a perfect user of words uses things," he transfers things into words so that they become "miracles from his hands."[16] For Whitman, the poet is not merely Emerson's language user who employs words to discover hidden meanings; he is a language shaper who uses discourse to refashion experience according to his own vision.

In Emerson we discover spiritual implications in an essentially mimetic depiction. His Boston stands as a palpably real place, grounded in historical fact and rooted to native geography. But in "Crossing Brooklyn Ferry," Whitman does not record the transformation of ideal into sociopolitical fact, nor does he discover the relationship between these two realms to reveal an immanent order. Instead, he transmutes the social and physical into the ideal. Not concerned with returning to first principles or original relations, as Emerson defined the poetic task, Whitman "presume[s] to write, as it were, upon things that exist not, and travel[s] by maps yet unmade, and a blank." His technique does not impose a new form *on* the world or discover a latent pattern *in* the world; rather, it enables him to create a new form *from* the world, to reproduce all in his own forms. The difference between Emerson and Whitman, in other words, is symptomatic of the shift in the romantic aesthetic that Roy Harvey Pearce has pointed out: a "gradual but nonetheless revolutionary shift in the meaning of 'invention' . . . from 'coming upon' something made and ordered by God, to 'making' and 'ordering'—transforming—something, anything into that which manifests above all man's power to make and to order."[17] In this vein, Emerson's poet performs a sacerdotal office of administering the mysteries of grace; Whitman, as poet, is a god himself.

Pointing out this distinction between Emerson's and Whitman's concepts of the poet in relation to reality does not gainsay the immense influence Emerson exerted on Whitman or the fact that they shared many ideas. Nonetheless, that distinction does suggest an es-

sential difference in the purposes of their writings with respect to urban pastoralism. In emphasizing a balance between society and
solitude, nature and the city, individual and community, Emerson
sought a perdurable reconciliation on both the spiritual and social
planes. The goal of equilibrium and synthesis was his concern. Whitman, however, was less interested in achieving such a union, even as
a poetic accomplishment. More important was the continual exercise
of imagination as it creates that noetic synthesis. If we were to identify
an emblem for Emerson's concerns, the balance would be no bad
choice, but for Whitman the central symbol could only be the open
road, denoting a continual becoming, "the endless process of Creative
thought."[18]

In "Brooklyn Ferry" that process is indicated by the title itself. The
poem is called not "Crossing on Brooklyn Ferry" but "Crossing
Brooklyn Ferry"—a leaping over or transcending of an actual ferry
ride. Whitman's ferry takes us on no literal journey but on a symbolic
one from the shores of waking consciousness to the realm of ideal and
thought, embodied and encountered in the poem. The pastoral city
it steams by is a metaphor for the formative, unifying imagination,
which the poet shares with and points to in all people.

As if to make this point explicit, Whitman uses the concluding
canto to echo the invocation of canto 1. Providing a final meditation
on the pastoral city as an inward realization, he declaims:

> Thrive, cities—bring your freight, bring your shows, ample and
>   sufficient rivers,
> Expand, being than which none else is perhaps more spiritual,
> Keep your places, objects than which none else is more lasting.
> You have waited, you always wait, you dumb, beautiful ministers,
> . . . .
> We use you, and do not cast you aside—we plant you permanently
>   within us,
> We fathom you not—we love you—there is perfection in you also,
> You furnish your parts toward eternity,
> Great or small, you furnish your parts toward the soul.
>
> (123–32)

Although Stephen Black has argued that Whitman here "seems to
sense some incompatibility between his unconscious vision and the
world outside," the conclusion of "Brooklyn Ferry" is not a reluctant,

half-formed expression of uncertainty.[19] It is a deliberate effort to distinguish private vision from public actualities. The reference to literal cities as dumb, beautiful ministers planted within reminds us that we have been in and are now leaving a world in which the phenomena of urban life assume a liquidity before the flame of imagination. The ritualistic quality of the incantatory language indicates that the poem is part of the timeless process whereby imagination expresses desire by forming ideals from the world around it.

In "Crossing Brooklyn Ferry" and in his other poems which synthesize nature and the city, Whitman removes the urban-pastoral ideal from time and places it at its point of origin: in the realm of ideal, in dream and thought, in the creative process within. Never confusing what the mind can achieve in a lasting fiction with what society can accomplish in history, Whitman builds an idyllic urban world that serves primarily to affirm the power of human imagination.

II

Although Whitman's prose writings suggest why he believed the urban idyll could obtain only in imagination, few hints of a similar explanation appear in his poetry, and the reason for such silence stems from Whitman's conception of poetry's purpose. In *Specimen Days*, he complained that among America's "popular poets the calibres of an age, the weak spots of its embankments, its sub-currents . . . are unerringly indicated." This was not to be the task of true poetry, which should concern itself with "the clear sun shining, and fresh air blowing—the strength and power of health," the radiant life, even if it be a life exclusively of the mind.[20] Whitman never understood, that is, that weak spots could be exposed in two ways: on the surface, to urge reform (something he placed no faith in); or in the depths, to reveal the contradictions and inadequacies of pervading ideas.

It was precisely this latter tack that Hawthorne took in some of his most compelling fiction, as he dramatized the limitations of urban pastoralism in the face of history. If Whitman wished to lift his readers to the plane they could never tread in fact—to the green city of imagination—Hawthorne sought to explore the gap between that ideal and actuality and to analyze the human response to that fissure.

Not that Hawthorne found the urban-pastoral ideal unattractive. His interest in it can be gauged by the frequency with which an image of reconciliation, or attempted reconciliation, of the natural and the urban occurs in his writings. His *American Notebooks* contains several verbal paintings of towns nestled amidst gently rolling hills and picturesque descriptions of nature's appearance in the city. The image occurs again in *The House of the Seven Gables* in the form of Judge Pyncheon's suburban home, which unites "country-air" with city conveniences and to which Phoebe and Holgrave retire in a personal, domestic version of rural-urban harmony.[21] In work after work, Hawthorne challenges assumptions regarding a moral contrast between city and country. Like Emerson, he recognized that both realms, in themselves, denied as much as they promised. If the city potentially could satisfy man's need as a social being, it nonetheless could crush the individual beneath a weight of conformity. Yet the open landscape, precisely because it promised unbounded freedom, could estrange the individual from his fellow men, as it does in "Young Goodman Brown." What so many of Hawthorne's characters discover is exactly this dual truth; hence, the continual movement of characters between country (or forest) and city in his fiction. In that shuffling, Hawthorne allegorically depicts the human quest for a middle position between the two environments while raising a question central to urban pastoralism: Is it possible to reconcile the individual's needs with the demands of society? Hawthorne was drawn to the possibility of reconciliation because it represented, again allegorically, the need for a social and psychological integration in life.

Though fascinated by the possibility, Hawthorne's allegorical imagination prevented him from viewing it optimistically. While this tendency to allegorize sometimes could lead him to those artistic eccentricities that Henry James and several twentieth-century critics have lamented as weaknesses, it nonetheless allowed Hawthorne to examine urban pastoralism with detachment. Because allegory, as Charles Feidelson has pointed out, preserves a "distinction between thought and things," Hawthorne was keenly aware of an unbreachable trough between physical facts and the spiritual world they could represent—a gap, in other words, between the ideal and the actual.[22] His allegorical method led him to perceive history as a record of man trapped in time, where change tyrannizes over efforts to conform material and social reality to an unchanging ideal. And Hawthorne had perhaps the most profound sense of history among his contemporaries. Accordingly, when he broached the subject of urban pastoralism, he seldom allowed the ideal to stand unqualified.[23]

A suggestive example occurs in a series of notebook entries he made

in 1850 during a visit to Boston. Although seemingly random jot-
tings, they form a paradigm of his ironic response to the American
hope of integrating nature and the city. Explaining that he takes a
special interest in cities, particularly their back "nooks and crannies,"
Hawthorne records three related descriptions of one such scene as it
appears through the back window of a house in the center of the city.
The first effectively delineates what amounts to a pastoral enclave.
Gazing out the window, Hawthorne finds his eyes resting on the
"grass-plots, already green" (it is May), between the intervals of
houses. As his vision is drawn to these green oases, he notes that they
contain a multitude of fruit trees beginning to leaf and that one of
them, a cherry tree, is "almost in full blossom." Enchanted by the little birds that "flutter and sing" about, he is particularly delighted and
surprised that such "little spots of fructifying earth" exist "here in the
heart of the city."[24] It appears as if nature has taken root and employed
its charms to create an island of repose, a world apart that strikes in
him a corresponding sense of peace and felicity.

When he returns to the same scene seven days later, the impression
and his mood are much the same at first. Once again he refers to the
soft, pastoral aura of this urban asylum, which seems to extend to the
houses themselves in the cheerful, domestic activities observable
through their windows. Yet now a perceptible difference accompanies
his response. He notes that, despite their sheltered location, these
idyllic retreats are subject to the blast of east wind which manages to
shake the "withering blossoms from the cherry-trees." Most striking,
however, is the subject he turns to in the next paragraph. "Quiet as
this prospect is," he explains, "there is a continual and near thunder
of wheels, proceeding from Washington-street. In a building not far
off, there is a hall for exhibitions; and, sometimes, in the evenings,
loud music is heard from it; or, if a diorama be exhibiting (that of
Bunker Hill, for-instance, or the burning of Moscow) an immense
racket of imitative cannon and musketry." With this noisy intrusion,
the urban idyll is broken, and the effect resembles the interrupted rural idyll which Leo Marx has pointed out in Hawthorne's Sleepy Hollow notes. In this case, however, the disruption is far more
devastating. Unlike the Sleepy Hollow episode, in which Hawthorne
can regain some composure when the train moves off, his experience
in the city does not allow even a qualified return to the earlier state.
For the intruder here is no mere machine invading a rural hollow; it
is the city itself, which envelops and contains these slight, grassy

plots. When the urban world penetrates their boundaries, it engen-
ders a much more sober mood that Hawthorne cannot shake off. Consequently, when he returns to the scene in the next entry, darker
imagery dominates. Now, he muses, "a heavy downfal of . . . gloom"
pervades the view as the chimneys of the houses appear to choke with
their own smoke. Over the entire scene "broods a parallelogram of
sombre sky," leading Hawthorne to solemn thoughts about mankind
and some "old acquaintances." One gentleman he had known ten
years ago to be in good health with "cheerful spirits" has become
"pale, thin, oldish, with a grave and care-or-pain worn brow." Another, formerly a successful commander of a revenue vessel, is now
without service and has begun to display a "desperate state of mind"
and a "recklessness" of demeanor.[25] With these thoughts of withered,
broken lives verging on death, Hawthorne concludes the entry.

In these passages, later incorporated in *The Blithedale Romance* as
Miles Coverdale's response to the city, Hawthorne fashions a pattern
of reversal and incongruity. Having begun with a moment of peace,
felicity, and wholeness matching his own internal state, he then subjects the scene and his feelings to qualification. Lost in repose for a
time, Hawthorne realizes that his idyllic moment cannot account for
all the facts of city life: its sounds, pace, movements, the frustrated
lives of its inhabitants, and most of all Hawthorne's own sense of the
past. Though genuine as an inner response, such urban idylls cannot
stand up against the full range of the city's forces. Its evanescence
turns the experience into an oblique commentary on the inadequacy
of urban pastoralism for interpreting social reality.

If Hawthorne suggests in these passages that a synthesis of nature
and city can be only an internal, momentary achievement, another
notebook entry indicates how he conceives of the actual relationship
between the urban and rural worlds and the ideational implications of
that relationship. Sometime between 1842 and 1844, Hawthorne jot-
ted down the following idea for a sketch:

> the devouring of the old country residences by the overgrown mons-
> ter of a city. For instance, Mr. Beekman's ancestral residence was
> originally several miles from the city of New-York; but the pavements
> kept creeping nearer and nearer; till now the house is removed, and
> a street runs directly through what was once its hall.

An interesting feature of this entry is that, as a sociological statement,
it is unusual for its time. While others warned that urban growth

threatened to suck the vitality out of country life, Hawthorne reveals his awareness of a danger that twentieth-century Americans have discovered all too clearly: the problem of urban sprawl. More than twenty years before Frederick Law Olmsted would defend American cities because they could be laid out over large spaces, Hawthorne intimates that attempts to extend cities into the open landscape might not produce a propitious blend of urban and pastoral. Instead, America could obliterate the rural world.[26]

Nevertheless, in this note Hawthorne does not merely make a sociological statement or draw the conventional distinction between the two ways of life. The presence of the word *monster* suggests that his allegorical imagination already is at work, for what is monstrous about the city, the entry implies, is its protean quality. That is, Hawthorne uses country and city here to denote two psychological states or ways of comprehending the world. The city in this case represents a forceful, aggressive, progressive way of thought, a commitment to change and an awareness of history, while the country residences signify an essentially static way of conceiving of reality. To say this does not imply that Hawthorne values one over the other as the more correct response. Each perspective has value, but the two stand as antithetical ways of responding to the world. Mutually exclusive, they cannot be synthesized as a paradigm for reality.

The patterns of incompatibility and disruption in these notebook entries constitute variations of a method Hawthorne would employ in his fiction to probe the meaning and viability of urban-pastoral visions. Nineteen years before recording his ironic impressions of pastoral enclaves in Boston, he had incorporated a simple form of the pattern in the story "Sights from a Steeple," which presents a naive narrator highly susceptible to urban-pastoral fantasies. In the first half of this sketch, that narrator exposes his own dreamy temperament while depicting the scene he observes from the steeple of a town church. Discovering "cultivated fields, villages, white country-seats, the waving lines of rivulets, little placid lakes," and, on an inlet of the adjacent sea, a town, he delineates a panorama that composes an enchanting blend of landscape and cityscape in delightful repose.[27] The dominant mood is matched by the placid felicity within the town itself. He notes how, along one avenue, stately mansions each have their own "carpet of verdant grass" stretching from the front steps to the street, and "ornamental trees . . . grow thrivingly among the brick and stone" (193). Everything about the scene possesses an idyllic air with no hurry, noise, or discord. Nothing seems capable of disturbing this vista, not even a passing troop of soldiers, who appear from the narrator's position to resemble merely the harmless "painted veterans that garrison the windows of a toy-shop" (195). In the course of the story, however, this charming medley of town and country is rendered discordant by a violent thunderstorm, which destroys the serenity of the scene, washes away its beauty, and causes the narrator to admit that he is part of a "tumult which I am powerless to direct or quell" (198).

Taken together, this early sketch and the 1850 notebook passages show Hawthorne working out his response to the ideal of rural and urban synthesis by adopting a conventional device from pastoral poetry. Substituting an urban middle landscape for a rural one, he then subjects it to intrusions from its two vulnerable borders: untamed nature in "Sights" and the intensity and volatility of city life in the notebooks. If this were the extent of Hawthorne's response to urban pastoralism, however, we might dismiss it as merely a modification of literary pastoralism. Yet only a year after "Sights" appeared, he published a tale that goes beyond this borrowed pattern to explore the contradictions of the ideal in the context of historical forces. That advanced stage of Hawthorne's complicated treatment of urban pastoralism forms a significant theme of "My Kinsman, Major Molineux."[28]

When "Molineux" appeared in *The Token* in 1832, Hawthorne's decision to sign it "by the author of 'Sights from a Steeple' " suggests that he intended some type of relationship between the two stories.[29] But if "Molineux" is a subsequent expansion of his ideas about urban pastoralism, it also is an "earlier" tale occurring "not far from a hundred years ago" (209). The choice of the older setting is strategic in that it adds a layer of significance to Hawthorne's treatment of the ideal. In grounding his story in the past, he implies, quite correctly, that the ideal is enveloped in American history. As Roy Harvey Pearce has explained, Hawthorne's reference to the events of the tale as a "temporary inflammation of the popular mind" (209) generalizes those incidents as part of "a class of occurrences" indigenous to the culture.[30] Additionally, Hawthorne purposely obfuscates the time frame of the tale to widen its historical range. Though the prefatory paragraph places the story ostensibly in the 1730s, the events themselves resemble those of 1765 during the Stamp Act riots, when the Sons of Liberty were tarring and feathering British loyalists. As several critics have noted, the insurgency in the tale represents a "type" of the American Revolution—the period in which the belief in American uniqueness began to congeal into a national passion.[31] "Molineux," then, is both a prelude to the American promise and a legacy of it in Hawthorne's own time. More than anything else, however, what indicates that the action of the tale is part of a recurring historical pattern, and that that pattern is Hawthorne's subject, is the journey of the story's protagonist, young Robin.

Hawthorne presents Robin as an archetypal innocent embodying America's hopeful attitude toward urban experience.[32] Anticipating the promised patronage of his uncle, the major, Robin fully expects his newly adopted city (apparently Boston) to conform to his predetermined image. Arriving from his rural home, he enters the city "with as eager an eye, as if he were entering London city" (210). Robin's idea of the town is engendered in part by his image of the major, who, as a representative of the British Crown, ostensibly wields power and commands authority. From Robin's perspective, the major and the town he inhabits represent the best of the European city transferred to America: order, deference, and a clearly defined social structure. But the youth also feels that this embryonic New England city will accommodate the values of pastoral America. Boston is to be another one of those mythical "lands of opportunity," possessing affinities with the open landscape, as Franklin's Philadelphia had.[33] Though a recognizable rustic, Robin anticipates full acceptance into urban society and so embodies, in microcosm, the culture's conviction that bucolic America can find a place in the hierarchical social order of the city.

Robin also thinks that the physical city will comport with his urban-pastoral image. Anticipating wide avenues and comely residences, he expects to find "the stillness of [his] native woods, here in [the] streets" of the town (226). Because Robin's mind, as Hawthorne says, tends to move easily between "fancy and reality," the rural and urban tend to blend in his imagination. Thus, when he looks at one large edifice, its columns assume the shape of "tall, bare stems of pines." So powerful is his imaginative version of the city, he must ask himself at one point, while thinking back on his country home, "Am I here, or there?" (223). Though knowing he is in town, he cannot differentiate it from his rural environment, expecting the former to be as comprehensible as the world he has left behind.

This undifferentiated response is precisely what makes Robin incapable of comprehending the events of the evening: the rude rebuffs and threats he receives from various townsmen, the advances of a "pretty mistress," the laughter echoing down the labyrinth of narrow streets, and the ominous appearance of a grotesque individual who later will emerge as the dual-complexioned rebel leader. Indeed, the city does not conform to Robin's expectations but resembles in these instances a horrific city of damnation, which threatens the individual at every step. It is important to recognize, however, that Hawthorne here does not present the city as morally polluted while exposing his protagonist's inability to see it as evil.[34] Only from Robin's naive perspective does the city appear malevolent and corrupt. Lacking a knowledge of urban life and subscribing to an idealized image of the city, he does not understand that these events, as Hawthorne explains in the prefatory paragraph, are part of a calculated, organized effort to punish supporters of the king. As a result, the city appears to Robin more opaque and ominous than it is—a discrepancy the informed reader is expected to discover.

To say that the city looks menacing to Robin in no way contradicts the point made earlier that he sees the city as an urban ideal. For even after his expectations are thwarted, even after he is disconcerted by the dual-complexioned stranger, he still indulges in the urban-pastoral impulse. When he looks at a moonbeam shining in a church, he thinks that, perhaps, "Nature, in that deep hour, [had] become a worshiper in the house, which man had builded," and the impression leads automatically to thoughts of "his native woods" and the rural religious services his father conducted (222–23). Robin repeatedly fluctuates between images of the city as benign and horrific. At any one point he can see it only one way or the other; he cannot bring these responses together, as the reader clearly must do, to form a mature idea of the city. Robin's either-or attitude embodies the poles between which the pendulum of action swings. Not until the climactic scene, in which Robin meets the major, does Hawthorne reconcile the images to reveal the illusion of urban pastoralism.

As Robin encounters the rebellious crowd led by the two-complexioned man and bearing Major Molineux "in tar-and-feathery dignity," Hawthorne builds a series of compelling parallels. The leader of the mass is "clad in a military dress," much like the major normally might wear, and fixes his glance upon Robin shortly before the major does the same. The most important parallel occurs when Hawthorne describes the major's countenance: "His face was pale as death, and far more ghastly; the broad forehead was contracted in his agony, so that his eyebrows formed one grizzled line; his eyes were red and wild, and the foam hung white upon his quivering lip" (228). The delineation is striking because it nearly duplicates that of the rebel leader, whose face, before being disguised, had displayed a bulging forehead, "deep and shaggy" eyebrows, and eyes that glowed "like fire in a cave" (213). The major and the head of the insurgents suddenly appear as mirror images of one another. How much of this Robin recognizes is uncertain, but as the crowd's laughter increases and spreads, Robin symbolically becomes a member of the throng by sending forth "a shout of laughter" that "was the loudest there" (230).

The significance of Robin's outburst rests in the series of parallels Hawthorne has constructed. From Robin's point of view, the major has been the focal point of his urban-pastoral projections, and the dual-complexioned man has constituted a threat. From the crowd's angle, however, everything is reversed. The rebel leader is their hero and vital center, and the major, as a representative of British rule, is the impediment they must remove to achieve their idea of urban felicity. Hawthorne reinforces this implication by portraying the insurgents as a train of "wild figures in the Indian dress, and many fantastic shapes without a model, giving the whole march a visionary air, as if a dream has broken forth" (227–28). Their autochthonic characteristics (Indian dress, shapes without models) suggest that the rebels are urban dwellers seeking a return to origins, but what connects them most to the pastoral ideal is the fact that the images here replicate those Hawthorne employs to depict the pastoral revelers in "The Maypole of Merrymount." The revelers of "Molineux," acting out their pastoral desires, are attempting to purge their colonial American city of European influences and an oppressive past. As a result, the rebels are enacting a version of urban pastoralism directly in conflict with Robin's. Their efforts foreshadow the post-Revolutionary emphasis on separation from Europe and symbolize the belief, so rampant in Hawthorne's day, that the invocation of natural forms would yield a new, purer, indigenous urban society in America. When Robin figuratively joins the crowd, therefore, he does so by temporarily adopting their perspective. He discovers that his own image of urban life is inadequate because it cannot account for all the facts of the city, especially its shifting values. Though Robin does not comprehend the full implications of his discovery, he does recognize his need to abandon innocent expectations in the face of an urban environment characterized by differentiation, diversity, and change.

For the reader, however, the ramifications of Robin's experience bulk larger. By making the center of the tale a conflict between two versions of urban pastoralism, Hawthorne reveals that the inadequacy of the impulse lies, ironically enough, in the impulse itself. Just as a person may have "several voices . . . as well as two complexions," as a kindly stranger who befriends Robin informs him near the end of the tale, so may the impulse take a number of forms (226). There is no way to tell which is correct. In fact, none is "correct," since any form in which the impulse manifests itself imposes partial values, requiring suppression of others that must surface as discontent. Such surfacing is precisely what occurs in "My Kinsman, Major Molineux." By identifying the crowd as part of the "living stream," Hawthorne suggests that the events of the tale constitute the very pattern of life. The conflict of forces within the story forms part of a recurring, timeless process in history. Hawthorne, that is, dramatizes in his own allegorical manner the idea that Karl Mannheim would set forth in more discursive terms over one hundred years later: the dialectical nature of culture in which new utopian ideals repeatedly impinge upon preceding ones. Since such a pattern invalidates any form of urban pastoralism as a final solution, the tale presents the urban ideal as ultimately delusive.

At the same time, Hawthorne shows that the ideal carries its own dangers in that it can materialize in dark, inhumane forms. In describing the major's fate as one of "agony" and "overwhelming humiliation" and in characterizing the conspirators as "fiends . . . trampling all on an old man's heart," he evokes our sympathy for Major Molineux and requires us to see the crowd's actions as cruel and reprehensible (228–30). By doing so, Hawthorne implies that an attempt to impose a version of the ideal can be more despotic than the order it seeks to subvert. For he understood that a system considered repressive can be overthrown only by a more potent and, hence, potentially indomitable power.

Logically, therefore, we must conclude that the conspirators' efforts are just as inadequate and deluded as Robin's had been, and Hawthorne suggests that part of his protagonist's growth consists of his half-conscious awareness of that fact. In joining the crowd, explains Hawthorne, Robin experiences a "perception of tremendous ridicule in the whole scene"—a ridicule applying not only to his kinsman's ignominy but also to the absurdity of the crowd's pretensions and "counterfeited pomp" (229–30). Robin's laugh, by its very intensity, may signal a saving recognition, but we do not know, and Hawthorne wisely refuses to be more specific. We can only *surmise* that Robin, by clinging to a stone post as the crowd moves off, may have achieved a mature distance from the delusion of urban pastoralism in general.

Despite the inadequacy of the ideal, however, Hawthorne does not renounce the urban world or dismiss its significance. The tale illustrates that the city does contain benefits. Because of his experience, Robin has taken a necessary step toward maturity and "may rise in the world, without the help of [his] kinsman, Major Molineux" (231). Yet Hawthorne does not overestimate the value of that experience. We do not know the extent of Robin's growth or whether he even will remain in Boston, and if he does, his rise is only a possibility. The city is neither good nor bad, neither benevolent nor brutal; it is potentially both. In that ambiguity of the city's double promise the story concludes.

As we might expect, "My Kinsman, Major Molineux" was not Hawthorne's last word on urban pastoralism. Taking it up in his notebooks and elaborating those ideas in *The Blithedale Romance*, Hawthorne was able to enrich his treatment even futher. While "Molineux" demonstrates that a rural attitude brought to the urban scene can mislead, *The Blithedale Romance* discloses that the city brought to the country is equally insufficient. The real achievement of *Blithedale*, however, lies in Hawthorne's choice of an urbane but finally limited first-person narrator. By creating Miles Coverdale as an embodiment of many of his own ideas, Hawthorne builds what Frederick Crews has called "an inner coherence of self-debate" in the novel.[35] And part of that self-debate comprises Hawthorne's examination of his own ironic response to urban pastoralism.

Hawthorne establishes that response by first focusing on the Blithedale communitarians, who are attempting to leave behind the competitive and corrupt urban world to build an agrarian community of brotherhood. Even in its beginnings the entire scheme possesses an ambiance of incongruity and artificiality, from Zenobia's hothouse flower to the presence of Hollingsworth, a blacksmith turned implacable reformer, with an appearance and disposition, as Coverdale says, "hammered out of iron."[36] It is Coverdale who recognizes the contradictions and absurdities of Blithedale, at least as far as they relate to the stated aims of the community. From the moment he arrives, he senses an insouciant, fantastic aura about the place. Though "our costumes,"he says, "bore no resemblance to the be-ribboned doublets, silk breeches and stockings, and slippers fashioned with artificial roses, that distinguished the pastoral people of poetry and the stage," he admits that "we were a living epitome of defunct fashions" (63–64). For the Blithedalers are nineteenth-century versions of courtiers masquerading as shepherds, playing at "a modern Arcadia" in an urban age (58).

Not that Coverdale totally lacked appreciation for Blithedale at the time of his involvement. Retrospectively he admits that even in his initial skepticism he "once had faith and force enough to form generous hopes of the world's destiny—yes!—and to do what in me lay for their accomplishment" (11). As he comes to know the community, particularly its contradictions and affectations, however, his skepticism grows. After Hollingsworth discloses his scheme to buy Blithedale and turn it into an asylum for criminal reform, Coverdale's hopes disappear. The unimproved terrain, he discovers, will not be replaced by the soft pastoralism of Blithedale but by another "city" on a hill, dominated by Hollingsworth's iron will. In a world where pastoralism is but a dream, the best that can be hoped is that the immersion in nature can form the basis of a life-giving return to the city.

This conclusion is exactly the one Coverdale adopts. As he leaves Blithedale and returns to Boston, his sense of the city is invested with a new vigor. Though he formerly had seen Boston as confining and had grown tired of the "hot-house warmth of a town residence," the city now takes as "strenuous a hold upon my mind . . . as if there could never be enough of it," and Coverdale creates a sustained, joyous tribute to its vitality:

> Beneath and around me, I heard the stir of the hotel; the loud voices of guests, landlord, or barkeeper; . . . the lighter feet of chambermaids scudding along the passages;—it is ridiculous to think what an interest they had for me. From the street, came the tumult of the pavements, pervading the whole house with a continual uproar. . . . A company of the city-soldiery, with a full military band, marched in front of the hotel, invisible to me, but stirringly audible both by its foot-tramp and the clangor of its instruments. Once or twice, all the city-bells jangled together, announcing a fire, which brought out the engine-men and their machines, like an army with its artillery rushing to battle. . . . In some public hall, not a great way off, there seemed to be an exhibition . . . winding up with . . . the applause of spectators, with clap of hands, and thump of sticks, and the ener-

getic pounding of their heels. All this was just as valuable, in its way, as the sighing of the breeze among the birch-trees, that overshadowed Eliot's pulpit. (146–47)

Alive with human warmth and activity, this urban diorama resembles, in tone and structure, Whitman's "Crossing Brooklyn Ferry," and if Hawthorne had not published *The Blithedale Romance* four years before Whitman's poem appeared, one would think he was parodying Whitman's urban catalogues. Significantly, both share much the same mood. In Coverdale's description, the actualities of the city in no way jostle with his pastoral inclinations, and while nature does not play a role in the scene, Coverdale's feelings about it do. The urban sounds seem to complement his recollections of the sighing breeze among the birches, as Coverdale brings to his description emotions which American writers usually reserve for their response to the open landscape. Though the passage is not urban pastoral in content, it is in tone.

Nevertheless, Coverdale remains true to what he has learned at Blithedale and to the ruling logic of his narrative. Even as he sketches this energetic idyll of the city, he does not pass over its more disagreeable facts: the implications of war in the presence of the soldiers (whom Coverdale does not transform into harmless toys, as did the narrator in "Sights from a Steeple") and the fact that a fire burns somewhere in town. Concluding his rapturous depiction, he accordingly draws back from its implications: "Yet I felt a hesitation about plunging into this muddy tide of human activity and pastime. It suited me better, for the present, to linger on the brink, or hover in the air above it" (147). As the reality of the city impinges upon him, he does not commit the same mistake he had made at Blithedale. In this case, the "muddy tide of human[ity]" recalls the last thing he had seen at the community: the pigs wallowing in the mud, epitomizing the simplemindedness of faith in the pastoral ideal. For a time, he too had allowed himself to believe that the community might achieve the bucolic dream, but he had been disappointed. Now he suddenly realizes that he is falling into the maw of a similar fantasy in the city. Though his idyllic response seems more realistic because it accounts for the facts of society, it nonetheless constitutes wishful thinking. As a personal, temporary indulgence, it cannot serve as a model for interpreting the city.

This detached, self-conscious response to the urban idyll characterizes Coverdale's attitude in the rest of the romance. Recognizing the inadequacy of any reform based on pastoral ideals, he decides to become a removed, "calm observer." "As regards human progress," he explains, "let them believe in it who can, and aid in it who choose!" (246). Although not abandoning his urban-pastoral inclinations, he adopts a disengaged attitude toward them. Thus, when he sits gazing through his window, drawn to the "nooks and crannies, where Nature, like a stray partridge, hides her head among the long-established haunts of men," he delineates an urban tableau in a manner closely paralleling that of Hawthorne's notebooks. The grass-plots, gardens, trees laden with "singularly large, luxuriant, and abundant" fruit, grapevines clambering up trellises, and warming sunshine are all there. Present, too, are the little birds and the scenes of domestic bliss. But as Hawthorne incorporates material from his notebooks, he alters the pattern to accommodate his narrator's awareness. Instead of having the noise of the city intrude, he has Coverdale qualify the idyll as he describes it by noting its artificiality. The gardens, in Coverdale's eyes, become only "apologies" for gardens, while the soil, he explains, "had doubtless been enriched to a more than natural fertility." He also spends more time commenting on the affectations of the inhabitants in the houses (148–52). It seems, then, that Coverdale reflects Hawthorne's attitude about pastoral fantasies in both country and city. Yet even as he brings Coverdale to his own point of view, Hawthorne steps back, and the result is like Melville's splitting apart of Ishmael and Ahab in *Moby-Dick*.

One day, while staring out the window (presumably to engage in one of his private urban idylls), Coverdale notices Priscilla in an apartment across the way. Startled, he grows even more surprised when, in another window, he sees Zenobia conversing with Westervelt, who is equivalent, in this instance, to the thoughts of death in Hawthorne's notebook passages. At this moment, Coverdale suddenly suspects that Zenobia has been collaborating with the mesmerist to secure his power over Priscilla and so remove the innocent as a threat to Zenobia's fortune and her interest in Hollingsworth. The irony of this discovery is that, in the midst of Coverdale's private musings, life has intruded. Westervelt is more than just a fact of the city who checks pastoral reveries. His very presence demands Coverdale's involvement. And it is here that Hawthorne suggests the flaw of detachment. If the ironic response to pastoral projections in the city saves one from delusion, it cannot insulate a person from responsibility for participation in the "muddy tide of human activity." The danger is that the ironic attitude, which perceives the inadequacy of public action, threatens to sever the individual from involvement in the "living stream," however polluted it may be. Disengagement and insight can lead to isolation and effeteness when they, too, go unchecked.

Unfortunately, this danger is exactly what befalls Coverdale. Conscious of the failure of action and skeptical of active involvement in idealistic schemes, Coverdale fails to act. In practical terms, he does nothing about what he has witnessed from his window, and his passivity becomes paralytic as the novel moves toward its close. By adopting a wholly cynical attitude toward pastoral reform, he has denied himself any kind of meaningful social involvement. He cannot save Priscilla either from Westervelt or from Hollingsworth, who "rescues" her from the mesmerist only after he has learned that Zenobia's fortune has been transferred to her half-sister. Moreover, Coverdale is powerless to prevent Zenobia from drowning herself over Hollingsworth's desertion of her. Nor have Zenobia's death and Priscilla's abduction made him aware of his position. Though he "suspects" his life to be empty as he relates these past events, at the close of his narrative he is far from understanding the need for active, sympathetic participation in life.

With *The Blithedale Romance,* Hawthorne reached the most sophisticated point in his treatment of urban pastoralism. By distancing himself from Coverdale, and thus from his own skepticism, he successfully defined a meaningful middle position, and we may summarize it as follows: The urban-pastoral ideal possesses value because it stimulates human action and growth, but its meaning cannot exist apart from an ironic awareness of the inherent delusion in the ideal. Eight years later in *The Marble Faun,* Hawthorne would return to the theme of urban greenness but only to backtrack old ground. For while the romance is set in Europe, the story of Donatello and Miriam again demonstrates the inadequacy of pastoral impulses as a check against the realities of urban life. Delineating no new position, *The Marble Faun* is an expanded version of "My Kinsman, Major Molineux," and we must look at other elements in the novel to define its power. But in *The Blithedale Romance,* the achievement is clear; it stands as the culmination of Hawthorne's ironic examination of urban pastoralism.

In fashioning a pattern of contradiction with overt social and political import, Hawthorne created a response to urban pastoralism that is, therefore, quite different from Whitman's. Yet if Whitman removed the ideal from history by turning it into an inward realization—and so separated it from the realm of politics—his approach does not depoliticize the ideal. On the contrary, Whitman's method contains political implications in that it democratically extends the ideal by making it the province of all who wish to imaginatively re-create the pastoral city of their dreams. Mythology and politics, as Whitman knew, can never be separated, because mythology always possesses political resonance. But Whitman did not assume that mythology can adequately chart social and political accomplishments. Eschewing that assumption, however, did not lead him to believe that Americans should escape into a realm of fantasy. As his own efforts as a caring wound dresser during the Civil War indicate, Whitman was no Miles Coverdale who retreated from the muddy human tide to dream of urban idylls. Like Hawthorne's fictions, Whitman's poems underscore the value of urban pastoralism even as they suggest its limitations. The difference between their positions was one of emphasis. Whitman celebrated the dynamic, creative plasticity of the ideal while implicitly reminding his readers that its fruition can be only imaginative; Hawthorne stressed the gap between social possibilities and the goals of the ideal while nonetheless acknowledging its inspirational force. Though employing different approaches, both Whitman and Hawthorne incorporated in their works a dual perspective that is at once skeptical and appreciative of the visionary synthesis of urbanity and rusticity. Neither prescribing nor proscribing a view of the ideal, both offer to the culture a perspective whose significance lies in its potential for stimulating a mature assessment of the values and inadequacies of urban pastoralism.

III

In the latter part of the nineteenth century, the literary treatment of urban pastoralism remained polarized. While popular writers continued to affirm the ideal without qualification, major writers who confronted the concept of an urban middle landscape did so with a sophistication and complexity paralleling that of Whitman and Hawthorne. Yet the two responses—the internalized and the ironic—did not appear with equal frequency. As the glow of transcendental romanticism faded, a tough-minded skepticism took over causing the ironic version to become dominant.

By way of illustration we can briefly turn to two works at the close of the century that embody this ironic response through the fates of their central characters. In *Sister Carrie* (1900) Theodore Dreiser makes the urban-pastoral impulse a central motif defining the life of his protagonist, but in doing so he envelops it in a pattern of reversal that undermines the viability of the ideal. Initially, Dreiser's method is subtle and barely suggestive. When Carrie meets Drouet on the train early in the novel, his remark that Lincoln Park is the first thing she must see in Chicago seems incidental. But when her sister, Minnie, repeats the suggestion shortly after Carrie's arrival, the reference becomes more than casual. Dreiser's decision to make Lincoln Park the first items on Carrie's itinerary is important because of the park's social significance. The oldest one in Chicago, it was undergoing substantial improvement in 1889 (the year Carrie arrives) as part of the park-planning movement in America. The pride Chicagoans took in Lincoln and in their entire park system is evident in an 1889 official report of the park commissioners that lauds "the splendid chain of parks which, linked together by broad boulevards, surround and crown the imperial city of Chicago as with a diadem of matchless pearls."[37] The hope that Lincoln Park evoked in Chicagoans symbolizes Carrie's expectations on her arrival and implicitly connects her "desire for all which was new and pleasing" in the city with the pastoral impulse in urban society at large.[38]

Only when she reencounters Drouet, however, does the connection between her urban odyssey and pastoral dreams become direct. In the rest of the novel Dreiser employs a collocation of verdant imagery to characterize Carrie's life in Chicago and New York as a search for greenness—the peace, felicity, freedom amidst security, and freshness traditionally associated with pastoralism. From the flat she shares with Drouet, strategically located on the edge of a park and appointed with a carpet displaying "large jardinières" of "gorgeous impossible flowers," to the trysts with Hurstwood at Jefferson Park, to the "lovely harbingers of spring" accompanying her rise in the theater, Carrie's life comprises a series of ad hoc urban idylls (69, 319). In her relation with Hurstwood the idea is especially striking. As Dreiser explains, to Carrie, Hurstwood represents the world of North Chicago and Lincoln Park, with its "broad lawns, now first freshening into green," where, she believes, "was neither care nor unsatisfied desire" (86). With Hurstwood, Carrie envisions an ideal relationship in which she and he will be as one. Carving out their own little existence in an eternal present, they will live in an idyllic realm unencumbered by complications yet providing a conduit to the city of fashion, wealth, and social prominence.

The irony of Carrie's position is that her goal remains unfulfilled, partly because the inexorable city crushes Hurstwood but also because Carrie's protean human nature repeatedly compels her to recast her dream of felicity. Near the close of the novel Dreiser emphasizes the point by explicitly connecting Carrie's fate to the theme of pastoral failure in the city:

> Though often disillusioned, she was still waiting for that halcyon day when she should be led forth among dreams become real. Ames had pointed out a farther step, but on and on beyond that, if accomplished, would lie others for her. It was forever to be the pursuit of that radiance of delight which tints the distant hilltops of the world.
>
> Oh, Carrie, Carrie! Oh, blind strivings of the human heart! Onward, onward, it saith. . . . Whether it be the tinkle of a lone sheep bell o'er some quiet landscape, or the glimmer of beauty in sylvan places, or the show of soul in some passing eye, the heart knows and makes answer, following. . . . Know, then, that for you is neither surfeit nor content. (369)

Dramatizing the illusionary nature of the pastoral quest in the city, Dreiser nonetheless does not dismiss the ideal as irrelevant. Despite Carrie's unending separation from greenness, the action of the novel reveals that the quest has promoted growth and some insight in Carrie, who has discovered the inadequacy of social and material success.

Not all writers who incorporated an ironic vision of urban pastoralism made it a central configuration of their work. At times the images of the frustrated urban idyll forms only a part of the imaginative pattern, as in Edith Wharton's *The House of Mirth* (1905). Yet in this novel Wharton succeeds in exposing the myth of the pastoral city as an attractive but ultimately illusory response to the urban scene.

Much of Wharton's novel consists of a scathing attack on a New York society totally devoted to the pursuit of wealth, power, and exploitation. The one exception in this scene is the heroine, Lily Bart, whose precarious financial position comports with her grace, tenderness, and emotional responsiveness to the needs of others. These very characteristics, however, make Lily a social outcast, a "rare flower," as Wharton calls her, in a despoiled urban garden, and the main action of *The House of Mirth* consists of Lily's slow ostracism from a world where such values jeopardize survival. Throughout, Wharton's primary concern seems to be social protest against an urban milieu that has moved away from simple values and virtues.

Near the conclusion of the novel, however, the mood changes when Lily reencounters Nettie Crane, a young consumptive who once had been a recipient of Lily's charitable work among the impoverished and who since has become a devoted mother married to a poor but loving laborer. In Nettie's apartment, Lily finds an outwardly meager life but one inwardly rich in love and "human fellowship." With her husband and child, Nettie has built what seems to Lily a "shelter" amidst the harshness of the city. Seeing the young mother hold her child and then feeling in her own arms the infant's tender motions and warmth, Lily senses that the "central truth of existence" lies in the humble scene she now witnesses.[39]

Juxtaposed with what Wharton calls the "rootlessness" of Lily's own life, Nettie's story, as Richard Poirier has suggested, "might be called a pastoral version of Lily's," for in Nettie, Wharton draws on an idea repeatedly found in sentimental versions of urban pastoralism: the popular notion of the home as pastoral enclave in the city.[40] Even as Wharton builds the image, however, it becomes apparent that she does not intend it as a plausible alternative to the dominant urban milieu. Nettie's life, despite its appeal, has "the frail audacious permanence of a bird's nest built on the edge of a cliff—a mere wisp of leaves and straw," which hangs tenuously over the urban "abyss" (517). Structurally, it occupies a similar position in the novel. Located on the margins of the plot, Nettie's enclave can be nothing more than a temporary asylum in the sophisticated, competitive, cosmopolitan environment to which Lily belongs. Consequently, as Lily ponders her lost possibilities, Wharton turns her heroine's mind to thoughts of death. That night, in a drugged stupor, Lily dies imagining that she holds Nettie's baby in her arms. The novel's final image—the darkened windows of Lily's apartment set against a morning that "rose mild and bright, with a promise of summer in the air" (523)—constitutes perhaps Wharton's most ironic, tragic comment on the tenuous appeal but final inadequacy of urban-pastoral projections.

In their sophisticated responses to urban pastoralism Wharton and Dreiser enhance the insights of Hawthorne and Whitman by drawing attention to the contradictions between the ideal and the urban realities that work against its fulfillment, even as they identify the value of urban pastoralism as a token of hope. For some writers who addressed this issue, however, more than the limitations of city life was acting against the achievement of a stable balance between pastoral values and urban activities. Lurking beneath their responses was a recognition that the very nature of history vis-à-vis the idea of America as a special place had to be reckoned with.

One writer at the turn of the century to seize upon this idea was Henry James. More than any of his novels, his *American Scene*, published three years after his return to America in 1904 following a twenty-year absence in Europe, merits close attention because it embodies a unique perspective on the contradictions besetting the American quest for the pastoral city. Coming near the end of his career and serving as a virtual capstone to his ideas about the meaning of America, this nonfictional work is James's most explicit and suggestive treatment of the relation between America's urban identify and the significance of the native landscape.

James explains in the opening pages that his homecoming and his efforts to recount that experience emanated from a dual purpose. The first might be said to embody the popular idea of America and its cities. James admits that, despite relishing his European experience, part of his reason for returning home stemmed from his feeling that abroad he had been "deprived to excess—that is for too long—of naturalism in *quantity*." Consequently, he seeks to recover the emotion one feels in that "strange conscious hush of the landscape," which for James includes the landscape of the city (New York) he had known in his youth. He seeks, that is, to build a bridge to the past, if only in imagination. Against this nostalgic, idealized intention, James balances a desire to report accurately what he finds. He will be, he says, a "restless analyst" probing for truth beneath the opaque veil of appearance.[41]

Although James initially comments on the sights of rural New England, his primary subject is the urban milieu, and he begins his analysis with his reaction to New York City. Approaching Manhattan from the south, he notes that the face of the city provides a "happily-excited" and "amused" view to the prodigal traveler, and in his description of the scene, as Alan Trachtenberg has commented, we hear reverberations of Whitman's "Crossing Brooklyn Ferry."[42] Just as Whitman imaginatively depicts a city which synthesizes nature and civilization, so does James feel that in this vista "nature and science were joyously romping together." The scene is so striking, notes James, that he feels as if New York might take as its "symbol, some collective presence of great circling and plunging, hovering and perching sea-birds, white-winged images of the spirit, of the restless freedom of the Bay" (73). It is as if James is testing Whitman's rhythmic imagery against the pulse of reality, and for a time he finds both beating in unison. For James discovers in Manhattan that same thrilling mood he had felt in the American landscape at large while visiting New England. The city seems to share with the rural scene that "beauty of light and air, the great scale of space" that is the defining trait of America. But what reinforces the connections between landscape and cityscape the most for James is the uneasiness he feels in the pres-ence of both. The bucolic charm of New England, he had noted, "might be the accident of one's situation"—in this case, his own "too long" separation from nature—and now he admits that his first impression of New York likewise "might just happen to proceed from the intellectual extravagance of the given observer" (15, 74). Since he seeks not only to present his response but also to discern its source, James here is speaking as the restless analyst. Does the origin of his feelings reside in the scene before him, he asks, or is it the result of his own wishful thinking? At first he is uncertain, but he is convinced that something in the scene affects him. He begins to identify that something only when he recognizes that its "appeal" stems from "a particular type of dauntless power" present in what he witnesses (74).

With that insight, the image of New York before him begins to change. Now it resembles some "monstrous organism" with its "sky-scrapers standing up . . . like extravagant pins in a cushion already overplanted" and its "immeasurable bridges" resembling "sheaths of pistons working at high pressure." He senses that he is watching some kind of growing monster, the very epitome of the industrial city in which nature appears to play no part. Yet James will not rest in the dichotomy. Even in his altered mood, he feels that "memory and the actual impression" keep investing New York with a "tone" that recalls the primary feature of America: its great geographical scale (75–76). Despite their difference, the skyscrapers and network of bridges and roadways, he senses, somehow are part of that quality.

Though nonplussed at first, James begins to penetrate the paradox when he visits his old neighborhood around Washington Square. Ar-riving at the square, he is shocked by a scene which has "the effect for me . . . of having been amputated of half of my history." Not only has his own birthplace been razed, but the old New York University build-ing has "vanished from the earth" (91). Suddenly James starts to understand the implications of the vast sense of power that struck him earlier while viewing the bridges and skyscrapers. For these structures do not signify the overwhelming of nature by an oppressive urban world. Rather, they seem no more permanent than his own vanished home—mere "growths" which have "arisen but to be 'picked,' in time, with a shears." They are only the evanescent results of the American "passion that, restless beyond all passion, is for ever seeking more pliable forms" (77).

What James discovers in New York is only one instance of a phenomenon he finds pervasive in America. Chicago, Boston, St. Louis, Baltimore, Washington, and Richmond convey a similar sense of impermanence which figures for James a vast "incoherence" at the center of urban culture. Most telling is James's conclusion about the cause for this instability. Ironically enough, he realizes, it emanates not from rampant urbanization but from the American landscape itself. In the "latent powers of freedom and space," the "expanse of the floor, [and] the material opportunity" promised by the vast stretches of land and resources, "the trap [has been] laid" (444, 465). Since the image of America as a fresh, inexhaustible garden has suggested the opportunity, previously unmatched in history, to commence life anew, city dwellers have dedicated themselves to a "perpetual repudiation of the past" (53). So committed to seizing the "immensity of the chance" offered by the continent—the fantastic possibility of fresh forms and new beginnings, the unique opportunity to build a distinctive, better urban society—Americans have become preoccupied with an endless urban renewal (55). In the process, however, urban America has created for itself no identity at all. Instead, Americans have denied themselves the permanence and stability necessary for a healthy urban society of "organic social relations." For James, this curious state signals only a powerful "loneliness" in cities resulting from "loose values" and a denial of continuing traditions (160). To put the matter another way, James is saying that the American pursuit of its urban identity via the pastoral promise of the native landscape has proceeded with a vigor that precludes any chance of a meaningful union between the two. Under his analytical eye, American cities display only an "inflated . . . hotel-spirit . . . exhaling modernity at every pore" and "squaring itself between an absent future and an absent past" in "an insistent testimony to waste" (461, 159–61).

The uniqueness of James's insight arises from the connection he draws between history and the urban-pastoral impulse. Unlike Hawthorne, James does not say that history invalidates the ideal as a model for social institutions or as a guide to personal felicity. Instead, he asserts, the very denial of historical continuity by the entire culture makes achievement of the ideal impossible. In his reversal of terms James provides an additional perspective on the ultimate contradictions of urban pastoralism even as he reinforces the conclusions of major writers before him. For the bottom line of James's prospectus identifies the ideal itself as its own obstacle. With Hawthorne, Dreiser, and Wharton, James forms part of a literary tradition that has located at the very center of the American scene the incongruities and limitations of urban pastoralism.

Epilogue
Nature and the Omnipresent City

Henry James's image of an America rushing toward an urban identity is today a historical fact. In 1800 less than 5 percent of Americans lived in cities; today 70 percent of our population is urban. We have become a nation of city dwellers, a reality we cannot deny. The way in which Americans as a whole have responded to this development, however, is difficult to gauge. No extensive survey has probed the subject on a national scale, and the magnitude of the task suggests that such data are not likely to be forthcoming. Yet if demographic patterns provide any indication, Americans in general seem to have reacted to mass urbanization by seeking some kind of compromise between city and country. For nearly half of our population today lives in suburbs.[1] Although the suburban trend has been so pronounced that historians and sociologists now argue that the suburb-city dichotomy has replaced the city-country conflict in native ideology, only a degree of truth inheres in this assertion.[2] While the polarity of city and suburb may be a new phenomenon, the context of history reminds us that this opposition is part of another larger one operating in America since the seventeenth century: the dichotomy between the corrupt, over-civilized, yet disordered city and the redeemed urban society integrated with nature.

Of course, we have found that the suburban form of urban pastoralism has provided no more final or satisfactory social answer to the synthesizing impulse than did the city on the hill. The political autonomy on which suburbanites insist, based on an inveterate faith in grass-roots democracy, has created, in the words of Robert Wood, an organizational fragmentation of "tiny, ineffectual governments which seem almost willfully bent on reproducing chaos." This isolation,

amounting to political irresponsibility, is symptomatic of a general neglect which Lewis Mumford has labeled the suburban "temptation to
retreat from unpleasant realities, to shirk public duties, and to find the
whole meaning of life in the most elemental social groups, the family
. . . or even the self-centered individual."[3] Instead of a blend of rural
and urban, suburban life too often has produced alien commuters using the central city as a mere economic tool.

Because the suburb has borne more than its share of criticism over
the past forty years, however, there is no need here to rehearse all of
its shortcomings. What needs to be emphasized is that the disinte-
grative effects of suburbanization are the product of an underlying ideology inherently based on division. Suburbs may create a rift in the
metropolitan social and political fabric, but they do so as outgrowths
of the American faith in the fresh landscape as a vehicle for creating
a new urban milieu separate and different from the old. Like the promoters for an urban-pastoral West, suburban dwellers have fashioned
alternative cities in a symbolic "west"—the environs of existing cities. In the face of a closed horizon in the twentieth century, it is perhaps predictable that Americans would reconceive the dream city of
the West in this way, attempting to redefine and remake established
cities at their peripheries. Neither pure reformation nor complete
abandonment of the old city, the suburb represents a compromised
form of urban pastoralism, in which the suburbanite seeks contact
with the larger urban scene even as he withdraws from it daily for rest
and familial satisfaction. The shortcomings of such a compromise are
not new problems but an exacerbation of old ones: territorial divisiveness and the separation of work and leisure that had begun in the early
nineteenth century with the advancement of the home as pastoral retreat in the city.

Although suburbanism may be the most pronounced—and problematic—manifestation of urban pastoralism in our own day, the impulse is not limited to this phase of American life. We find it in
business, in the wholesale abandoning of the inner city for the industrial park. We discover it at work again in government projects and
policies: in municipal zoning laws prohibiting the building of high-
rise apartments; in our national highway system, designed in part to
improve connections between cities and their rural hinterlands; and
in the federal Model Cities Program of the 1960s, dedicated to reno-
vating slums with new housing projects and miniature parks. While
these developments clearly have produced certain benefits, the irony

is that they have created other problems. We have found that zoning laws framed to reduce urban density have contributed to urban sprawl, that our highways have led to insuperable traffic problems and the slicing up of urban neighborhoods, and that urban renewal often has disrupted indigenous communal patterns. Like the tensions which our nineteenth-century artists embodied in their works, the contradictions resulting from modern policies illustrate the pitfalls of urban pastoralism when it is translated into sociopolitical structures.

These examples suggest that even in the more thoughtful and informed segments of society, Americans often have been willing to indulge in uncritical acceptance of the quest for an organic city. Whether the field is urban planning, sociology, or history, the ideal has retained a credibility far surpassing its value and feasibility.

A striking example of this phenomenon is Frank Lloyd Wright's Broadacre City, which Wright designed as a remedy for what he called the "hopelessly, helplessly, inorganic" condition of twentieth-century urban America. Wright conceived Broadacre as a decentralized industrial city spreading over the landscape to provide each citizen with a minimum of one acre of land. "I have called this city Broadacre City," he explained, "because it is a broad freedom for the individual, honestly democratic, based upon the ground." Subscribing to an urban version of the Jeffersonian ideal, he asserted that such an arrangement somehow would return true "individuality" and "democracy" to Americans by offering them an opportunity to recapture the "free life." For Wright, the organic city epitomized in the Broadacre plan was "not only the only democratic city; it is the only possible city looking towards any future for these United States."[4]

Although Broadacre City stands as one of the more quixotic designs of the present century, it does share several features with many modern urban plans: an emphasis on decentralization and increased opportunities for contact with nature and an effort to simplify the social patterns of urban life. As Nathan Glazer has pointed out, much of "what passes for city planning today is fundamentally a rejection of the big city and of all it means—its variety, its peculiarities, its richness of choice and experience—and a yearning for a bucolic society."[5] This oversimplification of the complexity of urban life is precisely the weakness that Percival and Paul Goodman identify in Wright's pastoral city. Though Wright "aims at the integration of urban and rural life," they note, he fails to account for the volatile, disruptive influences in the industrial sectors of the modern city. Yet having acknowledged the inherently protean quality of urban society, the Goodmans claim that they have discovered "the fundamental issues that every . . . physical plan must face and satisfy" and proceed to offer their own "model solutions" to the question of the organic commercial city.[6]

This tendency to evict urban pastoralism through the front door while slipping in another version of it through the back typifies much of the response to American cities over the past fifty years. In *The Death and Life of Great American Cities*, for instance, Jane Jacobs asserts that the Garden City and City Beautiful movements attempted to impose patterns intrinsically incompatible with the urban dynamic yet suggests that a meaningful life in the city can be created only in small organic neighborhood units combining urban and rural patterns. The writings of Lewis Mumford, perhaps the most astute urban historian of the twentieth century, reveal a similar substitution. Displaying an animus toward suburbs and most versions of urban renewal, Mumford nonetheless holds that cities are "biological species" and advocates development of the "balanced region," which will allow for "a wider diffusion of the instruments and processes of a rich human culture, and . . . the infusion into the city of the life-sustaining environment and life-directed interests of the countryside." Curiously, while Mumford recognizes the dangers of efforts to "seek a harmony too absolute" that denies "the essential human need for disharmony and conflict," his own theories of a healthy urban society emphasize a carefully calibrated, optimum balance of social and material elements from country and city.[7]

There is to be sure a difference between these critical projections of urban pastoralism and the unquestioning versions that appeared in the nineteenth century—a difference that, in one sense, brings modern urban theorists closer to the sophisticated responses to the ideal found in America's major writers. Both recognize the dangers in the ideal even as they assent to its appeal and value. There remains, nevertheless, an important distinction between the two perspectives. If modern urban theorists have questioned the goal of integrating rural and urban, they have done so by focusing on the inadequacy of a particular manifestation of the ideal while failing to question its underlying assumptions. As a result, they remain caught in the trap of searching for practical embodiments for an idealized image. Nineteenth-century artists such as Hawthorne, Dreiser, and James recognized that such versions were historically constituted and so incapable

of serving as final answers. While accepting the inspirational significance of America's urban-pastoral mythology, they sought to explore
the myth at its core to develop in the culture a capacity for self-ex-
amination that would be at once critical and therapeutic.

If the responses of nineteenth-century writers remain essentially
different from the heightened awareness found in certain sectors of
twentieth-century culture, those responses also are distinct from that
of modern authors who have confronted the meaning of urban pastoralism. Over the past seventy years the ironic response has continued to prevail, but in the process it has taken on more ominous, even
fatal implications. Dominated by the image of a modern America as
an omnipresent city, twentieth-century American literature has so
thoroughly circumscribed the ideal that it has denied even a temporary or inward realization of the dream. No longer perceived as socially inadequate but internally estimable, the ideal has become
anathema, as writers have depicted it yielding not garden cities but a
perverse amalgam of artificial urbanity and reckless primitivism.
From Eugene O'Neill's *The Hairy Ape* and F. Scott Fitzgerald's *The
Great Gatsby* to Richard Wright's *Native Son* and Saul Bellow's *Mr.
Sammler's Planet*, modern literature has made the motif of the urban
wilderness a staple of its fictional environments. Whether delineating
a blasted urban garden of ashes, a jungle-like Chicago, or a New York
where "jeweled doors" lead "from hypercivilized Byzantine luxury
straight into the state of nature," this century's imaginative writers repeatedly have conceived of America as a place where only an aberrant
version of the ideal can result.[8] Unable to give credence any longer to
the myth of America as a special place, they have decried the treach-
ery of the idea of the pastoral city and the spoliation of the natural
scene—and the American self—that has supplanted it. In place of an
ironic response with tragic or hopeful implications, we find primarily
a vast despair that tends to deny any value to the ideal and the human
experience in the city. Nor has this pessimistic vision of urban life
been limited to writers using urban-pastoral materials. From T. S.
Eliot and Nathanael West to Thomas Pynchon, Edward Albee, and
Norman Mailer, the pervading image has been one in which an atmosphere of doom, like an apocalyptic nightmare, hangs over the
modern city. Seldom, if ever, can we discover today the kind of complicated though balanced perspective of Hawthorne, Whitman, or
Dreiser.

To say this, however, is not to imply that *The Blithedale Romance* or

"Crossing Brooklyn Ferry" is somehow "superior" to *The Great Gatsby* or *The Hairy Ape*. Nor do the power and value of these and other works considered here reside primarily in the way they have responded to the urban-pastoral dream. Our most compelling authors have written from a purpose larger than that of simply addressing a single cultural issue or attempting to be useful by explaining our situation.

Nonetheless, by incorporating in their texts several versions of the qualified urban ideal, they have acted as a potentially valuable countervoice in the culture. Our best artists have confronted the myth of the idyllic city not to deracinate it but to probe its meaning for a nation continually devoted to acts of urban renewal. Although the shape of our cities ultimately rests in the hands of urban planners and city politicians and in the way each of us participates in the urban community, our artists have reminded us that we must do more than simply seek to reconceive or rebuild our cities. Their insights suggest that we need to examine our hopes for a more meaningful urban society in light of the tacit premises of our culture, including the mythology of the pastoral city that has played such an important role in our continuing history. For if we wish to change our situation, it may be necessary to produce new myths informed by a rigorous questioning of their value and limitations. Our major writers already have asked some of those qustions about America's urban-pastoral dream. We would not be amiss in following their lead as we look to the future of our cities.

Notes
Selected Bibliography
Index

Notes

Prologue

1 *The Journals and Miscellaneous Notebooks of Ralph Waldo Emerson,* ed.
William H. Gilman, Ralph H. Orth, et al. (Cambridge: Harvard Univ.
Press, 1960–1982), 15: 430.

2 Perry Miller, *Nature's Nation* (Cambridge: Belknap Press of Harvard
Univ. Press, 1967), p. 119. The terms "agrarian myth," "pastoral ideal,"
and "myth of the garden" are used respectively by Richard Hofstadter,
The Age of Reform: From Bryan to F.D.R. (1955; rpt. New York: Knopf,
1974); Leo Marx, *The Machine in the Garden: Technology and the Pastoral
Ideal in America* (1964; rpt. New York: Oxford Univ. Press, 1973); and
Henry Nash Smith, *Virgin Land: The American West as Symbol and Myth*
(New York: Vintage-Random House, 1950). A recent interesting dis-
cussion of this idea in relationship to the shaped landscape of America
is John Stilgoe's *Common Landscape of America, 1580 to 1845* (New
Haven: Yale Univ. Press, 1982).

3 Quoted in Harry Levin, *The Myth of the Golden Age in the Renaissance*
(Bloomington: Indiana Univ. Press, 1969), p. xv.

4 Carl Bridenbaugh, *Cities in the Wilderness: The First Century of Urban
Life in America, 1625–1742* (1938; rpt. New York: Capricorn, 1955) and
Cities in Revolt: Urban Life in America, 1743–1776 (New York: Knopf,
1955); Sam Bass Warner, Jr., *The Urban Wilderness: A History of the
American City* (New York: Harper & Row, 1972); Charles Glaab and A.
Theodore Brown, *A History of Urban America* (New York: Collier-Mac-
millan, 1967); John Reps, *The Making of Urban America: A History of
City Planning in the United States* (Princeton: Princeton Univ. Press,
1965) and *Cities of the American West: A History of Frontier Urban Plan-*

ning (Princeton: Princeton Univ. Press, 1979); and Richard Wade, *The Urban Frontier: The Rise of Western Cities, 1790–1830* (Cambridge: Harvard Univ. Press, 1959). In the past twenty-five years the number of full-length studies of American urban development has become legion, and a full bibliography probably would comprise a work as long as this study. Among the more valuable, in addition to those cited above, are Blake McKelvey, *The Urbanization of America, 1860–1915* (New Brunswick, N. J.: Rutgers Univ. Press, 1963); Gunther Barth, *City People: The Rise of Modern City Culture in Nineteenth-Century America* (New York: Oxford Univ. Press, 1980); and Sylvia Fries, *The Urban Idea in Colonial America* (Philadelphia: Temple Univ. Press, 1977).

5 Henry Tappan, *The Growth of Cities: A Discourse Delivered before the New York Geographical Society* (New York, 1855), pp. 24 and 16. Though less numerous than other types of urban history, there have been some important studies of the image or conception of the city in America. The most notable—and also the most one-sided—has been Morton White and Lucia White, *The Intellectual Versus the City* (1962; rpt. New York: New American Library, 1964). More balanced and wide-ranging are Anselm L. Strauss, *Images of the American City* (New York: Free Press of Glencoe, 1961); and Andrew Lees, *Cities Perceived: Urban Society in European and American Thought, 1820–1940* (New York: Columbia Univ. Press, 1985).

6 See, for example, discussions of the nineteenth-century ideal of the urban home as "rural" retreat in Marlene Stein Wortman, "Domesticating the Nineteenth-Century American City," in Jack Salzman, ed., *Prospects: An Annual of American Cultural Studies,* Vol. 3 (New York: Franklin, 1977), pp. 531–72; and Kirk Jeffrey, "The Family as Utopian Retreat from the City," in Sallie TeSelle, ed., *The Family, Communes, and Utopian Societies* (New York: Harper & Row, 1972), pp. 21–41.

7 Scott Donaldson, "City and Country: Marriage Proposals," *American Quarterly,* 20 (1968), 547–66; John L. Thomas, "Utopia for an Urban Age: Henry George, Henry Demarest Lloyd, Edward Bellamy," *Perspectives in American History,* 6 (1972), 135–63; and Peter Schmitt, *Back to Nature: The Arcadian Myth in Urban America* (New York: Oxford Univ. Press, 1969). See also Francisco Dal Co, "From Parks to the Region: Progressive Ideology and the Reform of the American City," in Giorgio Ciucci et al., *The American City: From the Civil War to the New Deal,* trans. Barbara Luigia La Penta (Cambridge: MIT Press, 1979), pp. 143–292; and Strauss, *Images of the American City,* pp. 206–45. Although Strauss notes that "reconciliation of rurality with urbanity" has been a

"persistent theme" in America since 1800, he devotes only five of the thirty-nine pages of his discussion to the period before the Progressive Era.

8 One of the few studies—and the only full-length one—to examine the idea of rural-urban integration in the antebellum period is Thomas Bender's *Toward an Urban Vision: Ideas and Institutions in Nineteenth-Century America* (Lexington: Univ. Press of Kentucky, 1975). Unfortunately, Bender limits the value of his book by focusing on New England mill towns, park planning, and the urban reform of Charles Loring Brace, thus neglecting the role of the ideal in other urban-reform efforts and in conceptions of the American West. Moreover, in arguing that the ideal of synthesis was unique to the nineteenth century (p. 17), Bender ignores the presence of urban pastoralism in the colonial period. For a somewhat related study, which discusses the way Americans in the early nineteenth century viewed the city as an intrinsic outgrowth of nature, see Bernard Rosenthal, *City of Nature: Journeys to Nature in the Age of American Romanticism* (Newark: Univ. of Delaware Press; London: Associated Univ. Presses, 1980). The only historian who has recognized a relation between rural ideals and positive conceptions of the city in colonial America is Sylvia Fries (*The Urban Idea in Colonial America*). However, Fries's book suffers from some of the same limitations as Bender's, particularly in its failure to examine the relation between early colonial ideas and the subsequent shape of urban-rural integration in the late eighteenth and the nineteenth and twentieth centuries.

9 "Letter to the Commissioners," 30 May 1800, in H. Paul Caemmerer, *The Life of Pierre Charles L'Enfant* (Washington, D.C.: National Republic, 1950), p. 398.

10 John Winthrop, *A Model of Christian Charity,* in *Winthrop Papers,* Massachusetts Historical Society Publications (Boston: Merrymount, 1929–47), 2: 283 and 295.

11 Peter O. Muller, "Everyday Life in Suburbia: A Review of Changing Social and Economic Forces that Shape Daily Rhythms within the Outer City," *American Quarterly,* 34 (1982), 265.

12 Charles Glaab, "The Historian and the American Urban Tradition," *Wisconsin Magazine of History,* 57 (Autumn 1963), 25.

13 Histories of utopian communities and communitarian ideals in America are numerous, and although few overtly identify an urban-pastoral component in these societies and theories, a number of historians have discussed utopian experiments in a way that points to the existence of the ideal in their social patterns and city designs. Two of the better general

discussions are Mark Halloway, *Heavens on Earth*, 2d ed. (New York: Dover, 1966); and Michael Fellman, *The Unbound Frame: Freedom and Community in Nineteenth-Century American Utopianism* (Westport, Conn.: Greenwood, 1973). On utopian communities and town planning see Arthur E. Bestor, *Backwoods Utopias* (Philadelphia: Univ. of Pennsylvania Press, 1971); Dolores Hayden, *Seven American Utopias* (Cambridge: MIT Press, 1976); and Reps, *Making of Urban America*, pp. 439–74. For interesting discussions of Bellamy and Olerich in this regard see, respectively, Thomas, "Utopia for an Urban Age," and Strauss, *Images of the American City*, pp. 207–9.

14 Marx, *Machine in the Garden*, pp. 3–11, 20–31, et passim. The description of cultural pastoralism in the next paragraph also draws on these pages.

15 *National Intelligencer*, 17 February 1815, p. 3 (n. pag.), cols. 2–3. The representativeness of Troup's method of depicting Jackson and his men is discussed by John William Ward, *Andrew Jackson: Symbol for an Age* (New York: Oxford Univ. Press, 1955), pp. 7–10 and 30–78.

16 Henry George, *Progress and Poverty* (1879; rpt. New York, 1881), pp. 244, 489, 491, and 350.

17 George, *Progress and Poverty*, pp. 405–6, 245, 390, 493, 405, and 409–10. See also Thomas, "Utopia for an Urban Age," pp. 150–52.

18 George, *Progess and Poverty*, pp. 417 and 423.

19 *The Vision of Columbus*, in *The Works of Joel Barlow* (Gainesville, Fla.: Scholars' Facsimilies & Reprints, 1970), 2: 301 (Bk. 7, lines 67–68), 304 (Bk. 7, lines 141, 144–46, 149–50), and 338 (Bk. 9, Argument).

20 Emerson, *Journals*, 11: 218. Several literary critics and one historian have noted this interest among major writers in a fusion of rural and urban: Janis Stout, *Sodoms in Eden: The City in American Fiction before 1860* (Westport, Conn.: Greenwood, 1976), pp. 95–114; David Weimer, *The City as Metaphor* (New York: Random House, 1966), pp. 25 and 75; Michel Cowan, *City of the West: Emerson, America, and Urban Metaphor* (New Haven: Yale Univ. Press, 1967), pp. 180–229; Bender, *Toward an Urban Vision*, pp. 13–15; and Leo Marx, "Pastoral Ideals and City Troubles," *Journal of General Education*, 20 (1968–69), 251–71. While Weimer makes only a passing comment, Stout and Cowan go into more detail regarding Hawthorne and Emerson respectively. Because of their focus, however, they say little about other romantics in regard to this question and ignore important differences among Whitman, Hawthorne, and Emerson in their responses to the idea of synthesizing nature and the city. Moreover, neither Cowan nor Stout considers the relation-

ship between the ideas of major artists and those of the culture at large. While Marx and Bender are the only individuals who have broached the question of that relation, their comments suffer from two major weaknesses: They are far too brief to deal adequately with the complexity and diversity of literary responses, and, more significantly, they mistakenly assert that major American artists have embraced the idea with the same unquestioning enthusiasm found in the general culture. Both also fail to distinguish pastoralism from the idea of rural-urban synthesis.

21 Michael Kammen, *People of Paradox: An Inquiry concerning the Origins of American Civilization* (1972; rpt. New York: Vintage-Random House, 1973), pp. 295 and 89.

22 *Civilization and Its Discontents*, trans. Joan Riviere, in *The Standard Edition of the Complete Psychological Works of Sigmund Freud*, ed. James Strachey (London: Hogarth, 1955), 21: 77 and 101. For Freud's discussion of the development of early communities see *Totem and Taboo*, trans. James Strachey, in *Standard Edition*, 13: 1–160.

23 Herbert Marcuse, *Eros and Civilization: A Philosophical Inquiry into Freud* (1955: rpt. Boston: Beacon, 1966), p. 18.

24 Heinz Kohut, *The Restoration of the Self* (New York: International Universities Press, 1977), pp. 5, 7, et passim. I do not wish to overemphasize Kohut's applicability here, since his psychology of the self is somewhat at odds with the drive psychology of Freud and Marcuse. In relation to repression, however, Kohut's discussion of self psychology becomes relevant to the point. As he explains, narcissistic personality disorders, with their accompanying loneliness, usually occur in environments where prohibitions and rivalries are lacking (p. 27). Since one goal of pure pastoralism is to eliminate such rivalries and to free the individual from social repression, it threatens to produce the kind of emotional void intrinsic to narcissistic disorders.

25 Freud, *Civilization and Its Discontents*, pp. 96 and 126–27.

26 Karl Mannheim, *Ideology and Utopia: An Introduction to the Sociology of Knowledge*, trans. Louis Wirth and Edward Shils (New York: Harcourt, Brace, 1936).

27 Carl Becker, *The Heavenly City of the Eighteenth-Century Philosophers* (New Haven: Yale Univ. Press, 1932).

28 Yehezkel Kaufmann, *The Religion of Israel*, trans. Moshe Greenberg (1937; rpt. Chicago: Univ. of Chicago Press, 1960), p. 351.

29 Kaufmann, *Religion of Israel*, pp. 345–46.

30 "Urban and the Crusades," ed. Dana Carleton Munro, pp. 7–8, in *Translations and Reprints from the Original Sources of European History*, Vol. 1

224

(Philadelphia, 1879). Although the ideal integration of Hebrew eschatology posited a future state never before achieved, the interrelation of city/court and landscape had been central to Jewish conceptions of environment even before the prophetic books. The Israelites apparently borrowed from the earlier Canaanite inhabitants of Jerusalem a cultic mythology identifying the health of the landscape with the conditions of the city and its rulers. Discovering in the Psalms remnants of this cultic worship, Aubrey Johnson has noted how the advent of nourishing rains and the general fertility of the countryside were linked to the well-being of the members of the Davidic dynasty residing in Jerusalem and the currents of the "cosmic sea," which Yahweh had subjugated. That sea, which appears again in Ezekiel, is said to originate beneath the Temple and flow into the Jordan Valley as a great fertilizing agent enriching the land (*Sacral Kingship in Ancient Israel* [Cardiff: Univ. of Wales Press, 1967], pp. 8–11, 13, and 101–9). Given such a close connection between city and countryside in Jewish thought, it is not surprising to find the prophets incorporating it in their projections of last things.

31 The figure of a reconstituted earth and the description of the New Jerusalem, itself identified with natural abundance, appear in Rev. 21 and 22.

32 Lactantius, *Divine Institutes*, trans. William Fletcher, Bk. 7, Chap. 24, in Alexander Roberts and James Donaldson, eds., *The Ante-Nicene Fathers*, Vol. 8 (New York: Scribner's, 1905); Irenaeus, *Against the Heresies*, trans. Alexander Roberts and W. H. Rambaut, Bk. 5, Chap. 35, in *Ante-Nicene Fathers*, Vol. 1.

33 On the role and shape of millennial expectations in the Middle Ages and early Reformation see Norman Cohn, *The Pursuit of the Millennium* (London: Heinemann, 1962), pp. 20–98 and 226–306; and Frank E. Manuel and Fritzie P. Manuel, *Utopian Thought in the Western World* (Cambridge: Belknap Press of Harvard Univ. Press, 1979), pp. 15–16 and 48. For the continuing interest in apocalypticism among the orthodox see the documents and the discussions accompanying them in Bernard McGinn, *Visions of the End: Apocalyptic Tradition in the Middle Ages* (New York: Columbia Univ. Press, 1979), pp. 37–141. Regarding the relation between prophetic tradition and the New World, Manuel and Manuel point out that Columbus himself "insisted that his 'execution of the affair of the Indies' was a fulfillment of prophecies in Isaiah" (p. 61).

34 George, *Progress and Poverty*, p. 496.

Chapter I. The Pastoral City of Man and God

1 *Utopia*, in *The Complete Works of St. Thomas More*, ed. Edward Surtz and J. H. Hexter (New Haven: Yale Univ. Press, 1965), 4: 137.

2 More, *Utopia*, pp. 115 and 125.

3 More, *Utopia*, pp. 147 and 195.

4 Lewis Mumford, *The City in History: Its Origins, Its Transformations, and Its Prospects* (New York: Harcourt, Brace, 1961), p. 326.

5 On the affinities between More's environmental ideals and classical tradition, particularly as embodied in the writings of other Renaissance humanists, see Wayne A. Rebhorn, "Thomas More's Enclosed Garden: *Utopia* and Renaissance Humanism," *English Literary Renaissance*, 6 (1976), 140–55. Rebhorn notes that other thinkers of the age anticipated More's ideas about environment, since a common humanist image of the good society was an enclosed garden, "especially a garden contained within an ideal palace or city."

6 Alistair Fox, *Thomas More: History and Providence* (Oxford: Blackwell, 1982), pp. 95, 159–60, 204–5, and 217. Fox points out, however, that More did not subscribe to the expectation of a renewed earth and millennial paradise. His position was closer to Augustine's in that More believed the apocalypse would bring the destruction of the earth and a purely spiritual reward for the faithful.

7 More, *Utopia*, pp. 203–5. In some classical writings this localism, under the success of Roman imperialism, did include an idea of universal order, but only when united to Judeo-Christian eschatology. See Lidia Storoni Mazzolani, *The Idea of the City in Roman Thought: From Walled City to Spiritual Commonwealth*, trans. S. O'Donnell (Bloomington: Indiana Univ. Press, 1970).

8 See, for example, Robbin Johnson, *More's "Utopia": Ideal and Illusion* (New Haven: Yale Univ. Press, 1969), pp. 69–132; Warren W. Wooden, "Anti-Scholastic Satire in Sir Thomas More's *Utopia*," *Sixteenth Century Journal*, 8, No. 2 (1977), 29–45; and George M. Logan, *The Meaning of More's* Utopia (Princeton: Princeton Univ. Press, 1983), pp. 218–53.

9 More, *Utopia*, p. 247; More himself briefly discusses his use of names in a letter to Peter Giles, in *Complete Works*, 4: 251.

10 On the centrality of this idea in More's thinking see J. H. Hexter, *More's "Utopia": The Biography of an Idea* (Princeton: Princeton Univ. Press, 1952), pp. 71–72; and Fox, *Thomas More*, pp. 51, 87, 151, et passim.

11 A recent discussion of this divided opinion appears in Ray Allen Bil-

226

lington, *Land of Savagery, Land of Promise* (New York: Norton, 1981), pp. 1–8.

12 *The Voyages of Columbus,* ed. Edward G. Bourne, in *Original Narratives of Early American History* (New York: Scribner's, 1906), 1: 125, 157, and 204.

13 Columbus, *Voyages,* pp. 214–15.

14 Cartier quoted in John Bartlet Brebner, *The Explorers of North America* (1933; rpt. Cleveland: World Publishing, 1964), pp. 106–7.

15 Hernando Cortes, Letter 2, in *Five Letters, 1519–1526,* trans. J. Bayard Morris (1929; rpt. New York: Norton, 1962), pp. 50–51 and 59.

16 Cortes, Letter 2, pp. 85–86.

17 Cortes, Letter 2, pp. 86–89.

18 Cortes, Letter 2, pp. 95–96.

19 Cortes, Letter 2, pp. 59, 93, 68 and 86–89.

20 Cortes, Letter 2, pp. 98, 44, and 114; Charles Braden, *Religious Aspects of the Conquest of Mexico* (New York: AMS, 1966), pp. 17–19. On the crusading motif in the letters see also Hugh Honour, *The New Golden Land: European Images of America from the Discoveries to the Present Time* (New York: Pantheon, 1975), p. 21.

21 Morris, Introduction, *Five Letters,* p. xliv.

22 De Mendieta's remarks quoted in Braden, *Religious Aspects of the Conquest of Mexico,* p. 76; see also John Leddy Phelan, *The Millennial Kingdom of the Franciscans in the New World,* 2d ed. (Berkeley: Univ. of California Press, 1970), pp. 72–77.

23 George Chapman, Ben Jonson, and John Marston, *Eastward Ho,* in *The Plays and Poems of George Chapman,* ed. Thomas Marc Parrott (London: Routledge; New York: Dutton, 1914), 2: 498–99 (Act 3, Scene 3).

24 William Wood, *New England's Prospect* (London, 1634), p. 47.

25 Tommaso Campanella, *City of the Sun: A Poetical Dialogue,* trans. Daniel J. Donno (Berkeley: Univ. of California Press, 1981), pp. 29 and 33–35.

26 Campanella, *City of the Sun,* pp. 83 and 49.

27 Campanella, *City of the Sun,* pp. 81 and 65.

28 Campanella, *City of the Sun,* p. 27.

29 Cortes, Letter 3, p. 220; for a summary of the various interpretations of the source for the name of Campanella's city see Bernardino Bonansea, *Tommaso Campanella: Renaissance Pioneer of Modern Thought* (Washington, D.C.: Catholic Univ. Press, 1969), p. 393, n. 54. On this question of sources, I by no means wish to claim that Cortes' letters are the only "true" source for Campanella's version of the ideal city. My concern instead is with identifying a relationship which bears on the question of credibility in conceptions of America.

30 Cortes, Letter 2, pp. 85–86 and 95–96; Campanella, *City of the Sun*, pp. 27 and 34.

31 Campanella, *City of the Sun*, pp. 51–53, 75, and 115.

32 Bonansea, *Tommaso Campanella*, p. 274.

33 *Monarchia Messiae* quoted in Bonansea, *Tommaso Campanella*, pp. 280–81; Campanella, *City of the Sun*, pp. 109 and 123.

34 Campanella, *City of the Sun*, pp. 121 and 125–27. On Campanella's vision of a divinely ordained millennial hegemony encompassing the whole world, see also Manuel and Manuel, *Utopian Thought in the Western World*, pp. 279–88.

35 Quoted in Honour, *New Golden Land*, p. 16.

36 William Strachey quoted in Edward D. Neill, *The English Colonization of America* (London, 1871), p. 51n; *Virginia's Cure*, pp. 6 and 19, in Peter Force, ed., *Tracts and Other Papers Relating Principally to the Origin, Settlement, and Progress of the Colonies of North America*, Vol. 3 (1836–46; rpt. Gloucester, Mass.: Peter Smith, 1963).

37 William Haller, *Foxe's Book of Martyrs and the Elect Nation* (London: Cape, 1963). Several historians have subsequently questioned Haller's thesis that John Foxe and other sixteenth-century Englishmen drew upon biblical tradition to define themselves as an elect people. See T. H. L. Parker, *English Reformers* (London: SCM, 1966), p. 681; and Katharine R. Firth, *The Apocalyptic Tradition in Reformation Britain* (London: Oxford Univ. Press, 1979), pp. 106–9. Although the extent of Haller's thesis probably needs to be tempered, the literature of the period clearly shows a repeated tendency to claim that God had singled out England for special favor and leadership. Cardinal Pole had announced to Queen Mary in 1554 that Britain was the vanguard of a divine plan whereby "the greatest part of the world had fetched the light of religion from England" (Haller, p. 19), and in his 1559 oration to Queen Elizabeth, John Hale proclaimed that "our natural mother England . . . hath been counted to be the surest, the richest, and of late also the most godly nation of the earth" owing to "all the gifts and benefits wherewith God and nature indued her" (John Foxe, *Acts and Monuments of these Latter and Perilous Days,*, ed. Stephen Cattley [London, 1837–41], 8: 673). Even dissenting William Bradford would begin his history of Plymouth by recalling that "the first breaking out of the light of the gospel [was] in our honourable nation of England" (*Of Plymouth Plantation*, ed. Samuel Eliot Morison [New York: Random House, 1952], p. 3).

38 Richard Hakluyt, *A Particular Discourse concerning the Great Necessity and Manifold Commodities* . . . , in William Huse Dunham, Jr., and Stanley Pargellis, eds., *Complaint and Reform in England, 1436–1714*

228

(New York: Oxford Univ. Press, 1938), p. 245; John White, *The Planter's Plea*, p. 12, in *Tracts and Other Papers*, Vol. 2.

39 White, *Planter's Plea*, p. 9; Twisse quoted in Neill, *English Colonization of America*, p. 178.

Chapter II. New England's Jerusalem

1 Thomas Shepard and John Allin, *A Defence of the Answer* (London, 1648), p. 8.

2 John Winthrop, *Journal or History of New England, 1630–1649*, ed. James Kendall Hosmer, in *Original Narratives of Early American History* (New York: Scribner's, 1908), 7: 47; Winthrop to John Winthrop, Jr., July 1630, in *Winthrop Papers*, 2: 307; Thomas Welde to former parishioners at Tarling, England, June/July 1632, in Everett Emerson, ed., *Letters from New England* (Amherst: Univ. of Massachusetts Press, 1976), p. 96; George Wiswall to George Rigby, 27 September 1638, in *Letters from New England*, p. 232; Cotton Mather, *Theopolis Americana* (Boston, 1710), p. 44.

3 Edward Johnson, *Wonder-Working Providence of Sions Savior in New England*, ed. J. Franklin Jameson, in *Original Narratives of Early American History* (New York: Scribner's, 1910), 10: 68, 210, and 248; John Higginson, *The Cause of God and His People in New England* (Cambridge, Mass., 1663), pp. 10–11; Peter Carroll, *Puritanism and the Wilderness: The Intellectual Significance of the New England Frontier, 1629–1700* (New York: Columbia Univ. Press, 1969), pp. 14–15; Sacvan Bercovitch, "New England's Errand Reappraised," in John Higham and Paul K. Conkin, eds., *New Directions in American Intellectual History* (Baltimore: Johns Hopkins Univ. Press, 1979), pp. 97–98.

4 *Winthrop Papers*, 2: 127 and 136; C. Mather, *Theopolis Americana*, p. 44.

5 Quoted in Mason I. Lowance, Jr., "Typology and the New England Way: Cotton Mather and the Exegesis of Biblical Types," *Early American Literature*, 4 (1969), 30–31.

6 *Winthrop Papers*, 2: 282–95.

7 For a different interpretation, see Fries, *Urban Idea in Colonial America*, pp. 36–37, who argues that by incorporating a hierarchical pattern the Puritans were attempting to establish a rural feudal order in opposition to the socio-economic fluidity of urban life. Such an interpretation, however, confuses phenomena with conceptions. While the growing mercantilism of the time undoubtedly disturbed old urban patterns, city

dwellers, as Carl Bridenbaugh has noted, were discovering new social distinctions and hierarchies (*Vexed and Troubled Englishmen* [New York: Oxford Univ. Press, 1968], p. 175). By contrast, Renaissance pronouncements about rural life reveal a deemphasis on hierarchy, associating that social pattern with court and city in opposition to the country. As children of the Renaissance and Reformation, Puritans tendentiously reached the same conclusion. For support they turned to John Foxe and John Calvin, the latter of whom spoke of hierarchies as desiderata of urban life and the order and peace of "all commonwealths." "Take these away," wrote Calvin, "and the whole discipline of cities collapses and dissolves" (*Institutes of the Christian Religion*, ed. John T. McNeill, trans. Ford Lewis Battles [Philadelphia: Westminster, 1967], Bk. 4, Chap. 20, Sec. 5).

8 Richard Slotkin, *Regeneration through Violence: The Mythology of the American Frontier, 1600–1860* (Middletown, Conn.: Wesleyan Univ. Press, 1973), p. 68.

9 Fries, *Urban Idea in Colonial America*, pp. 48–50 and 64–65. On the township pattern see also William Haller, Jr., *The Puritan Frontier: Town-Planting in New England Colonial Development* (New York: Columbia Univ. Press, 1951), pp. 27, 36, et passim; and Mumford, *City in History*, p. 232.

10 Quoted in Perry Miller, *The New England Mind: From Colony to Province* (1953; rpt. Cambridge: Harvard Univ. Press, 1966), p. 241.

11 Samuel Danforth, *A Brief Recognition of New England's Errand into the Wilderness* (Cambridge, Mass., 1671), pp. 1–3. On the same idea see Cotton Mather, *Magnalia Christi Americana*, 2 vols. (Hartford, Conn., 1855), 1: 68. Further elaboration of this concept appears in Carroll, *Puritanism and the Wilderness*, pp. 87–107; and Perry Miller, *Errand into the Wilderness* (1956; rpt. Cambridge: Harvard Univ. Press, 1969), pp. 1–22.

12 Mitchell quoted in Carroll, *Puritanism and the Wilderness*, p. 72; C. Mather, *Magnalia*, 1: 46.

13 For statements identifying the discovery and settlement of the Western Hemisphere as a sign of last things, see, for example, Neill, *English Colonization of America*, p. 177n; John Higginson, "An Attestation to the Church History of New England," in C. Mather, *Magnalia*, 1: 13; and Samuel Sewall, *Phaenomena quaedam Apocalyptica* (Boston, 1697), p. 3.

14 Regarding the renewed interest in millennialism resulting from new exegetical techniques, see Ernest Lee Tuveson, *Millennium and Utopia: A*

230

Study in the Background of the Idea of Progress (Berkeley: Univ. of California Press, 1949), pp. 75–78; James West Davidson, The Logic of Millennial Thought (New Haven: Yale Univ. Press, 1977), pp. 43–47; and R. G. Clouse, "The Rebirth of Millenarianism," in Peter Toon, ed., Puritans, the Millennium and the Future of Israel (London: James Clarke, 1970), pp. 42–65. The remark on the eighty books is cited by Toon, "Conclusions," p. 128.

15 Periodically the question has been raised concerning the degree to which seventeenth-century Puritans were premillennialists. Because there are indications that the Puritans believed in their own ability (aided by Providence) to usher in the millennium and because several of the millennialist documents, such as Edward Johnson's Wonder-Working Providence, declaim a spiritual chiliasm rather than a literal one, several historians have argued that these New Englanders cannot be categorized as premillennialists. (See, for example, Francis Bremer, The Puritan Experiment: New England Society from Bradford to Edwards [New York: St. Martin's, 1976], p. 137; David E. Smith, "Millenarian Scholarship in America," American Quarterly, 17 [1965], 535–49; and Joy Bourne Gilsdorf, "The Puritan Apocalypse: New England Eschatology in the Seventeenth Century," Diss. Yale Univ. 1964, passim.) Such conclusions, though, fail to consider that even these millennialist texts, including Johnson's, assert that the millennium is to be preceded by some final, providentially aided upheaval, such as Armageddon. Thus, the New Jerusalem can descend only after the world has undergone a radical extra-human alteration, an essential feature of premillennialism.

16 Johnson, Wonder-Working Providence, pp. 270, 33–35, and 25; Edward R. Lambert, History of the Colony of New Haven (New Haven, 1838), p. 50. Johnson's representativeness is discussed in Sacvan Bercovitch, "The Historiography of Johnson's Wonder-Working Providence," Essex Institute Historical Collections, 104 (1968), 139, and Charles L. Sanford, The Quest for Paradise: Europe and the American Moral Imagination (Urbana: Univ. of Illinois Press, 1961), p. 83.

17 For an illuminating discussion of these early millennialist texts see J. F. Maclear, "New England and the Fifth Monarchy: The Quest for the Millennium in Early American Puritanism," William and Mary Quarterly, 3d ser., 32 (1975), 223–60.

18 Sewall, Dedication "To the Honourable William Stroughton, Esq.," in Phaenomena; Diary, in Massachusetts Historical Society Collections, 5th ser. (Boston, 1878), 5: 340; Sacvan Bercovitch, The Puritan Origins of the American Self (New Haven: Yale Univ. Press, 1975), p. 62. For a

variety of reasons relating to his reading of the prophetic books, Sewall expected the New Jerusalem to descend, not in New England, but in Mexico (see *Phaenomena*, pp. 4–16). The important point, however, is that Sewall believed in the prophetic promise quite literally and did argue that America was to be the location of the renewed metropolis. This conviction and the tradition of imagery surrounding it help explain the somewhat curious tribute to Plum Island in the *Phaenomena* (p. 59). For years critics and historians, while largely ignoring the rest of the text, pointed to it as a sign of a new fondness for nature in New England. More recently, several commentators have argued that the tribute, though eloquent, is essentially insignificant or secondary to the main apocalyptic thrust of the book. But the tribute is neither insignificant nor primary. Rather, Sewall's pastoral depiction must be read in the context of his earlier encomium to the Mexican landscape. Both support his argument that the natural plenty of America testifies to its fitness for becoming the land of milk and honey promised as a concomitant of the millennial Jerusalem.

19 John Davenport, "Epistle to the Reader," in Increase Mather, *The Mystery of Israel's Salvation Explained and Applied* (London, 1669), sig. A5; Thomas Shepard, *The Parable of the Ten Virgins Opened & Applied* (London, 1660).

20 The citations here are from the following works respectively: Increase Mather, *The Day of Trouble is Near* (Cambridge, Mass., 1674), p. 29; Cotton Mather, *Things to be Look'd for* (Boston, 1691), p. 20; C. Mather, *Remarks Upon the Changes of a Dying World* (Boston, 1715), p. 15; C. Mather, *Magnalia*, 1: 46; I. Mather, *The Mystery of Israel's Salvation*, p. 65; I. Mather, *Discourse Concerning Faith and Fervency in Prayer . . .* (Boston, 1710), p. 57; C. Mather, "Triparadisus," MS. American Antiquarian Society, fol. 101; C. Mather, *The Present State of New England* (Boston, 1690), p. 35; C. Mather, *Theopolis Americana*, p. 4; and I. Mather, *A Discourse Concerning the Danger of Apostacy* (Boston, 1685), p. 77. For this summary of the Mathers' millennialism I have drawn on both the works cited above and I. Mather, *Ichabod* (Boston, 1702); I. Mather, *Heavens Alarm to the World* (Boston, 1681); C. Mather, *A Midnight Cry* (Boston, 1692); C. Mather, *Diary*, in Massachusetts Historical Society Collections, 7th ser. (Boston, 1912), 8: 54, 733, and 804; and Robert Middlekauff, *The Mathers: Three Generations of Puritan Intellectuals* (New York: Oxford Univ. Press, 1971), pp. 179–87 and 320–49.

21 C. Mather, *Magnalia*, 1: 330–31. Sacvan Bercovitch has argued, quite correctly I believe, that the entire *Magnalia* functions as an apocalyptic-

232

millennialist text which looks to the past glories of New England while tracing its movement toward cataclysm and the future glory promised for its chosen saints (*The American Jeremiad* [Madison: Univ. of Wisconsin Press, 1978], pp. 86–87).

22 *The Necessity of Reformation With the Expedients subservient thereunto, asserted,* Declaration of the Synod of Boston in 1679, in Williston Walker, ed., *The Creeds and Platforms of Congregationalism* (1893; rpt. Boston: Pilgrim Press, 1960), pp. 423–24; Robert G. Pope, *The Half-Way Covenant: Church Membership in Puritan New England* (Princeton: Princeton Univ. Press, 1969), pp. 236–38.

23 For the clergy's reticence on this subject see Mason I. Lowance, Jr., *The Language of Canaan: Metaphor and Symbol in New England from the Puritans to the Transcendentalists* (Cambridge: Harvard Univ. Press, 1980), pp. 57–63.

24 C. Mather, *Maganalia,* 1: 63.

25 Mather quoted in Sacvan Bercovitch, "Images of Myself: Cotton Mather in His Writings, 1683–1700," in Everett Emerson, ed., *Major Writers of Early American Literature* (Madison: Univ. of Wisconsin Press, 1972), p. 109.

26 Darrett Rutman, *Winthrop's Boston: Portrait of a Puritan Town* (Chapel Hill: Univ. of North Carolina Press, 1965), pp. 27–28 and 280–83.

27 William Hubbard, *A General History of New England,* in Massachusetts Historical Society Collections, 22d ser. (Boston, 1815), 6: 305.

28 Josselyn cited in Bernard Bailyn, *The New England Merchants in the Seventeenth Century* (1955; rpt. New York: Harper & Row, 1964), p. 97; Rutman, *Winthrop's Boston,* pp. 200 and 279.

29 Thomas Walley, *Balm in Gilead to Heal Sions Wounds* (Cambridge, Mass., 1669), pp. 8–9; Increase Mather, *Two Sermons Testifying Against the Sin of Drunkenness* (Cambridge, Mass., 1673), sig. A2; Bridenbaugh, *Cities in the Wilderness,* pp. 22, 97, and 387; Bailyn, *New England Merchants in the Seventeenth Century.*

30 C. Mather, *Diary,* 8: 451; Bailyn, *New England Merchants in the Seventeenth Century,* pp. 112–13; Bridenbaugh, *Cities in the Wilderness,* p. 70.

31 "Some Observations of God's Merciful Dealing with Us . . . ," in *The Collected Verse of William Bradford,* ed. Michael G. Runyan (St. Paul, Minn.: Colet, 1974), p. 224, lines 282–83.

32 Bradford, *Collected Verse,* pp. 166–73, lines 9–12, 13, and 16.

33 C. Mather, *Magnalia,* 1: 98, 103, 102, 121, and 296.

34 Stoddard's remark on King Philip's War is quoted in Perry Miller, "Solomon Stoddard, 1643–1729," *Harvard Theological Review,* 34 (1941),

281; Solomon Stoddard, *An Answer to Some Cases of Conscience Respecting the Country*, in *Magazine of History*, 14 (1917), 191.

35 Urian Oakes, *New-England Pleaded With* (Cambridge, Mass., 1673), p. 36; C. Mather, *Magnalia*, 2: 490.

36 Bailyn, *New England Merchants of the Seventeenth Century*, pp. 54, 98, and 112; Richard Bushman, *From Puritan to Yankee: Character and the Social Order in Connecticut, 1690–1765* (1967; rpt. New York: Norton, 1970), pp. 55–58 and 81; Michael Zuckerman, *Peaceable Kingdoms: New England Towns in the Eighteenth Century* (New York: Knopf, 1970), pp. 15, 18, 38, and 47; T. H. Breen, "Persistent Localism: English Social Change and the Shaping of New England Institutions," *William and Mary Quarterly*, 3d ser., 32 (1975), 3–28. The declaration of the General Court appears in C. Mather, *Magnalia*, 2: 335.

37 Miller, *Nature's Nation*, p. 48; see also Breen, "Persistent Localism," p. 21; and Zuckerman, *Peaceable Kingdoms*, p. 34. For a discussion of the Mather-Stoddard debate consult Miller, "Solomon Stoddard," pp. 299–316; and *New England Mind: From Colony to Province*, pp. 256–61 and 276–87.

38 Shepard, *Parable of the Ten Virgins*, pp. 15 and 28–29; C. Mather, *Things to be Look'd for*, pp. 52 and 56.

39 Davidson, *Logic of Millennial Thought*, p. 15.

40 C. Mather, *Diary*, 8: 733; John Colman, *The Distressed State of the Town of Boston Considered* (Boston, 1720); C. Mather, "Triparadisus," fols. 55 and 56.

41 Davidson, *Logic of Millennial Thought*, pp. 218–25 et passim; H. Richard Niebuhr, *The Kingdom of God in America* (1935; rpt. Hamden, Conn.: Shoe String, 1956), p. 148.

Chapter III. Civilization and the Order of Nature

1 R. G. Collingwood, *The Idea of Nature* (Oxford: Clarendon, 1945), pp. 8–11; Becker, *Heavenly City of the Eighteenth-Century Philosophers*, p. 51; "Epistle Intended for Sir Isaac Newton," in *The Poems of Alexander Pope*, ed. John Butt et al., Twickenham Edition (London: Methuen; New Haven: Yale Univ. Press, 1939–69), 6: 317.

2 Charron and Cumberland quoted in Lois Whitney, *Primitivism and the Idea of Progress* (Baltimore: Johns Hopkins Univ. Press, 1934), pp. 8 and 25.

3 Tindall quoted in Whitney, *Primitivism and the Idea of Progress*, p. 24; Becker, *Heavenly City of the Eighteenth-Century Philosophers*, p. 103. For

234

a discussion of Locke's influence on the English deists see John Orr, *English Deism: Its Roots and Its Fruits* (Grand Rapids, Mich.: Eerdmans, 1934), pp. 83–113.

4 Robert Nisbet, *History of the Idea of Progress* (New York: Basic Books, 1980); Leibniz quoted in Whitney, *Primitivism and the Idea of Progress*, p. xvii. Though its ideas largely have been superseded, see also J. B. Bury, *The Idea of Progress: An Inquiry into Its Origins and Growth* (London: Macmillan, 1920). For additional discussions of progressive inclinations in the thought of antiquity and the Middle Ages consult Ludwig Edelstein, *The Idea of Progress in Classical Antiquity* (Baltimore: Johns Hopkins Univ. Press, 1967); and Etienne Gilson, *The Spirit of Medieval Philosophy* (New York: Scribner's, 1936).

5 It should be noted, however, that the gap between millennialism and progressivism was not nearly as great as this discussion might imply. Rather, the idea of progress seems to have evolved in part from millennianist speculation. See Nisbet, *History of the Idea of Progress*, pp. 124–39; and Tuveson, *Millennium and Utopia*.

6 Perry Miller and Thomas H. Johnson, eds., *The Puritans*, rev. ed. (1938; rpt. New York: Harper & Row, 1963), pp. 47–48. I. Woodbridge Riley, *American Thought from Puritanism to Pragmatism*, 2d ed. (New York: Holt, 1923), p. 77. This does not mean that New England lagged behind the colonies to the south in exposure to the new sciences. On the contrary, interest in New England seems to have been keener, with someone like Cotton Mather actually being a member of the Royal Society. The main difference is that in New England the findings of the new science were synchronized with the dominant theology, thus retarding major transformation. See Miller, *New England Mind: From Colony to Province*, Chap. 26; and Middlekauff, *Mathers*, pp. 279–304.

7 "Letter from the Councill and Company of the hounourable Plantation of Virginia to the Lord Mayor, Aldermen and Companies of London," in Alexander Brown, ed., *The Genesis of the United States* (Boston, 1891), p. 253; *The New Life of Virginia*, p. 19, in *Tracts and Other Papers*, Vol. 1; Alexander Whitaker, *Good News from Virginia* (London, 1613), p. 23. On the religious role in southern colonization see Perry Miller, "Religion and Society in the Early Literature of Virginia," in *Errand into the Wilderness*, pp. 99–140; and Thomas Hall, *The Religious Background of American Culture* (Boston: Little, Brown, 1930), pp. 110–26.

8 Robert Beverley, *The History and Present State of Virginia*, ed. Louis B. Wright (Chapel Hill: Univ. of North Carolina Press, 1947), pp. 16 and 66.

9 Beverley, *History and Present State of Virginia*, pp. 86 and 57–58.

10 Beverley, *History and Present State of Virginia*, pp. 87–88 and 105.

11 Fries, *Urban Idea in Colonial America*, pp. 111–12; Louis Wright, "Robert Beverley II: Historian and Iconoclast," in *The First Gentlemen of Virginia* (1940; rpt. Charlottesville: Univ. of Virginia Press, 1964), p. 292. The statement by the commissioners appears in Edward M. Riley, "The Town Acts of Colonial Virginia," *Journal of Southern History*, 16 (1950), 321.

12 Beverley, *History and Present State of Virginia*, pp. 136, 146, 296, and 316.

13 Beverley, *History and Present State of Virginia*, p. 319.

14 Francis Makamie, *A Plain & Friendly Perswasive to the Inhabitants of Virginia and Maryland for Promoting Towns & Cohabitation*, in *Virginia Magazine of History and Biography*, 4 (1896–97), 262. For a reading of Beverley's *History* as an expression of the purely pastoral ideal see Marx, *Machine in the Garden*, pp. 75–88.

15 Beverley, *History and Present State of Virginia*, pp. 174–77.

16 Cadwallader Colden, *The History of the Five Indian Nations* . . . (Ithaca, N.Y.: Cornell Univ. Press, 1964), pp. xx-xxi.

17 To underscore Beverley's departure from the common assumptions of the previous century on this matter, compare his remarks with those of the Puritan John Eliot, who wrote in 1661 that the Indians were in "the condition of Barbarians, who are not yet come in either by themselves, or their Progenitors," to a civilized state and due form of "Government of the Lord" (*The Christian Commonwealth*, in Massachusetts Historical Society Collections, 3d ser. [Boston, 1846], 9: 146).

18 Beverley, *History and Present State of Virginia*, p. 233.

19 *The Complete Works of Ralph Waldo Emerson*, ed. E. W. Emerson (Boston: Houghton Mifflin, 1903), 1: 365.

20 *An Inquiry into the Original of Our Ideas of Beauty and Virtue*, Vol. 1 of *Collected Works of Francis Hutcheson*, ed. Bernard Fabian (Hildesheim, Germany: Olms, 1971); A. O. Lovejoy, " 'Nature' as Aesthetic Norm" and "The Chinese Origins of a Romanticism," *Essays in the History of Ideas* (Baltimore: Johns Hopkins Univ. Press, 1948), pp. 69–77 and 99–135; Edward Malins, *English Landscape and Literature*, 1660–1800 (London: Oxford Univ. Press, 1966).

21 Addison quoted in Maynard Mack, *The Garden and the City: Retirement and Politics in the Later Poetry of Pope* (Toronto: Univ. of Toronto Press, 1969), p. 24; Adam Smith, *An Inquiry into the Nature and Causes of the Wealth of Nations*, ed. Edwin Cannan (New York: Random House, 1937), Bk. 3, Chaps. 1 and 4; Paul H. Johnstone, "In Praise of Husban-

236

dry," *Agricultural History*, 11 (1937), 80–95; A. Whitney Griswold, *Farming and Democracy* (New York: Harcourt, Brace, 1948), p. 21 et passim; Marx, *Machine in the Garden*, pp. 88–103.

22 *The Writings of Benjamin Franklin*, ed. Albert H. Smyth (New York: Macmillan, 1906), 10: 117–18; *The Poems of Philip Freneau*, ed. Fred Lewis Pattee (Princeton: University Library, 1902–7), 3: 381–94, lines 2, 26, and 81–82; *The Writings of Thomas Jefferson*, ed. H. A. Washington (New York, 1853–54), 1: 403; Griswold, *Farming and Democracy*, pp. 14–15 and 36–37.

23 Freneau, *Poems*, 2: 380; Franklin, *Writings*, 9: 245–46; William D. Liddle, "Virtue and Liberty: An Inquiry into the Role of the Agrarian Myth in the Rhetoric of the American Revolutionary Era," *South Atlantic Quarterly*, 77 (1978), 15–38.

24 E. A. Gutkind, *Urban Development in Western Europe*, Vols. 5 and 6 of *International History of City Development* (New York: Free Press; London: Collier-Macmillan, 1964–72); U.S. Bureau of the Census, *A Century of Population Growth . . . 1790–1900* (Washington, D.C.: GPO, 1909), p. 11; Bureau of the Census, *Historical Statistics of the United States: Colonial Times to 1790* (Washington, D.C.: GPO, 1975), pp. 3 and 11–12. The figures 24 and 200,000 in all likelihood are misleadingly low because so many towns in 1790 were not incorporated. Census figures for that year, in fact, suggest that there were at minimum an additional 110 unincorporated towns with populations of 2,500 or greater (*Century of Population Growth*, pp. 188–200).

25 The Baltimore resident is quoted anonymously in Bridenbaugh, *Cities in Revolt*, p. 215.

26 For a discussion of the concept of civilization and its currency in America, see Charles A. Beard and Mary Beard, *The American Spirit*, Vol. 4 of *The Rise of American Civilization* (1942; rpt. New York: Macmillan, 1948); Chipman quoted in Rosenthal, *City of Nature*, p. 175.

27 Whitney, *Primitivism and the Idea of Progress*, passim.

28 Pope, "Epistle to Bathurst" and "Epistle to Burlington," in *Poems*, 3: 72–121 and 123–51; Richard Feingold, *Nature and Society: Later Eighteenth-Century Uses of the Pastoral and Georgic* (New Brunswick, N.J.: Rutgers Univ. Press, 1978), pp. 30–38; Max Byrd, *London Transformed: Images of the City in the Eighteenth Century* (New Haven: Yale Univ. Press, 1978), pp. 31–49.

29 John Dyer, "The Fleece," in *Poems*, 1761 (Menston, England: Scolar, 1971), pp. 51–188, lines 165–84, 306, 309–10, and 316–20; Feingold, *Nature and Society*, pp. 83–119.

30 Smith, *Wealth of Nations*, 3: 1 and 4; Arthur Young, "Importance of London to National Husbandry," *Annals of Agriculture*, 23 (1795), 271–73; Paolo Balsamo, "Thoughts on Great Cities," *Annals of Agriculture*, 13 (1790), 465–82.

31 Gutkind, *Urban Development in Western Europe*, 5: 131 and 262–63; Warwick Wroth, *The London Pleasure Gardens of the Eighteenth Century* (London, 1896); "Description of a City Shower," in *The Poems of Jonathan Swift*, ed. Harold Williams (Oxford: Clarendon, 1937), p. 139, lines 61–62.

32 Griswold, *Farming and Democracy*, pp. 50–51; Médéric Louis Elie Moreau de St. Méry, *American Journey*, trans. and ed. Kenneth Roberts and Anna M. Roberts (Garden City, N.Y.: Doubleday, 1947), p. 265. On the monstrous image of London at this time see Raymond Williams, *The Country and the City* (New York: Oxford Univ. Press, 1973), p. 146.

33 "Views of Great Cities," *London Magazine*, 28 (1759), 202.

34 Moreau de St. Méry, *American Journey*, pp. 168, 147, 77, and 79; *Colonial Panorama: Dr. Robert Honyman's Journal for March and April, 1775*, ed. Philip Padelford (San Marino, Cal.: Huntington Library, 1939), pp. 22 and 49.

35 Frances Wright, *Views of Society and Manners in America*, ed. Paul R. Baker (Cambridge: Harvard Univ. Press, 1963), pp. 249 and 13; A. Levasseur, *Lafayette in America in 1824 and 1825*, rpt. in part in Blake McKelvey, comp., *The City in American History* (London: Allen and Unwin; New York: Barnes and Noble, 1969), pp. 136–37.

36 Hector St. John de Crèvecoeur, *Letters from an American Farmer and Sketches of Eighteenth-Century America* (New York: New American Library, 1963), Letter 3, p. 65, and Letter 1, pp. 36–37.

37 Crèvecoeur, Letter 3, p. 75; Letter 2, p. 48; Letter 12, p. 195; Letter 1, p. 41.

38 Crèvecoeur, Letter 12, pp. 211 and 199–200.

39 Within the past fifteen years, students of Crèvecoeur increasingly have pointed out the ironic qualifications surrounding James and have asserted, quite correctly, that he is only a persona. While a few have gone so far as to call James an "incorrigible idealist and moral coward" and Crèvecoeur's "straw man," most critics now agree that Crèvecoeur uses the farmer's plight to undermine Enlightenment assumptions and assert the failure of the American ideal (see, for example, Elayne Antler Rapping, "Theory and Experience in Crèvecoeur's America," *American Quarterly*, 19 [1967], 707–18; Thomas Philbrick, *St. John de Crèvecoeur* [New York: Twayne, 1970], pp. 74–88; and Mary E. Rucker, "Crève-

238

coeur's *Letters* and Enlightenment Doctrine," *Early American Literature,* 13 [1978], 193–212). Unfortunately these revisionist efforts, in attempting to compensate for earlier simplistic responses to the *Letters,* have gone to the other extreme in arguing for a tidy ironic dichotomy between James and his creator. Assuming such a categorical distinction, however, ignores the function of the farmer as a persona—that is, as a literary device which embodies a perspective analogous to though different from the author's. Although qualifying Farmer James's suppositions, Crèvecoeur, as I argue, does not repudiate but redefines them.

40 Crèvecoeur, Letter 3, pp. 60 and 74.

41 Crèvecoeur, *Sketches,* Chap. 4, p. 299; Chap. 1, pp. 238–39. Although the letters published in 1925 as *Sketches* were written concurrently with those published in 1782 and though five of the former were included in the 1784 and 1787 French editions of the *Letters,* a substantial difference exists between the narrator of the *Sketches* and Farmer James. As Thomas Philbrick points out, the farmer of the *Sketches* "is a James *manqué,* a characterization . . . between the plowman of reality and the farmer of feelings" (*St. John de Crèvecoeur,* p. 113). That is, the narrator of the *Sketches* adopts a rationalistic, realistic response to agriculture characteristic of Crèvecoeur himself.

42 Albert E. Stone, Jr., Forward, in Crèvecoeur, *Letters,* p. xvi.

43 Several points need to be made regarding the narrator of Letters 4 through 8. Although recognizing narrative voice in the *Letters* as belonging to a persona, critics generally assume that, except in Letter 11, which Crèvecoeur explicitly attributes to one Ivan Al—z, the voice is consistent and belongs to James. Only Russel Nye ("Michael-Guillaume St. Jean de Crèvecoeur: *Letters from an American Farmer,*" in Hennig Cohen, ed., *Landmarks of American Writing* [New York: Basic Books, 1969], p. 35) and Mary Rucker have noted a shift in Letter 4, asserting that with that letter Crèvecoeur himself replaces the farmer as narrator. While Nye does not elaborate on what allows us to recognize that alteration, Rucker writes that "the depth of intellection and breadth of subject matter" in the letters on Nantucket and Martha's Vineyard indicate that the speaker is Crèvecoeur ("Crèvecoeur's *Letters* and Enlightenment Doctrine," p. 199). Insofar as they recognize the narrative displacement, these observations accord with my position, though they oversimplify by ignoring the text's literary, fictive status. Just as we would not equate author and narrator in an eighteenth-century epistolary novel, so must we understand that the narrator of Letters 4 through 8 is not Crèvecoeur

but another persona. The confusion results from the fact that the narrator of this section is much more credible than James. While the farmer and his exclusively rural vision are finally undermined, no such qualification encumbers this second persona. Consequently, his position, we can reasonably assume, more closely parallels Crèvecoeur's. But the two men are not the same, and assuming that they are fails to appreciate Crèvecoeur's effective manipulation of perspective. In the following discussion I assume such a distinction, though for convenience I refer to this second persona as "Crèvecoeur."

44 Crèvecoeur, Letter 4, p. 106; Letter 8, p. 152.

45 Crèvecoeur, Letter 4, pp. 104–9; Letter 7, p. 140.

46 Bridenbaugh, *Cities in Revolt*, p. 3n; Crèvecoeur, Letter 5, p. 125.

47 Crèvecoeur, Letter 4, pp. 104–7 and 119; Letter 8, p. 149.

48 Crèvecoeur, Letter 4, p. 119; Letter 8, p. 159.

49 Crèvecoeur, Letter 6, p. 137; Letter 8, p. 154.

50 Crèvecoeur, Letter 9, pp. 160–63; Letter 7, p. 141.

51 Jean Beranger, "The Desire for Communication: Narrator and Narratee in *Letters from an American Farmer,*" *Early American Literature*, 12 (1977), 81.

52 Crèvecoeur, Letter 13, p. 195. Cecelia Tichi, *New World, New Earth: Environmental Reform in American Literature from the Puritans through Whitman* (New Haven: Yale Univ. Press, 1979), pp. 103–5, also argues that Crèvecoeur looked beyond an exclusively agrarian America to champion urban development and social change in his unpublished essay "The Rock of Lisbon."

53 *Gentleman's Progress: The Itinerarium of Dr. Alexander Hamilton*, 1744, ed. Carl Bridenbaugh (Chapel Hill: Univ. of North Carolina Press, 1948), p. 54.

54 Hamilton, *Itinerarium*, pp. 3, 16, and 55–56.

55 Hamilton, *Itinerarium*, pp. 65, 165–66, 107, 41, and 18.

56 Hamilton, *Itinerarium*, pp. 18 and 44.

57 Quoted in Christopher Tunnard and Henry Hope Reed, *American Skyline: The Growth and Form of Our Cities and Towns* (1953; rpt. New York: New American Library, 1956), p. 56.

58 For a full discussion of the developments leading to the choice of the Federal City's location see Wilhelmus Bryan, *A History of the National Capital* (New York: Macmillan, 1914), Vol. 1, Chaps. 1, 2, and 6; and John Reps, *Monumental Washington: The Planning and Development of the Capital Center* (Princeton: Princeton Univ. Press, 1967), pp. 1–5.

59 L'Enfant to Jefferson, 11 March 1791, in Saul K. Padover, ed., *Thomas Jefferson and the National Capital* (Washington, D.C.: GPO, 1946), p. 47; L'Enfant to Hamilton quoted in Elizabeth S. Kite, *L'Enfant and Washington, 1791–1792* (New York: Arno and New York Times Books, 1970), p. 16; L'Enfant, "Letter to the Commissioners," pp. 398 and 406.

60 William Penn, "Some Account of the Province of Pennsylvania," in Albert Cook Meyer, ed., *Narratives of Early Pennsylvania West New Jersey and Delaware*, in *Original Narratives of Early American History* (New York: Scribner's, 1912), 13: 205; Penn, *Fruits of Solitude* (Chicago: Donnelley, 1906), p. 51.

61 The best case is made by Fries, who compares Holme's plan to Penn's 1681 "Instructions" for laying out the town and argues that Penn "did not in fact anticipate an urban place but rather the recovery of a [rural] world rapidly receding into the memories of many Englishmen" (*Urban Idea in Colonial America*, pp. 79ff.). For a contrary view consult Reps, *Making of Urban America*, pp. 158ff.

62 William Penn, "Letter to the Committee of the Free Society of Trades," in *Narratives of Early Pennsylvania West New Jersey and Delaware*, p. 243; Glaab and Brown, *History of Urban America*, pp. 6–7.

63 L'Enfant to Jefferson, 26 February 1792, in Kite, *L'Enfant and Washington*, p. 150. On L'Enfant's background see Caemmerer, *Life of Pierre Charles L'Enfant*, pp. 1–13; and Reps, *Monumental Washington*, pp. 5–9.

64 Kite, *L'Enfant and Washington*, pp. 36–37 and 15; Penn, "Letter to the Committee," pp. 239–40; Tichi, *New World, New Earth*, p. 70.

65 Kite, *L'Enfant and Washington*, pp. 47–48 and 63–64.

66 Pierre Charles L'Enfant, "Observations Explanatory of the Plan [of the Federal City]," in Kite, *L'Enfant and Washington*, pp. 62–65; "Letter to the Commissioners," p. 401; L'Enfant's remarks on the presidential house appear in Kite, p. 18. The relation between landscape theory and L'Enfant's concern with prospects and vistas in the city is discussed by J. P. Dougherty, "Baroque and Picturesque Motifs in L'Enfant's Design for the Federal Capital," *American Quarterly*, 26 (1974), 32–36.

67 L'Enfant, "Letter to the Commissioners," p. 400; "Report to Washington," circa June 1791, in Kite, *L'Enfant and Washington*, p. 54.

68 L'Enfant, "Memorials," in Columbia Historical Society Records, 2 (1899), 83. L'Enfant's remark on the democratic symbolism of his plan is quoted in Mumford, *City in History*, p. 403.

69 Reps, *Making of Urban America*, p. 263; Tunnard and Reed, *American Skyline*, p. 54; Caemmerer, *Life of Pierre Charles L'Enfant*, pp. 338–45.

70 "Account of the Federal Procession," *Columbian Magazine*, 2 (1788), 396–400.

71 Philip Freneau, "The Rising Glory of America" (1809 version), in *Poems*, 1: 71, lines 282–88.

72 Philip Freneau, "The Rising Glory of America" (1772 version), in *Poems*, 1: 59–60, lines 197 and 214–16.

73 Freneau, "Rising Glory" (1772), p. 74, lines 538–41; p. 77, lines 609–12; and pp. 80–81, lines 676–82.

74 David Humphreys, "Future State of the Western Territory," in *The Columbian Muse* (Philadelphia, 1794), p. 164, lines 110, 112, and 87–92. Significantly, Humphrey's word are almost a verbatim borrowing of lines from Pope's *Windsor-Forest*.

75 Jefferson, *Writings*, 4: 572; Lattimore quoted in Reps, *Making of Urban America*, p. 321; Bridenbaugh, *Cities in Revolt*, pp. 244–45, 339–40, et passim.

76 Franklin to Mathew Carey, 16 August 1786, in *Writings*, 9: 533–34. For a discussion of Franklin's revisions and his role in the decision to publish the uncompleted *Autobiography* see Max Farrand, Introduction, *Benjamin Franklin's Memoirs: A Parallel Text Edition* (Berkeley: Univ. of California Press, 1949); and Bruce Granger, *Benjamin Franklin: An American Man of Letters* (Ithaca, N.Y.: Cornell Univ. Press, 1964), pp. 214–17.

77 Robert Sayre, *The Examined Self: Benjamin Franklin, Henry Adams, Henry James* (Princeton: Princeton Univ. Press, 1964), p. 6; *The Autobiography of Benjamin Franklin*, ed. Leonard W. Labaree et al. (New Haven: Yale Univ. Press, 1964), p. 135.

78 Hugh Dawson, "Fathers and Sons: Franklin's 'Memoirs' as Myth and Metaphor," *Early American Literature*, 14 (1979–80), 270–72. Concerning Locke's early influence on Franklin see Arthur Bernon Tourtellot, *Benjamin Franklin: The Shaping of Genius: The Early Years* (Garden City, N.Y.: Doubleday, 1977), pp. 212–19.

79 Franklin, *Autobiography*, pp. 95–107 and 70.

80 Franklin, *Autobiography*, pp. 54 and 51.

81 Franklin, *Autobiography*, pp. 72–75.

82 Franklin, *Writings*, 3: 73.

83 Franklin, *Autobiography*, pp. 75–78.

84 On the tone of the *Autobiography* see, for example, Robert H. Bell, "Benjamin Franklin's 'Perfect Character,' " *Eighteenth-Century Life*, 5, No. 2 (Winter 1978), 23.

85 Franklin, *Autobiography*, p. 111.

242

86 Peter Gay, "The Enlightenment," in C. Vann Woodward, ed., *The Comparative Approach to American History* (New York: Basic Books, 1968), p. 41.

87 Franklin, *Autobiography*, pp. 125–26 and 164.

88 Rex Burns, *Success in America: The Yeoman Dream and the Industrial Revolution* (Amherst: Univ. of Massachusetts Press, 1976), p. 1; Franklin, *Autobiography*, pp. 148–56.

89 Norman Fiering, "Benjamin Franklin and the Way to Virtue," *American Quarterly*, 30 (1978), 219; Franklin, *Autobiography*, pp. 149–57.

90 Franklin, *Autobiography*, pp. 171–75, 181–87, 195, and 202–4.

91 Freneau, *Poems*, 2: 227; Thomas Pownall, *Memorial* (London, 1783), pp. 137–38; Franklin, *Writings*, 3: 50 and 6: 395.

Chapter IV. Landscape as Cityscape

1 Emerson, *Works*, 1: 371; Mills quoted in Helen Marr Gallagher, *Robert Mills: Architect of the Washington Monument, 1781–1855* (New York: Columbia Univ. Press, 1935), p. 156; "Great Cities," *Putnam's*, 5 (January–July 1855), 254–63.

2 Census Bureau, *Historical Statistics*, pp. 11–12; Superintendent of the United States Census, *Statistical View of the United States . . . Beginning with 1790* (Washington, D.C., 1854), pp. 192–93; Jeffrey G. Williamson and Joseph A. Swanson, "The Growth of Cities in the American Northeast, 1820–1870," *Explorations in Entrepreneurial History*, 2d ser., 4 (Supplement 1966), 3–101. Although the rise in urbanization was most pronounced in the Northeast, the South also experienced a substantial increase in the number and size of its cities. From 1790 to 1850 southerners watched the number of places with 2,500 or more rise from 5 to 41. Of this total in 1850, 10 cities contained over 10,000 inhabitants, and New Orleans, with 116,000, stood as the fifth largest city in America (T. Lynn Smith, "The Emergence of Cities," in Rupert B. Vance and Nicholas J. Demerath, eds., *The Urban South*, [1954; rpt. Freeport, N.Y.: Books for Libraries, 1971], p. 28). Such statistics indicate that we cannot think of this period as one marked by a simple dichotomy of agrarian South versus urban North. The growth of cities was a pervasive phenomenon significantly altering the contours of the entire American scene.

3 Amory Mayo, *Symbols of the Capital; or, Civilization in New York* (New York, 1859), pp. 12 and 20; Edwin Chapin, *Moral Aspects of City Life*, 2d ed. (New York, 1854), p. 42.

4 Fitz-Hugh Ludlow, "The American Metropolis," *Atlantic Monthly*, 15 (January–June 1865), 75–77.

5 Charles Caldwell, "Thoughts on the Moral and Other Indirect Influences of Rail-Roads," *New England Magazine*, 2 (1832), 291–92; *Report of Israel D. Andrews, on the Trade and Commerce of the British North American Colonies* (Washington, D.C., 1853), rpt. in part in Charles Glaab, ed., *The American City: A Documentary History* (Homewood, Ill.: Dorsey, 1963), pp. 71–79.

6 "Cities and Parks," *Atlantic Monthly*, 7 (January–June 1861), 418.

7 Mayo, *Symbols of the Capital*, pp. 40–43.

8 "Cities and Parks," p. 420; Chapin, *Moral Aspects of City Life*, pp. 14 and 19; Chapin, *Humanity in the City* (1854; rpt. New York: Arno, 1974), p. 22.

9 Glaab and Brown, *History of Urban America*, pp. 84, 94, 95, and 161; Eliot quoted in Theodore Hammett, "Two Mobs of Jacksonian Boston: Ideology and Interest," *Journal of American History*, 62 (1975–76), 845.

10 Wortman, "Domesticating the Nineteenth-Century American City," p. 534; Glaab and Brown, *History of Urban America*, pp. 86–87; "Cities and Parks," p. 416.

11 Chapin, *Moral Aspects of City Life*, pp. 177–78.

12 *The Diary of Philip Hone*, ed. Allan Nevins (New York: Dodd, Mead, 1927), 2: 785; Kimball quoted in Bender, *Toward an Urban Vision*, p. 108; "Our New Atlantis," *Putnam's*, 5 (January–July 1855), 379.

13 *The Letters of Ralph Waldo Emerson*, ed. Ralph L. Rusk (New York: Columbia Univ. Press, 1966), 1: 350; "Present Population and Future Prospects of the Western Country," *Western Monthly Review*, 1 (May 1827–April 1828), 332. In his study of antebellum popular thought, Lewis O. Saum has argued that because only a few of the letters and diaries written by average Americans at this time use the phrase "garden of the world" to describe the tramontane region, that image of the West was not widely held (*The Popular Mood of Pre–Civil War America* [Westport, Conn.: Greenwood, 1980], pp. 201–5). Though Saum may be correct in part, what he fails to recognize is that the reappearance of this exact wording, even in the few instances he cites, suggests the idea was well enough established to serve as a catch phrase in the vocabularly of common people.

14 Superintendent of the Census, *Statistical View*, p. 192. The reporter is quoted in Glaab and Brown, *History of Urban America*, p. 33.

15 John Greenleaf Whittier, *The Stranger in Lowell* (Boston, 1845), p. 136; "Great Cities," pp. 255–56; Smith, *Virgin Land*, pp. 253–60.

16 The best discussion of Scott's thought appears in Charles Glaab, "Jesup W. Scott and a West of Cities," *Ohio History*, 73 (1964), 3–12; but see also, Smith, *Virgin Land*, pp. 183–86.

17 Jesup Scott, "Internal Trade," *The Hesperian, or Western Monthly Magazine*, 2 (November 1838– April 1839), 42–49.

18 Jesup Scott, "Internal Trade of the United States," *Hunt's Merchants' Magazine*, 9 (July–December 1843), 31–37. See also Scott's "The Progress of the West," *Hunt's*, 14 (January–July 1846), 163–65; and "Westward the Star of Empire," *DeBow's Review*, 27 (July–December 1859), 125–36.

19 Smith, *Virgin Land*, pp. 38–44. The only modern, full-length study of Gilpin's life and thought is Thomas Karnes, *William Gilpin: Western Nationalist* (Austin: Univ. of Texas Press, 1970); but consult also Charles Glaab, "Visions of Metropolis: William Gilpin and Theories of City Growth in the American West," *Wisconsin Magazine of History*, 45 (1961–62), 21–31.

20 William Gilpin, *Central Gold Region* (Philadelphia, 1860), pp. 120, 35–36, 20, 82, and 131–33.

21 Gilpin, *Central Gold Region*, p. 20.

22 Gilpin, *Central Gold Region*, pp. 132–33, and 127.

23 Daniel Drake, *Natural and Statistical View; or, Picture of Cincinnati and the Miami Country* (Cincinnati, 1815), pp. 226 and 26.

24 Drake, *Natural and Statistical View*, pp. 228 and 231; *Pittsburgh Mercury* quoted in Richard C. Wade, *The Urban Frontier: The Rise of Western Cities, 1790–1830* (Cambridge: Harvard Univ. Press, 1959), pp. 322–23; Ben Casseday, *The History of Louisville from Its Earliest Settlement till the Year 1852* (Louisville, 1852), pp. 15 and 252.

25 S. Waterhouse, "Missouri—St. Louis, the Commercial Center of North America," *Hunt's Merchant's Magazine*, 55 (1866), 53–61; William Bross, *History of Chicago: Historical and Commercial Statistics . . . Republished from the* Daily Democratic Press [from 1852 to 1876] (Chicago, 1876), pp. 6–7; Charles C. Spalding, *Annals of the City of Kansas* (Kansas City, 1859), pp. 28 and 111.

26 Timothy Flint, *A Condensed Geography and History of the Western States or Mississippi Valley*, 2 vols. (Gainesville, Fla.: Scholars' Facsimiles & Reprints, 1970), 2: 157–58.

27 Drake, *Natural and Statistical View*, p. 227; Gilpin, *Central Gold Region*, p. 103.

28 Glaab, "Jesup W. Scott," p. 3; C. W. Dana, *The Great West; or, The Garden of the World* (Philadelphia, 1857), pp. 172–73.

29 Lane quoted in Wade, *Urban Frontier*, p. 270.

30 Jesup Scott, "Our American Lake Cities," *Hunt's Merchants' Magazine*, 31 (July–December 1854), 410–12; "The Growth of Cities in the United States," *Western Journal and Civilian*, 5 (October 1850–March 1851), 284–85; Bross, *History of Chicago*, p. 66.

31 Dana, *Great West*, pp. 173–74; John Peyton, *Over the Alleghenies*, rpt. in part in Warren S. Tryon, ed., *A Mirror for Americans* (Chicago: Univ. of Chicago Press, 1952), 3: 605; Charles Hoffman, *A Winter in the West*, rpt. in part in *Mirror for Americans*, 3: 551–52; Timothy Flint, *Recollections of the Last Ten Years*, ed. C. Hartley Grattan (New York: Knopf, 1932), pp. 20–21; "Beautiful Description of Cincinnati," *Western Monthly Review and Literary Journal*, 1 (1836), 285.

32 "Chicago," *Western Monthly Review and Literary Journal*, 1 (1836), 247; "Pittsburgh: Its Trade and Manufactures," *Hunt's Merchants' Magazine*, 17 (July–December 1847), 589–90; Cassedy, *History of Louisville*, pp. 210–15.

33 "Pittsburgh: Its Trade and Manufactures," p. 591.

34 Sara Lippincott, *New Life in New Lands*, rpt. in part in *Mirror for Americans*, 3: 646.

Chapter V. Organic Cities

1 Quoted in Wade, *Urban Frontier*, p. 319.

2 Emerson, *Journals*, 3: 286.

3 "Cities and Parks," p. 416. On the Jeffersonian undergirdings of antebellum urban reform see Albert Fein, "The American City: The Ideal and the Real," in Edgar Kaufmann, Jr., ed., *The Rise of American Architecture* (New York: Praeger, 1970), pp. 51 and 79.

4 Horace Bushnell, "City Plans," in *Work and Play; or, Literary Varieties* (New York, 1864), pp. 333 and 336. For a discussion of contemporary scientific theories concerning the need for fresh air and greenery in cities see Glaab and Brown, *History of Urban America*, pp. 70–71; and George Collins and Christiane Collins, *Camillo Sitte and the Birth of Modern City Planning* (New York: Random House, 1965), pp. 192–94.

5 John Reps, "William Penn and the Planning of Philadelphia," *Town Planning Review*, 27 (1956–57), 36–37; Downing quoted in Reps, *Monumental Washington*, p. 53.

6 Frederick Law Olmsted, Jr., and Theodora Kimball, eds., *Frederick Law Olmsted, Landscape Architect* (New York: Putnam's, 1922–28), 2: 20–21. For Bryant's role in fomenting interest in a central park see Allan

Nevins, *The Evening Post: A Century of Journalism* (New York: Boni & Liveright, 1922), pp. 192–207. For Downing see his "A Talk about Public Parks and Gardens," *Horticulturist*, 3 (July 1848–June 1849), 153–58; and "The New York Park," *Horticulturist*, 6 (1851), 345–49.

7 The objection is quoted in Frederick Law Olmsted, "Public Parks and the Enlargement of Towns," in *Civilizing American Cities: A Selection of Frederick Law Olmsted's Writings on City Landscapes*, ed. S. B. Sutton (Cambridge: MIT Press, 1971), p. 87. The objection from the *Journal of Commerce* is cited in Nevins, *Evening Post*, p. 197.

8 Kingsland's letter appears in Olmsted and Kimball, *Frederick Law Olmsted*, 2: 25; "Architecture in the United States," *American Journal of Science and the Arts*, 17 (January–July 1830), 108; Tappan, *Growth of Cities*, pp. 35–36.

9 Chapin, *Humanity in the City*, pp. 18–19.

10 John Todd, *The Moral Influence, Dangers and Duties, Connected with Great Cities* (Northampton, Mass., 1841), p. 26; Parker quoted in Daniel Aaron, *Men of Good Hope: A Story of American Progressives* (New York: Oxford Univ. Press, 1951), p. 41; Chapin, *Moral Aspects of City Life*, pp. 180–81; White and White, *Intellectual Versus the City*, p. 228.

11 Horace Bushnell, *Christian Nurture* (New Haven: Yale Univ. Press, 1967), pp. 20 and 22. On the secular legacy of the jeremiad see Bercovitch, *American Jeremiad*, pp. 132–75. A useful discussion of Bushnell's response to excessive individualism appears in R. W. B. Lewis, *The American Adam* (1955; rpt. Chicago: Univ. of Chicago Press, 1975), pp. 66–73.

12 Chapin, *Moral Aspects of City Life*, pp. 138 and 61; Timothy L. Smith, *Revivalism and Social Reform in Mid-Nineteenth-Century America* (New York: Abingdon, 1957).

13 Bender, *Toward an Urban Vision*, p. 135; Robert S. Pickett, *Houses of Refuge: Origins of Juvenile Reform in New York State, 1815–1857* (Syracuse, N.Y.: Syracuse Univ. Press, 1969); David J. Rothman, *The Discovery of the Asylum: Social Order and Disorder in the New Republic* (Boston: Little, Brown, 1971).

14 Mayo, *Symbols of the Capital*, pp. 31–33; Horace Greeley, *Hints toward Reforms*, in *Lectures, Addresses, and Other Writings* (New York, 1850), pp. 314 and 360.

15 Parker quoted in Aaron, *Men of Good Hope*, pp. 38 and 49.

16 John L. Thomas, "Romantic Reform in America, 1815–1865," *American Quarterly*, 17 (1965), 659–70.

17 Chapin, *Humanity in the City*, pp. 144–45; Bushnell, *Christian Nurture*, p. 88 et passim.

18 Mayo, *Symbols of the Capital*, p. 296; Chapin, *Humanity in the City*, p. 150; de Grandfort quoted in Bayrd Still, *Mirror for Gotham* (New York: New York Univ. Press, 1956), p. 135.

19 Freneau, *Poems*, 3: 386; Chapin, *Humanity in the City*, p. 149. For Brace, see Thomas, "Romantic Reform in America," pp. 666–68; and Bender, *Toward an Urban Vision*, pp. 143–50.

20 Martha Read, *Monima; or, The Beggar Girl* (New York, 1802); Sarah Hale, *Traits of American Life* (Philadelphia, 1835); Hale, *Sketches of American Character* (Boston, 1838); A. J. Graves, *Girlhood and Womanhood* (Boston, 1844); Catharine Sedgwick, *Married or Single?* 2 vols. (New York, 1857); Sedgwick, *Clarence; or, A Tale of Our Times*, 2 vols. (Philadelphia, 1830); Emma Southwood, *The Mother-in-Law* (New York, 1851). For a discussion of family life as treated in popular fiction of this time, see Stout, *Sodoms in Eden*, Chap. 1; Herbert Ross Brown, *The Sentimental Novel in America* (Durham, N.C.: Duke Univ. Press, 1940), pp. 283–84 et passim; and Adrienne Siegel, *The Image of the American City in Popular Literature, 1820–1870* (Port Washington, N.Y.: Kennikat, 1981), pp. 68–70.

21 Jeffrey, "Family as Utopian Retreat from the City," pp. 21–41. The belief that the proper environment for a healthy family was one closer to nature is, of course, still with us today in the cult of the suburb. As such it constitutes what Daniel Boorstin has called a "pseudo-event"—a mental construct which, despite evidence to the contrary, becomes an image of reality for mass consumption (*The Image: A Guide to Pseudo-Events in America* [1962; rpt. New York: Harper, 1964].

22 Mayo, *Symbols of the Capital*, pp. 296–97; Maria Cummins, *The Lamplighter* (New York, [1844]); Ann Douglas, *The Feminization of American Culture* (New York: Knopf, 1977), pp. 17–117; Wortman, "Domesticating the Nineteenth-Century American City," pp. 535, 541, et passim; Jeffrey, "Family as Utopian Retreat from the City," pp. 22 and 28–29. Another source for this tendency to identify the home as a virtuous asylum in the city may have been Charles Dickens, whose novels enjoyed immense popularity in America. As Alexander Welsh has noted, the home as a private sanctuary forms a recurrent motif in novels such as *Bleak House, David Copperfield,* and *Great Expectations* (*The City of Dickens* [Oxford: Clarendon, 1971], p. 31).

23 Mayo, *Symbols of the Capital*, p. 296; Chapin, *Humanity in the City*, p.

248

149 and 151; Bushnell, *Christian Nurture*, p. 348; Wortman, "Domesticating the Nineteenth-Century American City," p. 535.

24 Chapin, *Humanity in the City*, p. 175; Mayo, *Symbols of the Capital*, p. 243; Wortman, "Domesticating the Nineteenth-Century American City," p. 545; Daniel Levine, *Varieties of Reform Thought* (Madison: State Historical Society of Wisconsin, 1964), p. 4. Several historians have noted the ironic polarities generated by the cult of domesticity: Jeffrey, "Family as Utopian Retreat from the City," p. 37; and Nancy F. Cott, *The Bonds of Womanhood: "Woman's Sphere" in New England, 1780–1835* (New Haven: Yale Univ. Press, 1977), pp. 69–70.

25 Levine, *Varieties of Reform Thought*, p. 5.

26 *The Correspondence of Emerson and Carlyle*, ed. Joseph Slater (New York: Columbia Univ. Press, 1964), p. 283; Emerson, *Journals*, 10: 30; *Young Emerson Speaks: Unpublished Discourses on Many Subjects*, ed. Arthur Cushman McGiffert, Jr. (Boston: Houghton Mifflin, 1938), p. 99; *Works*, 3: 182–83.

27 Emerson, *Works*, 1: 10, 31, and 369 and 7: 31–32. Joel Porte, *Representative Man: Ralph Waldo Emerson in His Time* (New York: Oxford Univ. Press, 1979), pp. 55–63 and 247–52, provides an enlightening discussion of Emerson's monetary concerns while noting that "Although Emerson scholars have generally given short shrift to such . . . pecuniary dealings, Emerson himself was careful not to make that mistake."

28 Emerson, *Journals*, 15: 430; Cowan, *City of the West*, pp. 1, 3, and 23.

29 Emerson, *Journals*, 13: 241; *Works*, 7: 15 and 10; Stephen Whicher, *Freedom and Fate: An Inner Life of Ralph Waldo Emerson* (Philadelphia: Univ. of Pennsylvania Press, 1953), p. 131.

30 Emerson, *Journals*, 7: 14 and 439. For a discussion of Emerson's evolving desire "to effect a mediation of country solitude and the society of the city," see Sherman Paul, *Emerson's Angle of Vision* (1952; rpt. Cambridge: Harvard Univ. Press, 1965), pp. 199ff.

31 *Correspondence of Emerson and Carlyle*, pp. 355 and 421; Paul, *Emerson's Angle of Vision*, p. 79; Emerson, *Journals*, 11: 395 and 9: 226; *Works*, 1: 83.

32 Emerson, *Works*, 1: 36; *Journals*, 7: 288.

33 Emerson, *Journals*, 14: 286 and 4: 297–98; *Works*, 12: 297 and 1: 82. Emerson's ideas of the relationship among reason, understanding, and memory are discussed in Paul, *Emerson's Angle of Vision*, pp. 125 and 157; and Vivian C. Hopkins, *Spires of Form: A Study of Emerson's Aesthetic Theory* (Cambridge: Harvard Univ. Press, 1951), pp. 30ff.

34 Emerson, *Journals*, 7: 348 and 374–75 and 5: 176; *Works*, 1: 34–35.

35 Emerson, *Works*, 1: 387, 366, 276, 281, 74, and 255 and 3: 261. *Journals*, 9: 284.

36 Emerson, *Journals*, 7: 81; 3: 269; and 4: 96; *Works*, 1: 112. See also Cowan, *City of the West*, pp. 200–205.

37 Emerson, *Works*, 1: 30 and 3: 18.

38 Emerson, *Journals*, 11: 218.

39 Emerson, *Works*, 4: 61.

40 Emerson, "Boston," *Works*, 12: 183, 185–86, 191, and 204–5. Cowan (*City of the West*, pp. 253–61) briefly discusses this essay from a somewhat related perspective.

41 Emerson, "Boston," pp. 190, 185–86, and 197 for citations in the previous two paragraphs.

42 Emerson, "Boston," pp. 192, 196, 204, and 207–9.

43 Emerson, "Boston," p. 208; Cowan, *City of the West*, p. 199–200.

44 Emerson, "Boston," pp. 195, 200–201, and 203.

45 Emerson, "Boston," pp. 188, 187, and 200 for citations in the previous two paragraphs.

46 Emerson, *Works*, 8: 34.

47 Emerson, *Works*, 1: 230 and 3: 86; *Journals*, 13: 48 and 2: 321. For Emerson's ideas on the relation between thought and social action see Paul, *Emerson's Angle of Vision*, pp. 132–64; and Gay Wilson Allen, *Waldo Emerson: A Biography* (New York: Viking, 1981), p. xii.

48 Emerson, *Works*, 1: 268, 285–86, and 248.

49 Emerson, *Works*, 2: 58–59 and 1: 395; Thomas, "Romantic Reform in America," p. 674.

50 Frederick Law Olmsted, *Mount Royal, Montreal* (New York, 1881), p. 23; *Walks and Talks of an American Farmer in England* (1852; rpt. Ann Arbor: Univ. of Michigan Press, 1967), p. 95; Olmsted to Frederick Kingsbury, June 1846, in Olmsted and Kimball, *Frederick Law Olmsted*, 1: 77. For Olmsted's intellectual relationship with Emerson consult Laura Wood Roper, *FLO: A Biography of Frederick Law Olmsted* (Baltimore: Johns Hopkins Univ. Press, 1973), pp. 11, 63–64, et passim.

51 Olmsted, "Autobiographical Passages," in Olmsted and Kimball, *Frederick Law Olmsted*, 1: 46; Olmsted's remarks on the "real prophets" quoted in Roper, *FLO*, p. 40.

52 "Autobiographical Fragment" and "Report to the Brooklyn Park Commissioners," in *Landscape into Cityscape: Frederick Law Olmsted's Plans for a Greater New York City*, ed. Albert Fein (Ithaca, N.Y.: Cornell Univ. Press, 1967), pp. 52 and 160, respectively.

53 Olmsted quoted in Julius Fabos et al., *Frederick Law Olmsted, Sr., Founder*

of Landscape Architecture in America (Amherst: Univ. of Massachusetts Press, 1968), p. 47; Olmsted, "Public Parks and the Enlargement of Towns," p. 70; Olmsted to Kingsbury, p. 77.

54 Olmsted and Kimball, *Frederick Law Olmsted,* 2: 45–46.

55 Frederick Law Olmsted and Calvert Vaux, "Greensward: Description of a Plan for the Improvement of Central Park," in Olmsted and Kimball, *Frederick Law Olmsted,* 2: 214–33; Fabos et al., *Frederick Law Olmsted, Sr.,* pp. 18–20; Olmsted, "Public Parks and the Enlargement of Towns," p. 82.

56 Olmsted and Kimball, *Frederick Law Olmsted,* 2: 250 and 45 and 1: 68; Fabos et al., *Frederick Law Olmsted, Sr.,* p. 47; Olmsted, "Public Parks and the Enlargement of Towns," p. 77.

57 Geoffrey Blodgett, "Frederick Law Olmsted: Landscape Architecture as Conservative Reform," *Journal of American History,* 62 (1975–76), 869–89; see also Robert Lewis, "Frontier and Civilization in the Thought of Frederick Law Olmsted," *American Quarterly,* 29 (1977), 385–403.

58 Meath quoted in Blodgett, "Frederick Law Olmsted," p. 888n. For a discussion of the park-planning movement in this period and the impetus provided by Central Park, see Fabos et al., *Frederick Law Olmsted, Sr.,* p. 3; Fein, "American City," p. 93; Glaab and Brown, *History of Urban America,* pp. 178 and 255–56; and Schmitt, *Back to Nature,* pp. 59–60 and 70–76.

59 Peter Hales, *Silver Cities: The Photography of American Urbanization, 1839–1915* (Philadelphia: Temple Univ. Press, 1984), pp. 102–12; J. P. Craig, *Tally Ho! Coaching through Chicago's Parks and Boulevards* (Chicago, 1888), quoted in *Silver Cities,* p. 108.

60 *North Chicago: Its Advantages, Resources, and Probable Future* (Chicago, 1873), p. 8; Adna F. Weber, *The Growth of Cities in the Nineteenth Century* (New York, 1899), p. 475.

61 Park quoted in Glaab and Brown, *History of Urban America,* p. 251; George, *Progress and Poverty,* p. 397; Levine, *Varieties of Reform Thought,* pp. 12–33.

Chapter VI. Urban Pastoralism and Literary Dissent

1 F. O. Matthiessen, *American Renaissance* (1941; rpt. New York: Oxford Univ. Press, 1974), p. x; Michael Bell, *The Development of American Romance: The Sacrifice of Relation* (Chicago: Univ. of Chicago Press, 1980), p. 30.

2 *Leaves of Grass,* ed. Sculley Bradley and Harold W. Blodgett, Vol. 9 of

The Collected Writings of Walt Whitman, gen. eds. Gay Wilson Allen and Sculley Bradley (New York: New York Univ. Press, 1961–84), p. 19, line 83. Subsequent references to Whitman's *Leaves* will be to this edition and will appear in the text by line number.

3   See, for example, James E. Miller, Jr., *Walt Whitman* (New York: Twayne, 1962), p. 134; Bradley and Blodgett, *Leaves of Grass,* p. 313n; and Rosenthal, *City of Nature,* p. 226.

4   Richard Chase, *Walt Whitman Reconsidered* (New York: Sloane, 1955), p. 87.

5   Walt Whitman, *Democratic Vistas,* in *Prose Works 1892,* ed. Floyd Stovall, Vols. 7 and 8 of *Collected Writings,* 2: 419 and 370–72.

6   Walt Whitman, *Notes Left Over,* in *Prose Works,* 2: 525.

7   See, for example, Stephen Tanner, "Walt Whitman as Urban Transcendentalist," *South Dakota Review,* 14, No. 2 (Summer 1976), 8; and Burton Pike, *The Image of the City in Modern Literature* (Princeton: Princeton Univ. Press, 1981), pp. 77–86. Though noting that Whitman is aware "that the [urban] reality he wishes for is the opposite of the reality he sees" and that his poetic cities "are private," Pike goes on to assert that Whitman, like Hart Crane, engages in his poems of the city in an "intense act of will bent towards a future better than the present."

8   Walt Whitman, "Poets to Come," in *Leaves of Grass,* p. 14, line 6.

9   Walt Whitman, *Specimen Days,* in *Prose Works,* 1: 262.

10 For Whitman's early interest and involvement in reform, consult Gay Wilson Allen, *Solitary Singer,* rev. ed. (1955; rpt. New York: New York Univ. Press, 1967), p. 394; and Chase, *Walt Whitman Reconsidered,* pp. 29–30. The theory of Whitman's alienation is offered by Chase, p. 50. Brief discussions of the poet's antireformist stance after 1850 appear in Allen, p. 394; and Floyd Stovall, *The Foreground of Leaves of Grass* (Charlottesville: Univ. of Virginia Press, 1974), p. 158.

11 Quoted in Stovall, *Foreground of Leaves of Grass,* p. 277.

12 See, for example, Stanley K. Cauffman, Jr., " 'Crossing Brooklyn Ferry': A Note on the Catalogue Technique in Whitman's Poetry," *Modern Philogy,,* 51 (August 1953–May 1954), 229; and Marx, *Machine in the Garden,* p. 222.

13 Edwin Miller, *Walt Whitman's Poetry: A Psychological Journey* (New York: New York Univ. Press, 1968), p. 201.

14 Gay Wilson Allen has written that "the idea of becoming disembodied, all spirit," was a "powerful stimulus" to the creation of "Crossing Brooklyn Ferry" and forms a leitmotif of the poem (*Solitary Singer,* p. 257).

15 Whitman, *Notes Left Over,* pp. 516–17.

16 Walt Whitman, *The Primer of Words*, in *Daybooks and Notebooks*, ed. William White (New York: New York Univ. Pres, 1978), 3: 740.

17 Whitman, *Democratic Vistas*, p. 391; Roy Harvey Pearce, *The Continuity of American Poetry* (Princeton: Princeton Univ. Press, 1961), p. 41.

18 Whitman, *Specimen Days*, p. 259. In fairness to Emerson it should be noted that in his private moments he occasionally doubted whether the urban-pastoral ideal could be embodied in actual society. In one journal entry he recorded, "I wish to have rural strength & religion for my children & I wish city facility & polish. I find with chagrin that I cannot have both" (*Journals*, 9: 87).

19 Stephen Black, *Walt Whitman's Journey into Chaos* (Princeton: Princeton Univ. Press, 1975), p. 165.

20 Whitman, *Specimen Days*, p. 232.

21 See *The American Notebooks*, ed. Claude M. Simpson, Vol. 8 of *The Centenary Edition of the Works of Nathaniel Hawthorne*, gen. eds. William Charvat, Roy Harvey Pearce, and Claude M. Simpson (Columbus: Ohio State Univ. Press, 1962–85), pp. 101–2, 327, 496–97, and 506–7; *The House of the Seven Gables*, Vol. 2 of *Centenary Edition*, p. 128.

22 Charles Feidelson, *Symbolism and American Literature* (Chicago: Univ. of Chicago Press, 1953), p. 15.

23 An exception would seem to be the conclusion to *The House of the Seven Gables*, where Phoebe and Holgrave appear to shake free from the curse of the past and retire to the Pyncheon suburban home. However, Hawthorne employs several means that compel us to look beyond this overtly simple solution. For one thing, Phoebe and Holgrave's final position recalls the cult of urban domesticity and its saccharine version of urban pastoralism. Then, too, as John Caldwell Stubbs points out, "the comic and pathetic love of Hepzibah and Clifford suggests something of a mockery of such an easy solution" in that the qualified success of this couple "points up the artificiality of the complete and easy solution of Holgrave and Phoebe" (*The Pursuit of Form: A Study of Hawthorne and the Romance* [Urbana: Univ. of Illinois Press, 1970], pp. 44 and 114). Even Holgrave recognizes the inadequacy of his position by calling his decision to accommodate himself to a middle path "especially unpardonable in this dwelling of so much hereditary misfortune" (315). It is essentially false because it denies Hawthorne's assertion in the preface that "the wrongdoing of one generation lives into the successive ones" (2). As Nina Baym argues, "there is no way to interpret the conclusion as triumphant within the logic of the story" (*The Shape of Hawthorne's Career* [Ithaca, N.Y.: Cornell Univ. Press, 1976], p. 171).

24 Hawthorne, *American Notebooks*, pp. 496–97.

25 Hawthorne, *American Notebooks*, pp. 506–9; Marx, *Machine in the Garden*, pp. 11–15.

26 Hawthorne, *American Notebooks*, p. 239; see Olmsted's "Observations on the Progress of Improvements in Street Plans . . . ," rpt. in part in *Civilizing American Cities*, pp. 23–42.

27 Hawthorne, "Sights from a Steeple," in *Twice-Told Tales*, Vol. 9 of *Centenary Edition*, p. 192. Subsequent references appear in the text.

28 Although "Molineaux" was published about a year after "Sights," it is uncertain which story actually was written first. Hawthorne apparently sent Samuel Goodrich the manuscript of "Molineux" in December 1829, but according to Arlin Turner, in May 1830 Hawthorne submitted two "new pieces," one of which was "Sights" (*Nathaniel Hawthorne: A Biography* [New York: Oxford Univ. Press, 1980], pp. 53–54). Whether "Sights" was new in the sense of being just composed or new in being freshly sent—and thus written between 1825 and 1829—is unclear. The greater polish and complexity of "Molineux," however, suggest it was written after "Sights."

29 Though both stories first appeared in *The Token*, "Sights" later was included in *Twice-Told Tales* while "Molineux" was reprinted in *The Snow-Image*. All references to "Molineux" are from The Snow-Image *and Uncollected Tales*, Vol. 11 of *Centenary Edition*.

30 Roy Harvey Pearce, "Hawthorne and the Sense of the Past or, the Immortality of Major Molineux," *English Literary History*, 21 (1954), 330.

31 Neal Frank Doubleday discusses the historical setting of "Molineux" in *Hawthorne's Early Tales: A Critical Study* (Durham, N.C.: Duke Univ. Press, 1972), pp. 228–29. See also Pearce, "Hawthorne and the Sense of the Past," p. 329; and Daniel Hoffman, *Form and Fable in American Fiction* (New York: Oxford Univ. Press, 1961), p. 118.

32 Several critics have pointed out the archetypal Americanism of this story and have read it as an allegory of "bucolic America" being transformed into "urbanized Europe": Stout, *Sodoms in Eden*, pp. 12–13 and 94–95; and Sidney H. Bremer, "Exploding the Myth of Rural America and Urban Europe," *Studies in Short Fiction*, 18 (1981), 49–57. So far as they go, such interpretations are undoubtedly correct, though they tend to reduce the tale to dramatic reportage. Hawthorne's interest in the American city involved much more than just documenting the change from agrarianism to urbanism as an inevitable part of native experience. As we have seen, Hawthorne's contemporaries were quite conscious of America's urban development and welcomed it. Nor was Hawthorne unaware of this response.

33 Three critics have cited the parallels between Franklin's *Autobiography*

254

and "Molineux": Julian Smith, "Coming of Age in America: Young Ben Franklin and Robin Molineux," *American Quarterly*, 17 (1965), 550–58; A. B. England, "Robin Molineux and Young Ben: A Reconsideration," *Journal of American Studies*, 6 (1972), 181–88; and Denis M. Murphy, "Poor Robin and Shrewd Ben: Hawthorne's Kinsman," *Studies in Short Fiction*, 15 (1978), 185–90. Moreover, Murphy argues that Robin's midnight adventure is "a delusive mockery of the Franklin ideal." While such parallels are suggestive, Smith, England, and Murphy, I believe, exaggerate them, in that Robin's position differs sharply from Franklin's. Robin journeys from country to city, while Franklin moves from an older city to a developing one. Additionally, Franklin expects to earn his place in Philadelphia, while Robin anticipates favor through patronage. While one could argue that Hawthorne sought to undermine the message of the *Autobiography* by suggesting that in his own age of increasing urbanization it was no longer possible to tame the city through individual effort, the setting Hawthorne chose problematizes such an interpretation. If reversal were his point, a contemporary setting would have been more appropriate. Rather than read "Molineux" as a direct satire of Franklin's success story, we need to see it as a qualification of a particular response to urban life of which Franklin's *Autobiography* is only one example.

34 Those who have interpreted the city of "Molineux" as horrific and hellish include Arthur L. Broes, "Journey into Moral Darkness: 'My Kinsman, Major Molineux' as Allegory," *Nineteenth-Century Fiction*, 19 (1964–65), 171–84; Carl Dennis, "How to Live in Hell: The Bleak Vision of *My Kinsman, Major Molineux*," *University of Kansas City Review*, 37 (1971), 250–58; and Stout, *Sodoms in Eden*, pp. 94–95.

35 Frederick Crews, *Sins of the Fathers* (New York: Oxford Univ. Press, 1966), p. 195.

36 Nathaniel Hawthorne, *The Blithedale Romance*, Vol. 3 of *Centenary Edition*, p. 28; subsequent references appear in the text.

37 *Report of the Commissioners and a History of Lincoln Park*, comp. I. J. Bryan (Chicago, 1889), p. 14.

38 Theodore Dreiser, *Sister Carrie*, ed. Donald Pizer (New York: Norton, 1970), p. 17. Although the new Pennsylvania edition of *Sister Carrie* (gen. ed. Neda M. Westlake [Philadelphia: Univ. of Pennsylvania Press, 1981]) provides a very different "authoritative" version of the novel, the controversial editorial decisions on which it is based—as well as, I believe, some dubious conceptions of the relationship between intention and the process of composition—make it more a debatable than definitive edition and so not the best choice for textual analysis and reference.

All citations, therefore, are to the Norton edition, which relies on the original 1900 version authorized for publication by Dreiser.

39 Edith Wharton, *The House of Mirth* (New York: Scribner's, 1905), pp. 511 and 517. Subsequent citations to this edition appear in the text.

40 Richard Poirier, *A World Elsewhere: The Place of Style in American Literature* (1966; rpt. New York: Oxford Univ. Press, 1973), p. 233.

41 Henry James, *The American Scene* (Bloomington: Indiana Univ. Press, 1968), pp. 15 and 7. Subsequent citations are given in the text.

42 Alan Trachtenberg, "*The American Scene:* Versions of the City," *Massachusetts Review*, 8 (1967), 288–89. James had read Whitman as early as 1865, and by the time he returned from Europe, he was calling the poet "a very great genius" (Leon Edel, *Henry James* [Philadelphia: Lippincott, 1953–72], 5: 255).

Epilogue

1 Margaret S. Marsh and Samuel Kaplan, "The Lure of the Suburbs," in Philip C. Dolce, ed., *Suburbia: The American Dream and Dilemma* (Garden City, N.Y.: Anchor-Doubleday, 1976), p. 37.

2 See, for example, Strauss, *Images of the American City*, p. 246; and David C. Thorns, *Suburbia* (London: MacGibbon and Kee, 1972), p. 11.

3 Robert Wood, *Suburbia: Its People and Their Politics* (Boston: Houghton Mifflin; Cambridge: Riverside, 1959), p. 12; Mumford, *City in History*, p. 494.

4 Frank Lloyd Wright, *An Autobiography* (New York: Duell, Sloan and Pearce, 1943), p. 320; *Architecture and Modern Life*, with Baker Brownell (New York: Harper, 1937), pp. 317–18 and 321.

5 Nathan Glazer, "Why City Planning Is Obsolete," *Architectural Forum*, 109 (July 1958), 96. Interestingly enough, Glazer is reticent about the dangers accompanying the alternative he advocates—increased urban density.

6 Percival Goodman and Paul Goodman, *Communitas* (Chicago: Univ. of Chicago Press, 1947), pp. 48 and v. The Goodmans' plans appear on pp. 60–123.

7 Jane Jacobs, *The Death and Life of Great American Cities* (New York: Random House, 1961); Mumford, *City in History*, p. 129 et passim; and *The Culture of Cities* (New York: Harcourt, Brace, 1938), pp. 346, 401, and 485.

8 Saul Bellow, *Mr. Sammler's Planet* (New York: Viking, 1970), p. 7.

Selected Bibliography

This bibliography is designed as an aid to those interested in further study of American attitudes toward urban development. It is intended not as a comprehensive list but as a starting point.

Because American conceptions of the city have been tied inextricably to events and ideas extending beyond native boundaries, included among the resources are works dealing with European developments. The first section is devoted primarily to relevant studies in urban history and sociology, although also included are the few sources directly addressing the subject of general attitudes toward urbanization. Since those attitudes often have been outgrowths of other religious, political, economic, and environmental beliefs, the second section lists works in the history of ideas which I have found useful. Because of the emphasis of this study, grouped together under a separate heading are works devoted to the subject of the city in literature. The last section lists other general sources that can provide important background information for understanding the role of urbanization in American life and writing.

Urban Studies

Baldassare, Mark. *The Growth Dilemma: Residents' Views and Local Population Change in the United States.* Berkeley: Univ. of California Press, 1981.

Barth, Gunther. *City People: The Rise of Modern City Culture in Nineteenth-Century America.* New York: Oxford Univ. Press, 1980.

Bender, Thomas. *Toward an Urban Vision: Ideas and Institutions in Nineteenth-Century America.* Lexington: Univ. of Kentucky Press, 1975.

Bridenbaugh, Carl. *Cities in Revolt: Urban Life in America, 1743–1776.* New York: Knopf, 1955.

Bridenbaugh, Carl. *Cities in the Wilderness: The First Century of Urban Life in America, 1625–1742.* 1938; rpt. New York: Capricorn, 1955.

Ciucci, Giorgio, et al. *The American City: From the Civil War to the New Deal.* Trans. Barbara Luigia La Penta. Cambridge: MIT Press, 1979.

Dolce, Philip C., ed. *Suburbia: The American Dream and Dilemma.* Garden City, N.Y.: Anchor-Doubleday, 1976.

Donaldson, Scott. "City and Country: Marriage Proposals." *American Quarterly,* 20 (1968), 547–66.

Frick, Frank S. *The City in Ancient Israel.* Missoula, Mont.: Scholars Press, 1977.

Fries, Sylvia Doughty. *The Urban Idea in Colonial America.* Philadelphia: Temple Univ. Press, 1977.

Glaab, Charles N. "The Historian and the American Urban Tradition." *Wisconsin Magazine of History,* 57 (Autumn 1963), 12–25.

Glaab, Charles N., and A. Theodore Brown. *A History of Urban America.* New York: Collier-Macmillan, 1967.

Green, Constance McLaughlin. *The Rise of Urban America.* New York: Harper & Row, 1965.

Gutkind, E. A. *Urban Development in Western Europe.* Vols. 5 and 6 of *International History of City Development.* New York: Free Press; London: Collier-Macmillan, 1964–72.

Hales, Peter B. *Silver Cities: The Photography of American Urbanization, 1839–1915.* Philadelphia: Temple Univ. Press, 1984.

Haller, William, Jr. *The Puritan Frontier: Town-Planting in New England Colonial Development.* New York: Columbia Univ. Press, 1951.

Hatt, Paul K., and Albert J. Reiss, Jr., eds. *Cities and Society.* New York: Free Press of Glencoe, 1951.

Lees, Andrew. *Cities Perceived: Urban Society in European and American Thought, 1820–1940.* New York: Columbia Univ. Press, 1985.

McKelvey, Blake. *The Urbanization of America, 1860–1915.* New Brunswick, N.J.: Rutgers Univ. Press, 1963.

Mumford, Lewis. *The City in History: Its Origins, Its Transformations, and Its Prospects.* New York: Harcourt, Brace, 1961.

Nash, Gary B. *The Urban Crucible: Social Change, Political Consciousness, and the Origins of the American Revolution.* Cambridge: Harvard Univ. Press, 1979.

Pred, Allan. *The Spatial Dynamics of U.S. Urban-Industrial Growth, 1800–1914.* Cambridge: MIT Press, 1966.

Reps, John W. *The Forgotten Frontier: Urban Planning in the American West before 1890.* Columbia: Univ. of Missouri Press, 1981.

Reps, John W. *The Making of Urban America: A History of City Planning in the United States.* Princeton: Princeton Univ. Press, 1965.

Rutman, Darrett B. *Winthrop's Boston: Portrait of a Puritan Town.* Chapel Hill: Univ. of North Carolina Press, 1965.

Schmitt, Peter. *Back to Nature: The Arcadian Myth in Urban America.* New York: Oxford Univ. Press, 1969.

Spirn, Anne Whiston. *The Granite Garden: Urban Nature and Human Design.* New York: Basic Books, 1984.

Storoni Mazzolani, Lidia. *The Idea of the City in Roman Thought: From Walled City to Spiritual Commonwealth.* Trans. S. O'Donnell. Bloomington: Indiana Univ. Press, 1970.

Strauss, Anselm L. *Images of the American City.* New York: Free Press of Glencoe, 1961.

Thorns, David C. *Suburbia.* London: MacGibbon & Kee, 1972.

Tunnard, Christopher, and Henry Hope Reed. *American Skyline: The Growth and Form of Our Cities and Towns.* 1953; rpt. New York: New American Library, 1956.

Vance, Rupert B., and Nicholas J. Demerath, eds. *The Urban South.* 1954; rpt. Freeport, N.Y.: Books for Libraries, 1971.

Wade, Richard C. *The Urban Frontier: The Rise of Western Cities, 1790–1830.* Cambridge: Harvard Univ. Press, 1959.

White, Morton, and Lucia White. *The Intellectual Versus the City.* 1962; rpt. New York: New American Library, 1964.

Wood, Robert C. *Suburbia: Its People and Their Politics.* Boston: Houghton Mifflin; Cambridge: Riverside, 1959.

Wortman, Marlene Stein. "Domesticating the Nineteenth-Century American City." In *Prospects: An Annual of American Cultural Studies.* Vol. 3. Ed. Jack Salzman. New York: Franklin, 1977. Pp. 531–72.

Zuckerman, Michael. *Peaceable Kingdoms: New England Towns in the Eighteenth Century.* New York: Knopf, 1970.

History of Ideas

Bailyn, Bernard. *The Ideological Origins of the American Revolution.* Cambridge: Harvard Univ. Press, 1967.

Baldwin, Leland D. *The American Quest for the City of God.* Macon, Ga.: Mercer Univ. Press, 1981.

Baritz, Loren. *City on a Hill: A History of Ideas and Myths in America.* New York: Wiley, 1964.

Beard, Charles A., and Mary Beard. *The American Spirit.* Vol. 4 of *The Rise of American Civilization.* 1942; rpt. New York: Macmillan, 1948.

Becker, Carl L. *The Heavenly City of the Eighteenth-Century Philosophers.* New Haven: Yale Univ. Press, 1932.

Bercovitch, Sacvan. *The American Jeremiad.* Madison: Univ. of Wisconsin Press, 1978.

Bercovitch, Sacvan. *The Puritan Origins of the American Self.* New Haven: Yale Univ. Press, 1975.

Billington, Ray Allen. *Land of Savagery, Land of Promise: The European Image of the American Frontier in the Nineteenth Century.* New York: Norton, 1981.

Burns, Rex. *Success in America: The Yeoman Dream and the Industrial Revolution.* Amherst: Univ. of Massachusetts Press, 1976.

Carroll, Peter. *Puritanism and the Wilderness: The Intellectual Significance of the New England Frontier, 1629–1700.* New York: Columbia Univ. Press, 1969.

Cohn, Norman. *The Pursuit of the Millennium.* London: Heinemann, 1962.

Davidson, James West. *The Logic of Millennial Thought: Eighteenth-Century New England.* New Haven: Yale Univ. Press, 1977.

Douglas, Ann. *The Feminization of American Culture.* New York: Knopf, 1977.

Griswold, A. Whitney. *Farming and Democracy.* New York: Harcourt, Brace, 1948.

Haller, William. *Foxe's Book of Martyrs and the Elect Nation.* London: Cape, 1963.

Honour, Hugh. *The New Golden Land: European Images of America from the Discoveries to the Present Time.* New York: Pantheon, 1975.

Kammen, Michael. *People of Paradox: An Inquiry concerning the Origins of American Civilization.* 1972; rpt. New York: Vintage-Random House, 1973.

Levine, Daniel. *Varieties of Reform Thought.* Madison: State Historical Society of Wisconsin, 1964.

Lewis, R. W. B. *The American Adam: Innocence, Tragedy, and Tradition in the Nineteenth Century.* 1955; rpt. Chicago: Univ. of Chicago Press, 1975.

McGinn, Bernard. *Visions of the End: Apocalyptic Tradition in the Middle Ages.* New York: Columbia Univ. Press, 1979.

Manuel, Frank E., and Fritzie P. Manuel. *Utopian Thought in the Western World.* Cambridge: Belknap Press of Harvard Univ. Press, 1979.

Marx, Leo. *The Machine in the Garden: Technology and the Pastoral Ideal in America.* 1964; rpt. New York: Oxford Univ. Press, 1973.

Meyer, Donald. *The Democratic Enlightenment.* New York: Putnam's, 1976.

Meyers, Marvin. *The Jacksonian Persuasion: Politics and Belief.* 1957; rpt. Stanford: Stanford Univ. Press, 1960.

Miller, Perry. *Nature's Nation.* Cambridge: Belknap Press of Harvard Univ. Press, 1967.

Miller, Perry. *The New England Mind: From Colony to Province.* 1953; rpt. Cambridge: Harvard Univ. Press, 1966.

Nash, Roderick. *Wilderness and the American Mind.* New Haven: Yale Univ. Press, 1967.

Nisbet, Robert. *History of the Idea of Progress.* New York: Basic Books, 1980.

Riley, I. Woodbridge. *American Thought from Puritanism to Pragmatism and Beyond.* 2d ed. New York: Holt, 1923.

Sanford, Charles L. *The Quest for Paradise: Europe and the American Moral Imagination.* Urbana: Univ. of Illinois Press, 1961.

Saum, Lewis O. *The Popular Mood of Pre–Civil War America.* Westport, Conn.: Greenwood, 1980.

Slotkin, Richard. *Regeneration through Violence: The Mythology of the American Frontier, 1600–1860.* Middletown, Conn.: Wesleyan Univ. Press, 1973.

Smith, Henry Nash. *Virgin Land: The American West as Symbol and Myth.* New York: Vintage-Random House, 1950.

Tichi, Cecelia. *New World, New Earth: Environmental Reform in American Literature from the Puritans through Whitman.* New Haven: Yale Univ. Press, 1979.

Tuveson, Ernest Lee. *Millennium and Utopia: A Study in the Background of the Idea of Progress.* Berkeley: Univ. of California Press, 1949.

Tuveson, Ernest Lee. *Redeemer Nation: The Idea of America's Millennial Role.* Chicago: Univ. of Chicago Press, 1968.

Whitney, Lois. *Primitivism and the Idea of Progress.* Baltimore: Johns Hopkins Univ. Press, 1934.

The City in Literature

Bender, Thomas. "James Fenimore Cooper and the City." *New York History,* 51 (1970), 287–305.

Bremer, Sidney H., "Exploding the Myth of Rural America and Urban Europe: 'My Kinsman, Major Molineux' and 'The Paradise of Bachelors and the Tartarus of Maids.' " *Studies in Short Fiction,* 18 (1981), 49–57.

Byrd, Max. *London Transformed: Images of the City in the Eighteenth Century.* New Haven: Yale Univ. Press, 1978.

Chaffin, J. Thomas, Jr. "Give Me Faces and Streets: Walt Whitman and the City." *Walt Whitman Review*, 23 (1977), 109–20.

Cowan, Michael H. *City of the West: Emerson, America, and Urban Metaphor.* New Haven: Yale Univ. Press, 1967.

Dunlap, George. *The City in the American Novel, 1789–1900.* 1934; rpt. New York: Russell & Russell, 1965.

Feingold, Richard. *Nature and Society: Later Eighteenth-Century Uses of the Pastoral and Georgic.* New Brunswick, N.J.: Rutgers Univ. Press, 1978.

Gelfant, Blanche. *The American City Novel.* 1954; rpt. Norman: Univ. of Oklahoma Press, 1970.

Mack, Maynard. *The Garden and the City: Retirement and Politics in the Later Poetry of Pope.* Toronto: Univ. of Toronto Press, 1969.

Pike, Burton. *The Image of the City in Modern Literature.* Princeton: Princeton Univ. Press, 1981.

Rosenthal, Bernard. *City of Nature: Journeys to Nature in the Age of American Romanticism.* Newark, N.J.: Univ. of Delaware Press; London: Associated Univ. Presses, 1980.

Siegel, Adrienne. *The Image of the American City in Popular Literature, 1820–1870.* Port Washington, N.Y.: Kennikat, 1981.

Stout, Janis. *Sodoms in Eden: The City in American Fiction before 1860.* Westport, Conn.: Greenwood, 1976.

Tanner, Stephen. "Walt Whitman as Urban Transcendentalist." *South Dakota Review*, 14, No. 2 (Summer 1976), 6–18.

Thomas, M. Wynn. "Walt Whitman and Mannahatta-New York." *American Quarterly*, 34 (1982), 362–78.

Trachtenberg, Alan. "*The American Scene:* Versions of the City." *Massachusetts Review*, 8 (1967), 281–95.

Weimer, David. *The City as Metaphor.* New York: Random House, 1966.

Welsh, Alexander. *The City of Dickens.* Oxford: Clarendon, 1971.

Williams, Raymond. *The Country and the City.* New York: Oxford Univ. Press, 1973.

General

Bailyn, Bernard. *The New England Merchants in the Seventeenth Century.* 1955; rpt. New York: Harper & Row, 1964.

Bremer, Francis J. *The Puritan Experiment: New England Society from Bradford to Edwards.* New York: St. Martin's, 1976.

Bridenbaugh, Carl. *Vexed and Troubled Englishmen.* New York: Oxford Univ. Press, 1968.

Brown, Herbert Ross. *The Sentimental Novel in America.* Durham, N.C.: Duke Univ. Press, 1940.

Buchard, John, and Albert Bush-Brown. *The Architecture of America: A Social and Cultural History.* Abridged ed. Boston: Little, Brown, 1966.

Bushman, Richard. *From Puritan to Yankee: Character and the Social Order in Connecticut, 1690–1765.* 1967; rpt. New York: Norton, 1970.

Cott, Nancy F. *The Bonds of Womanhood: "Woman's Sphere" in New England, 1780–1835.* New Haven: Yale Univ. Press, 1977.

Elliott, Emory. *Power and the Pulpit in Puritan New England.* Princeton: Princeton Univ. Press, 1975.

Fussell, Edwin. *Frontier: American Literature and the American West.* Princeton: Princeton Univ. Press, 1965.

Haller, William. *The Rise of Puritanism.* New York: Columbia Univ. Press, 1938.

Hofstadter, Richard. *The Age of Reform: From Bryan to F.D.R.* 1955; rpt. New York: Knopf, 1974.

Kimble, George. *Geography in the Middle Ages.* London: Methuen, 1938.

Mannheim, Karl. *Ideology and Utopia: An Introduction to the Sociology of Knowledge.* Trans. Louis Wirth and Edward Shils. New York: Harcourt, Brace, 1936.

Potter, David. *People of Plenty: Economic Abundance and the American Character.* Chicago: Univ. of Chicago Press, 1954.

Smith, Timothy L. *Revivalism and Social Reform in Mid-Nineteenth-Century America.* New York: Abingdon, 1957.

Taylor, Walter F. *The Economic Novel in America.* Chapel Hill: Univ. of North Carolina Press, 1942.

TeSelle, Sallie, ed. *The Family, Communes, and Utopian Societies.* New York: Harper & Row, 1972.

Index